THE SCHOOLS HISTORY PROJECT · OFFICIAL TEXT

S·H·P

CRIME PUNISHMENT THROUGH TIME

an SHP development study

DISCOVERING THE PAST FOR GCSE

Ian Dawson

Series Editor: Colin Shephard

D0727318

JOHN MURRAY

The Schools History Project

This project was set up by the Schools Council in 1972. Its main aim was to suggest suitable objectives for history teachers, and to promote the use of appropriate materials and teaching methods for their realisation. This involved a reconsideration of the nature of history and its relevance in secondary schools, the design of a syllabus framework which shows the uses of history in the education of adolescents, and the setting up of appropriate examinations.

Since 1978 the project has been based at Trinity and All Saints' College, Leeds. It is now self-funding and with the advent of the National Curriculum it has expanded its publications to provide courses for Key Stage 3, and for a range of GCSE and A level syllabuses. The project provides INSET for all aspects of National Curriculum, GCSE and A level history.

Note: The wording and sentence structure of some written sources have been adapted and simplified to make them accessible to all pupils, while faithfully preserving the sense of the original.

Words printed in SMALL CAPITALS are defined in the Glossary on page 212.

Series consultants

Terry Fiehn
Tim Lomas
Martin and Jenny Tucker

© Ian Dawson 1999

First published in 1999
by John Murray (Publishers) Ltd
50 Albemarle Street
London W1X 4BD

Layouts by Liz Rowe
Artwork by Mike Humphries, Oxford Illustrators, Tony Randell, Steve Smith
Colour separations by Colourscript
Typeset in 10½/12pt Walbaum Book by Wearset, Boldon, Tyne and Wear
Printed and bound by the University Press, Cambridge

A catalogue entry for this title is available from the British Library

ISBN 0-7195-5261-3
Teachers' Resource Book ISBN 0-7195-5262-1

Acknowledgements

Cover: *t* British Library, London/Bridgeman Art Library, London, *bl* Ann Ronan/Image Select, *br* Harris Museum and Art Gallery, Preston, Lancs/Bridgeman Art Library, London; **p.19** Scala; **p.24** *t* Universiteitsbibliotheek Gent (ms. 236); **p.24** *b* E.T. Archive; **p.25** Private Collection/Bridgeman Art Library, London; **p.26** The British Library (ms. Cott. Claud. B.IV f.59); **p.28** Ancient Art & Architecture Collection; **p.30** *l & r* Handschriften und Inkunabel Sammlung, Benediktinerabtei Lambach (Cod. Cml LXXIII f. 64v & 72); **p.36** Dean & Chapter of Durham Cathedral; **p.37** E.T. Archive; **p.43** The British Library (ms. Roy. 10.E.IV f.187); **p.45** The Master and Fellows of University College, Oxford (ms. 165, p.8), photo supplied by Bodleian Library, Oxford; **p.47** The Kobal Collection; **p.48** The Pierpont Morgan Library/Art Resource, New York; **p.49** By permission of the Syndics of Cambridge University Library (ms. Ee.3.59 f.4r); **p.56** *l* The British Library (ms. Roy.18.E.1 f.175); **p.56** *r* Mary Evans Picture Library; **p.58** Norfolk Museums Service (Norwich Castle Museum)/Bridgeman Art Library, London; **p.60** The British Library (ms. C.18.d.1); **p.61** The British Library (ms. C.18.d.1); **p.62** Mary Evans Picture Library; **p.63** Mary Evans Picture Library; **p.64** Mary Evans Picture Library; **p.66** Lauros-Giraudon/Bridgeman Art Library, London; **p.67** Mary Evans Picture Library; **p.73** *t* The British Library (Huth 114), *b* The British Library (C.40.c.20); **p.74** Mary Evans Picture Library; **p.75** Mary Evans Picture Library; **p.77** Fotomas Index; **p.82** The British Library (G.2393); **p.83** Mary Evans Picture Library; **p.84** *l & r* Mary Evans/Bruce Castle Museum; **p.88** Mary Evans Picture Library; **p.102** *t & b* Mary Evans Picture Library; **p.108** Mary Evans Picture Library; **p.110** Mary Evans Picture Library; **p.113** *t* John Frost Historical Newspaper Service, *bl & br* Bedfordshire & Luton Archives and Records Service; **p.115** Mary Evans Picture Library; **p.118** *t* Mary Evans Picture Library, *b* National Library of Australia, Canberra/Bridgeman Art Library, London; **p.122** *t* Nottingham City Council, Leisure and Community Services, Central Library, Nottingham, *b* Galleries of Justice Museum, Nottingham **p.123** *t* Mary Evans Picture Library, *b* Galleries of Justice Museum, Nottingham; **p.126** *all* Mary Evans Picture Library; **p.123** *all* Mary Evans Picture Library; **p.127** *all* Mary Evans Picture Library; **p.130** Mary Evans Picture Library; **p.131** Bedfordshire & Luton Archives and Records Service; **p.132** Lauros-Giraudon/Bridgeman Art Library, London; **p.133** *l* Private Collection/Bridgeman Art Library, London, *c & r* Mary Evans Picture Library; **p.134** *all* Mary Evans Picture Library; **p.136** *t* Punch, *bl, bc & br* Mary Evans Picture Library **p.137** *t & br* Punch, *bl* Mary Evans Picture Library; **p.140** Mary Evans Picture Library; **p.144** Mary Evans Picture Library; **p.147** Mary Evans/Tom Morgan; **p.148** E.T. Archive; **p.149** Public Record Office, Image Library; **p.152** Mary Evans Picture Library; **p.153** Hulton Getty; **p.155** Hulton Getty; **p.164** *t* Hulton Getty, *b* John Frost Historical Newspaper Service; **p.165** John Frost Historical Newspaper Service; **p.166** Mary Evans Picture Library; **p.167** John Frost Historical Newspaper Service; **p.173** *t* Dave Cheskin/PA News, *b* Popperfoto/Reuter; **p.178** *t & b* © BBC **p.179** *t* Popperfoto, *b* Michael Stephens/PA News; **p.181** *l* Nils Jorgensen/Rex Features, *r* Today/Rex Features; **p.184** Mary Evans Picture Library; **p.185** Popperfoto; **p.204** E.T. Archive; **p.208** Mary Evans Picture Library; **p.209** Popperfoto; **p.211** Rex Features.

b = bottom, *c* = centre, *l* = left, *r* = right, *t* = top.

Every effort has been made to contact copyright holders, and the publishers apologise for any omissions which they will be pleased to rectify at the earliest opportunity.

Contents

● ● ● ● ● ● ● ● ● ● ● ● ● ● ● ● ● ● ● ●

What do you think about crime and punishment?

CRIME INCREASING!

CRIMES ARE OFTEN in the news. A particularly shocking crime or an increase in crime can lead to heated discussion.

- Is crime becoming more violent?
- Are punishments harsh enough?
- Should criminals be locked away for longer?
- Does prison do any good?
- Should CAPITAL PUNISHMENT be brought back?

Often people simply voice their ideas or prejudices without really knowing the facts behind what they are saying. This course should help you to avoid that. You can understand more about crime and punishment today if you explore how past events have created the present-day police, prisons and crimes.

You can also untangle some of the ideas people have about crime and punishment today if you compare them with the ideas and attitudes people had in the past.

However, before plunging back into the past – and all that blood and torture that some of you may be looking forward to but others may be relieved to know isn't here – try answering these questions which tease out what **you think** about crime and punishment today. You could use them as the basis for an opinion poll among your family, friends and neighbours.

At the end of the book, try answering these questions again to see if you still agree with the answers you give now.

SURVEY 1
What are *your* attitudes to crime and punishment?

① **Why are criminals punished?**
- Ⓐ Revenge: to satisfy the victims or their families
- Ⓑ To deter others who might commit the same crime
- Ⓒ To help the criminal reform
- Ⓓ To keep them off the streets

② **Which policies would do most to reduce crime?**
- Ⓐ Tough prison sentences
- Ⓑ More police on the streets
- Ⓒ Reducing unemployment
- Ⓓ Stricter family discipline

③ **Should capital punishment be brought back?**
- Ⓐ Yes, for all murders
- Ⓑ Yes, for some murders
- Ⓒ No

④ **Should other physical punishments, such as whipping, be used against criminals?**
- Ⓐ Yes
- Ⓑ No

⑤ **Should criminals who are convicted three times serve a life sentence for the third offence, whatever it is?**
- Ⓐ Yes
- Ⓑ No

⑥ **Should the police carry guns?**
- Ⓐ Yes, all the time
- Ⓑ Only in some areas
- Ⓒ No, unless there is a dangerous situation to deal with

⑦ **Which of these is the most important cause of crime?**
- Ⓐ Greed
- Ⓑ Poverty
- Ⓒ A criminal upbringing
- Ⓓ Weak character
- Ⓔ Other (Be specific)

SURVEY 2
What do you *know* about crime and punishment in Britain today?

This quiz is based on the British Crime Survey carried out by the government and published in January 1998. Your teacher can tell you the results.

Crime and punishment in Britain today...

1 Is crime
   Ⓐ increasing rapidly
   Ⓑ increasing a little
   Ⓒ decreasing?

2 Is violent crime
   Ⓐ 50%
   Ⓑ 35%
   Ⓒ 15%
   Ⓓ 6% of all crime?

3 What percentage of these criminals are sent to prison after being convicted?
   Ⓐ Rapists
   Ⓑ Burglars
   Ⓒ Muggers

4 What percentage of our laws deal with crimes as opposed to regulations about health, safety and education?
   Ⓐ 2%
   Ⓑ 10%
   Ⓒ 50%

5 How many murders were there in 1996?
   Ⓐ 2473
   Ⓑ 1542
   Ⓒ 680
   Ⓓ 286

6 Are men or women more likely to be attacked by a stranger?

7 Who is most likely to be mugged – a pensioner or a person under 29?

8 How would you punish this criminal?

A 23-year-old man has been convicted of breaking into a pensioner's home while the owner was out. He took a video recorder worth £150 and a TV which he left damaged nearby. He has previous convictions for burglary. What sentence do you think he was given?

   Ⓐ Prison
   Ⓑ Suspended prison sentence
   Ⓒ Fine
   Ⓓ PROBATION
   Ⓔ COMMUNITY SERVICE
   Ⓕ Tagging
   Ⓖ DISCHARGE

9 The police solve the majority of violent crimes. True or false?

■ TASK

Arguments about crime and punishment are all around you – in newspaper and magazine articles, TV features and local radio reports.

During this course, compile a crime and punishment datafile. It could be an electronic file on disk or a physical one that you keep in a shoe box or plastic file!

In your datafile you should collect all the stories, articles and sources you can regarding:

■ crime
■ punishment
■ policing.

You could work in groups and assign one research task to each group member to research.

At the end of the course this datafile will come in particularly useful. Your syllabus might also ask you to look at protest. If so, then collect a datafile of stories, articles or sources about protest and the treatment of protesters in Britain and in other countries.

What is a development study?

A DEVELOPMENT STUDY investigates a topic over a long period of time, looking at changes and continuities.

Periods

In this development study you will be examining how crime and punishment have changed over 2500 years. You will look at five different periods.

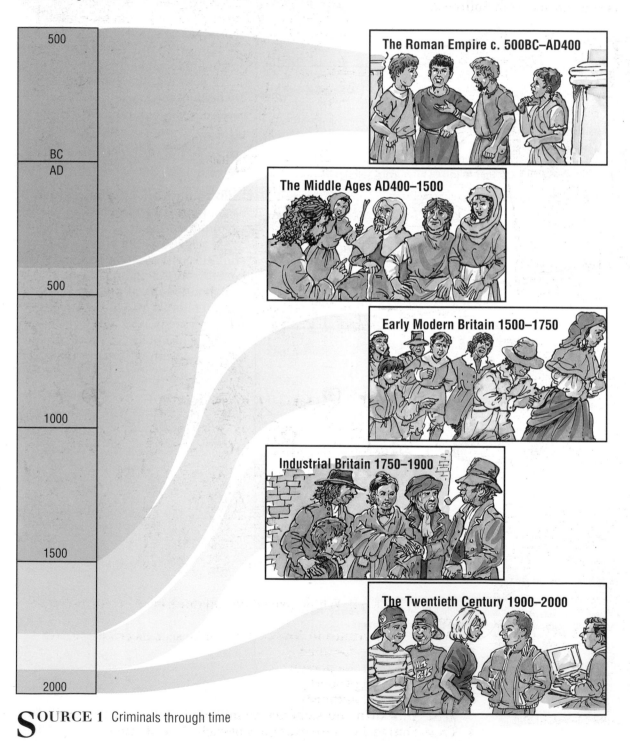

SOURCE 1 Criminals through time

Types of crime

There has been much continuity in types of crime. In each period minor theft has been by far the most common crime. Source 1 shows thieves from each period. Violent crimes such as murder have been a small, but very alarming, part of crime in all periods. However, in each period there have been many other kinds of crime as you can see from Source 2.

Pickpocketing

Riot

Highway robbery

Smuggling

Car theft

Witchcraft

POACHING

Theft and assault

SOURCE 2 Crimes through time

1. Look at Source 2. Which period do you think each crime comes from?
2. Which of the crimes in Source 2 would be seen as crimes today?
3. Crimes can be classified as:
   a) crimes against the person
   b) crimes against property
   c) crimes against authority
   Write your own one-sentence definition of each class of crime.
4. From Source 2 choose examples of each class of crime.

Types of punishment

In this course you will investigate how criminals were punished in each period. This has changed a lot over time. Source 3 shows punishments that have been used at different times.

5. Imagine each of the thieves in Source 1 has been found guilty of stealing goods worth a week's wages. How might they have been punished?

6. Which of the punishments in Source 3 are used in Britain today?

7. In which periods do you think each punishment in Source 3 might have been used?

SOURCE 3 Punishments through time

Reasons for punishment

In this course you are not only interested in what punishments were used at different times. You are also interested in **why** those punishments were used.

8. Look at the reasons for punishments in Source 4. Which would have made sense in each period in Source 1?
9. Which reasons explain the kinds of punishments we have today?

Policing and law enforcement

An important part of the history of crime and punishment is the story of how people tried to enforce the law and catch criminals. Source 5 shows you people whose job it was to stop crime in different periods.

10. Which of the law enforcers in Source 5 do you think belong to each period in Source 1?

Punishment should reform criminals, educate them, make them better people.

Punishment should prevent the criminal committing more crimes.

Punishment should be violent, bloody and public to frighten other people so they will not commit crimes.

Punishment should pay back the criminals for their crimes and avenge their victims — an eye for an eye, a life for a life.

Punishment of crimes against property should be harsh to protect the property of the rich and of landowners.

Punishment should help the criminal reach Heaven in the next life.

Punishment should be cheap.

SOURCE 4 Reasons for punishments

SOURCE 5 Law enforcers through time

Factors causing change and continuity

Through this development study you will be finding out how different factors have affected crime and punishment. Sometimes these factors caused change. Sometimes they prevented change. The table shows some of the most important factors you will come across.

11. Make your own large copy of this table. As you work through the development study use it to record examples of how each factor affected crime, punishment and policing.

Factors	Crime	Punishment	Policing
Government			
Religion			
Poverty			
Social change			
War			
Individuals			
Ideas and attitudes			
Others			

The big picture: crime and punishment over time

By the end of the course you are aiming to build up the big picture – to see how crime and punishment have changed over 2500 years. These are the key questions you will be interested in:

■ How have **types of crime** changed over time?
■ How have **punishments** changed over time?
■ **Who decided** laws and punishments in different periods?
■ How have the **ideas about crime and punishment** changed?
■ How have **methods of crime prevention and law enforcement** changed over time? How effective have they been?
■ Why has **protest** sometimes been allowed by the government, but at other times punished as a crime?

... and the close up: crime and punishment in each period

As well as the big picture, you will need to get close-ups through case studies from each period. You will think about:

■ What crime is being committed? Is it a new one or a continuing one?
■ What is the motivation of the person committing the crime?
■ Would it be regarded as a crime today? If so, would it be seen as a severe crime or a lesser crime?
■ How were offenders of different crimes punished? Compare the severity of punishments for a variety of crimes.
■ Why were they punished in these particular ways? What do the punishments tell us about the attitudes of people in that period?

1

CRIME AND PUNISHMENT IN THE ROMAN EMPIRE

The rational Romans: Why didn't they conquer crime?

THINK OF THE Romans and what images spring into your mind? Wealthy people living in comfortable villas with central heating? An efficient army? Rational thinkers and planners who built well-organised towns and straight roads that ran for hundreds of miles?

The Romans were an efficient and rational people. Their leaders were ruthless. You might think this would make them ideally suited for the task of conquering crime and yet they were not able to. This short chapter explores the Romans' approach to crime and punishment.

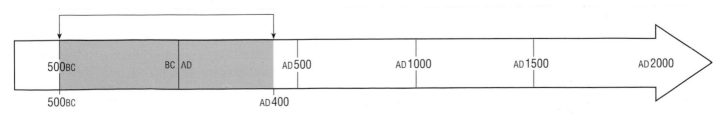

500BC   BC | AD   AD 500   AD 1000   AD 1500   AD 2000

500BC   AD 400

How did the Romans try to prevent crime?

Murder in Rome

'I had a brother called Lucius. One evening we dined with a friend and afterwards, as night fell, we left for home. When we reached the Forum, Caeso and a band of young troublemakers began to follow us. At first they laughed at us and insulted us. Rich young men who have drunk too much enjoy insulting the poor.

Lucius became angry and told Caeso what he thought of him. Caeso, who hated anyone standing up to him, ran up to Lucius and kicked him and beat him. I shouted for help and did all I could to defend my brother so Caeso turned on me, leaving Lucius lying dead in the street. He beat me until I too was motionless and speechless on the ground and he thought that I was dead.

Caeso went away rejoicing, as if he had conquered an enemy in war. As for us, some passers-by picked us up, covered in blood though we were, and carried us home, my brother being dead and I half-dead.'

■ TASK

That story was told by Marcus Volscius in about 460BC. The question is: 'what happened next?' Here are three alternative endings to this story. Think about what you already know about the Roman Empire. Do you think that the Romans had good laws? What sorts of punishments do you think that they used? Then decide which of these endings was the real one.

A
Caeso was arrested by the police and was imprisoned. At the trial Volscius repeated his evidence. Caeso was allowed to question him. The jury decided that Caeso was guilty and he was executed by being thrown off the highest cliff in Rome.

B
Caeso was taken by the police to the Emperor because he was a nobleman. The truth was decided by Caeso holding a red-hot iron bar. His hand was bandaged. Three days later Caeso's hand was still badly blistered. He was guilty. The sentence was death but because he was a nobleman he was sent into EXILE, many miles away from Rome.

C
Volscius had to gather the evidence against Caeso himself. He took the evidence to a judge who decided that there should be a trial. Volscius and Caeso hired lawyers and the case was heard by a jury of Roman citizens who decided both whether Caeso was guilty and what the punishment should be. He was guilty. The sentence was death but because he was a nobleman he was sent into exile, many miles away from Rome.

What did happen next?
The exercise on the next page will help you work that out for yourself – if your teacher hasn't told you already! On pages 12–13 you will find a bird's-eye view of the streets of Rome. In the illustration you can find scenes telling you about crime in Rome, about methods of preventing crime and about punishments. You should be able to work out from that what would have been the most likely ending.

■ TASK

1. Match descriptions 1–16 with the events shown in the picture on pages 12–13. All the descriptions are based on real events. Your teacher can give you a copy of the picture to mark.
2. Make three lists:
   a) crimes
   b) punishments
   c) methods of policing.
3. Using the information you have gathered from Source 1, suggest answers to questions a–e opposite. You will study these questions in more detail later, but you may already have a good idea of the answers.

a) Was there a great deal of crime or was it kept under control?
b) Were Roman laws simple or detailed, covering every aspect of life?
c) Did the Romans have a police force to investigate crimes and catch criminals?
d) Did the Romans have trials with lawyers, juries and evidence?
e) Did the Romans have a complex system of punishments with fines, prison sentences and executions?
4. Does this information help you decide which story ending opposite was most likely?

Descriptions

1. Anyone who deliberately burned down a building was bound, whipped and burned at the stake. If the fire had been accidental he had to repair the damage.

2. The VIGILES were fire-fighters who patrolled the city, especially at night to prevent fires breaking out and to arrest anyone who caused a fire.

3. The vigiles were also used to chase and capture runaway slaves.

4. Wealthy people travelled with a guard of slaves, especially at night, to protect them from robbery or attack.

5. City officials called AEDILES checked that householders kept the streets outside their homes clean.

6. Aediles inspected shops to check that, for example, the bread being sold was the correct weight.

7. Landlords could be prosecuted if their buildings fell down.

8. Windows were barred to prevent burglaries.

9. Prisoners of war were used as slave-labour on new buildings such as the Colosseum.

10. Murderers were sentenced to death in the arena, fighting as gladiators until everyone had been killed.

11. Noblemen sentenced to death were not executed. They were allowed to leave the city and go into exile outside the Roman Empire.

12. Theft of clothes was common while people were at the public baths.

13. Groups of youths, often from wealthy families, roamed the streets at night, looking for a fight.

14. Fighting between supporters of teams of chariot racers was common. The greatest rivals were the supporters of the Greens and the Blues.

15. Those who had been burgled had to try to stop the thief themselves, with the help of their friends, or collect evidence if they thought they knew who the thief was.

16. There were often protests against appalling housing, high taxes and food shortages which led to riots.

The streets of Rome

This picture shows various aspects of Roman crime, punishment and policing. Try to match the descriptions 1–16 on the previous page with the events shown in this picture.

SOURCE 1 An artist's reconstruction of Rome, c. AD75–80

So … how did the Romans tackle the problem of crime?

The Task on page 11 helped you discover for yourself the main methods Roman governments used to tackle crime – and what methods they did not try! This page gives you more detail about these so you can firm up your conclusions about Roman laws, policing, trials and punishments.

■ TASK

Correct or incorrect?

A. Roman laws covered every aspect of Roman life.

B. The Roman police force's main task was to investigate crimes.

C. Roman punishments were often violent.

1. Two of the statements A–C are correct. Read pages 14–17, then decide:
a) Which two are correct?
b) What evidence proves they are correct?
2. a) Rewrite the incorrect statement so it is correct.
b) What evidence proves your new statement is correct?
3. Copy and complete the chart below by listing one similarity and one difference between Roman methods and those used in Britain today.

	Similarities with Britain today	Differences from Britain today
Laws		
Police		
Trials		
Punishments		

4. Look back to page 10. Which story ending do you now think was the correct one?

Roman laws – from the Twelve Tables to Justinian

Roman laws dealt with every possible crime, from the ASSASSINATION of the Emperor to everyday crimes such as street theft and burglary – even selling under-weight bread in the market.

There were also laws designed to make Rome a better place to live in. Laws laid down that householders had to keep pavements and streets clean outside their homes. Dumping waste in the River Tiber (where drinking water came from) was illegal and so was starting fires – there was always great danger of fire spreading rapidly and destroying hundreds of homes.

The first recorded Roman laws were the Twelve Tables, which were written down around 450BC. Children learned them by heart at school. Over the next 1000 years many new laws were added as rulers tried to stop crimes. As the Roman Empire grew many of these laws spread to other parts of the Empire such as Britain.

The greatest Roman law code was the work of the Emperor Justinian in AD533. Justinian brought all the different laws together, simplifying and organising them into one system. This was a great achievement but Justinian's *Digest of the Roman Laws* was still one and a half times the length of the Bible!

Roman policing – the vigiles

In the early years of Rome there was no police force in the city. If a Roman was attacked or robbed, then he had to catch the criminal himself, with help from friends and neighbours. This often led to more violence.

In AD6 the Emperor Augustus set up forces to police Rome (see Source 2). However, the situation did not change much. Most were occupied with fire fighting. The core of the police were riot troops.

Roman trials and juries

Minor crime

Theft was regarded as a minor crime because it did not affect the ruler or the majority of the people. If you were burgled in Ancient Rome you could not expect any help from the people in Source 2. You had to find the criminal yourself. You had to collect the evidence. You had to summon the accused to the MAGISTRATE'S COURT.

At the court a judge was chosen – he was not a lawyer although he could take advice from lawyers – and both sides presented their evidence. Then the judge reached his decision.

Major crime

There was a different system for more serious cases such as murder. Cases were tried by magistrates with a jury. Anyone could bring a case to court for trial. When the suspect appeared, both sides gave evidence and the jury decided if he or she was guilty. The magistrate then decided the sentence.

Therefore there were three basic principles at work in Roman trials:

■ any Roman citizen could bring a case to court
■ the defendant was innocent until proved guilty
■ the defendant had the right to present evidence.

Praetorian Guard
The Emperor's household guards. They were used only in emergencies to protect the Emperor from riots.

Vigiles (7000 men)
Their main duty was preventing and putting out fires. On patrol at night, they tried to stop crimes or chased runaway slaves.

Urban cohorts (3000 soldiers)
Their main job was to keep order by stopping riots. They did not patrol the streets.

S**OURCE 2** Roman policing: the forces of law and order in Rome from c. AD6 to c. 400

What about Britain?

The Romans spread their ideas about law around their Empire. The Roman legal writer Ulpian said that the duty of the governor of a province such as Britain was: 'to see that the province is peaceful and quiet. This will not be difficult, if he acts diligently to search for wicked men and remove them from the province; he must search for temple-robbers, BRIGANDS, kidnappers, thieves and punish anyone committing these offences.'

So in Britain:

- Roman laws were introduced.
- Magistrates dealt with minor cases in local courts but all important cases were sent to the Governor's courts in the chief towns.
- The task of policing the villages and towns was taken on by the legionaries.
- Just as in the city of Rome itself, anyone who had been robbed in Roman Britain had to investigate and supply evidence himself. When the victim had the evidence, he took it to the local centurion who summoned the accused person to court to put his side of the case.

Roman punishments

The big idea of Roman punishment was to deter potential criminals by harsh punishment. How you were punished depended on who you were. Source 3 summarises punishments for different groups of people.

Prison sentences were not used as punishments. Prisons were only for people in debt or those awaiting trial or execution.

Over time, Roman punishments became more violent, including amputation of limbs, death by pouring molten lead down the convicted person's throat and CRUCIFIXION for those, like Christians and Jews, who refused to recognise the Emperor as a god. Anyone convicted of PATRICIDE (killing their father) was tied in a sack containing snakes and thrown into the river to drown.

Citizens (ordinary Romans)

Citizens could be put to death for serious crimes, such as

Arson   Attacking the Emperor

Robbing temples   Stealing farm animals

Punishment for lesser crimes, such as theft or selling under-weight bread, included

Whipping   Confiscation of property

Repaying the cost of goods

Nobles

Nobles could be sentenced to death for serious crimes but they were allowed to go into exile and avoid execution.

Slaves

All the slaves in a household were crucified if one of them murdered or tried to murder their master.

Slaves could give evidence at a trial, but only if they had been tortured first!

Legionaries

Legionaries who ran away in battle faced execution. One in every ten men from the legions that they ran away from was chosen by lot and also executed. This decimation was carried out ruthlessly.

SOURCE 3 Some Roman punishments

The most violent punishments were reserved for those who rebelled against the Empire.

After a revolt by thousands of runaway slaves led by Spartacus, 6000 captured prisoners were crucified and their bodies hung alongside the roads into Rome.

Christians who refused to worship Roman gods were executed, some by crucifixion, others were thrown to the beasts in the Colosseum.

After Jews rebelled against Rome, one million were killed and thousands more were transported as slaves to die in the games as gladiators.

1. Why were some crimes punished more harshly than others?
2. Why were some groups of people punished more harshly than others?

Why did they use these methods?

It will be clear from pages 10–16 that the Romans did *try* to solve the problem of crime. However, what may have struck you most is the things they did not do!

■ The government did little to improve the problems of poverty and overcrowded housing which played a part in causing crime.
■ The government did not establish an effective police force. The government did not see it as its job to catch criminals. Besides, a police force would have been too expensive. So if the criminals were not caught, then even the best trials and the most ferocious punishments could not work because they only dealt with a small proportion of criminals.

However, this is looking at events from our modern perspective. What the historian must try to do is see things from the perspective of the time.

Here is an imaginary scene. The leaders of Rome are debating how they will deal with crime.

3. How does this explain why Romans did not use police and prisons?
4. Why were executions common?

Was Rome riddled with crime?

SOURCE 1 GIVES one (wealthy) Roman's descriptions of crime in Ancient Rome. How accurate is this? How much crime was there really in Rome? Historians don't agree.

SOURCE 1 Three extracts from Juvenal's *Satire III*. Juvenal was a Roman author, writing c. AD100

"A

Although we try to hurry through the streets of Rome we are blocked by a surging crowd in front and by a dense mass of people pressing from behind. One man digs an elbow into me, another knocks me with a hard sedan-pole. One bangs a beam, another a wine-cask against my head. My legs are plastered in mud. Huge feet trample me from every side and a soldier plants his hobnails on my toes.

B
Nor are these the only terrors. When your house is shut, when bar and chain have made fast your shop and all is silent, you will be robbed by a burglar or perhaps a cut-throat will do for you with cold steel.

C
And now think of the perils of the night. A drunken bully, who has not killed that night, will get no sleep until he has been in a brawl. Yet however reckless the fellow may be, however full of wine and young blood, he avoids anyone with a large retinue of attendants, with torches and lamps in their hands. Yet he pays no respect to me, escorted home by the moon or by the scant light of a candle. The fellow stands up against me and bids me halt. Obey, I must. What else can you do when attacked by a madman stronger than yourself? Having been cuffed and pounded into a jelly I beg to be allowed home with a few teeth still in my head. **"**

SOURCE 2 T. W. Africa, 'Urban Violence in Imperial Rome', *Journal of Interdisciplinary Studies*, 1971

" *Crime was commonplace ... the city was plagued with housebreakers, pickpockets, petty thieves and muggers.* **"**

SOURCE 3 R. MacMullen, *Enemies of the Roman Order*, 1967

" *... crime posed no insuperable problem ... On the whole we hear little of people attacked or of houses broken into in the accounts of the time.* **"**

Why can historians have such different views? The most important reason is that there are **no** statistics to tell us about Roman crime. We have no idea how many crimes were committed each year or whether the numbers of crimes increased or decreased over the years.

Without statistics we have to depend on the descriptions of writers like Juvenal (Source 1). Juvenal's Rome is seething with dangers. But should we believe him?

Reasons why we should believe Juvenal
Juvenal did live in Rome and described the life around him. There must have been some truth in his descriptions or no one would have listened to his ideas.

Reasons why we should not believe Juvenal
Juvenal thought the government needed reforming and wanted a return to the 'good old days' which he believed had been more peaceful. Therefore he exaggerated the amount of crime to persuade his readers to agree with him.

Other writers tell us about spectacular and unusual crimes; for example, in AD80 Rome was plagued by a gang of contract killers who murdered victims for money, using poisoned needles. But as for everyday crime, we have very little evidence to go on. People certainly feared crime, but they have feared it in every period. Through this course you will see that people's fear of crime often exceeds the actual amount of crime.

What we can say is that conditions in Rome were probably ideal for crime.

- Rome was the biggest city of its day. Up to one million people were crammed tightly into the teeming, bustling metropolis. There was plenty of opportunity for crime.
- The government did not see it as its job to prevent or deal with minor crimes, so no effective police force was set up to deal with everyday crimes. This made it more likely that criminals would get away with crime.
- In Rome there were extremes of wealth alongside extremes of poverty. Human nature does not change and there will always be those who are greedy or desperate, or jealous enough to steal from others. Food shortages (as a result of bad harvests) sometimes drove normally law-abiding people to crime to help their families.

■ TASK

Work in pairs.

Using pages 9–19 you have to prepare a leaflet giving a guide to Roman crime and punishment for someone who is coming to live in Rome for the first time. You will need to tell them:

- how much of a problem crime is in Rome – what to watch out for or avoid
- how criminals are caught and tried – you could give them an example to help make your point
- how criminals are punished – and why they are punished in this way.

SOURCE 4 This wall painting shows the fighting that broke out at the gladiatorial games in AD59. The Roman historian, Tacitus, described the fighting in *The Annals of Imperial Rome*

66 *In AD59 there was a serious fight between the people of two Roman towns, Nuceria and Pompeii. It began at a gladiatorial show. Both sides shouted taunts at each other, then the abuse led to stone throwing and then swords were drawn. The people of Pompeii, where the show was held, came off better. Many Nucerians were wounded. Many died, leaving bereaved parents and children.* 99

This illustration is one of the few pictures of violence from this period, but sports hooliganism like this was also common in Rome itself, especially between the supporters of the top chariot-racing teams, the Greens and the Blues.

Summary: Crime and punishment in the Roman Empire

YOU WILL FIND a summary at the end of most of the chapters in this book. Each one follows a similar pattern so you can look for changes and continuities across time.

Types of crime

The Romans had to tackle a wide range of crimes because they made such a wide range of laws. Their laws dealt with all levels of crime from trying to assassinate the Emperor to selling under-weight bread in the market. They seem to have had all the kinds of crimes that later societies knew, for example: murder, ARSON and theft. We do not know which crimes were the most common because there are no records, but if the pattern of crime was similar to later times, then the most common crime would have been petty theft, with only a minority of crimes being violent. The Romans also had to deal with the crime of rebellion as a result of having conquered such a large empire.

Causes of crime in Ancient Rome

The pictures below show some of the reasons why crime was a problem in Rome and the Roman Empire.

1. List the causes of crime shown here.
2. Which of these reasons still cause crime today?

Obstacles to crime!
Solving the problems of crime in Ancient Rome

This is another illustration that you will have to get used to! You will find one at the end of Chapters 2, 4 and 7. You can compare these illustrations and get an overview of the whole topic. These 'obstacle courses' illustrate the main theme of the book: How did people in each period try to solve the problem of crime?

Different methods have been used at different times and here you can see the Roman methods. The barriers are the methods the Romans tried to use to prevent crime – methods of catching criminals, trials and punishments. As you can see, these methods were not successful because criminals were still able to steal through and commit their crimes.

3. Which methods did the Romans rely on most to stop crime?
4. Why did the Romans choose these methods rather than others?
5. The next chapter deals with the Middle Ages. During the Middle Ages a more thorough system of courts developed. Do you expect this barrier to have a major impact on crime?

Attitudes to crime and punishment

Roman attitudes can be summarised like this:

- governments regarded riots and rebellions as the most serious crimes
- laws and courts were needed to protect people against criminals
- trials had to be conducted properly so that the DEFENDANT was given a fair trial
- governments could not afford to pay for a detective police force or prisons so people were expected to collect evidence and bring cases to court themselves
- punishments were made harsh in an attempt to deter criminals.

What methods did they use to tackle crime in Ancient Rome?

The table below summarises the methods the Romans used to try to prevent crime.

6. What were the main weaknesses in Rome's fight against crime?
7. Which of these methods were most likely to prevent crime?

Rome and the future

There were three key principles of Roman law that are still part of the British legal system today:

- defendants must know the charges against them
- both accuser and defendant must come to the court
- defendants must have the chance to give their evidence to defend themselves.

■ TASK

Write an essay with the title: 'Why didn't the Romans conquer crime?'. You can get a sheet from your teacher to help you plan the essay.

		What did they do?
Laws		Laws were made by the Emperor and the Senate. They were written down in detail, often updated and covered all aspects of crime.
Policing		There was no effective police force in Rome but the Emperor's guard protected the Emperor and stopped riots. The army acted as a police force in the provinces of the Empire.
Trials		Victims of crime had to collect evidence and bring the accused to court. They could hire trained lawyers if they could afford them. Juries decided serious cases; judges decided less serious ones.
Punishments		Punishments were harsh and often violent. Executions were common although noblemen were allowed to go into exile to escape execution. Prisons were not used except for debtors.

2 CRIME AND PUNISHMENT 400–1500

• • • • • • • • • • • • • • •

The murderous Middle Ages: Did medieval kings really try to solve the problem of crime?

BY AD400 ROME was losing control of her Empire. The legions withdrew from Britain, Spain and the German frontiers to defend Rome from attacks. The Romans called the attackers barbarians because they had never adopted Roman ways of life or laws. Some of them, the Angles and Saxons from northern Europe, settled in Britain and created their own small kingdoms.

This was the beginning of the period known as the Middle Ages. Most films and TV programmes we see about the Middle Ages show us a caricature of the period: bloody punishments, battles and violence – all this driven by kings and noblemen whose only motives were greed and power (as in cartoon **a**). It's easy to think that medieval kings were more interested in breaking laws than making laws or catching and punishing criminals. This chapter challenges that stereotype (as in cartoon **b**).

■ **Part 2.1** investigates the early Middle Ages: 400–1100. **Was Saxon justice harsh and superstitious?**
■ **Part 2.2** investigates the later Middle Ages: 1100–1500. **Did kings improve the legal system in the later Middle Ages?**

a

> I need money. Go and steal some for me. And if you come back with nothing, I'll chop off your head.

b

> This man must have a fair trial. Otherwise my kingdom will be in chaos.

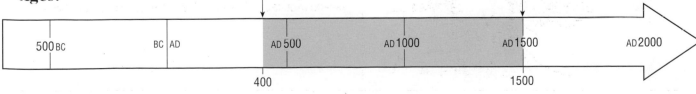

500 BC   BC AD   AD 500   AD 1000   AD 1500   AD 2000

400   1500

The main developments: 400–1500

THIS SPREAD SUMMARISES the main developments in crime and punishment that you will be studying in more detail in this chapter.

Down the side of each page you can see the main features of crime and punishment at each end of the Middle Ages.

The Saxon period 400–1100

Crime

Most crime was theft of money, food and belongings, usually of low value. Violent crimes were a small minority of cases.

Policing

The victims of crime were expected to find the criminal themselves, calling out fellow-villagers to chase criminals (the HUE AND CRY). Adult men were grouped into tens called TITHINGS. If one of them broke the law the others had to bring him to court.

Punishments

Criminals paid compensation to their victims. This was called a WERGILD – the blood price. By 1100 executions and other physical punishments ordered by the government were more common.

Trials

Juries of local people decided whether the accused was innocent or guilty. If they could not decide then the accused underwent TRIAL BY ORDEAL where God decided whether he or she was guilty. A series of courts developed, from royal courts and shire courts held twice a year to deal with serious cases to village or manor courts held by every landowner.

SOURCE 1 The execution of the Duke of Somerset in 1471. Somerset and others had rebelled against King Edward IV but were beaten in battle. Edward IV showed no mercy because he wanted to deter others from rebelling

SOURCE 2 The execution of rebels in 1450. Thousands of people had gathered in Kent protesting about poor government, military defeats in France and lawlessness. The rebels looted London until driven out by the Londoners. Most rebels were pardoned but some were executed on the charge of TREASON for daring to criticise the King

■ TASK

1. Compare the descriptions of crime, policing, trials and punishments, in the Saxon period and the later Middle Ages. Which of the four areas saw:
   a) the most continuity
   b) the most change?
2. Does the information on these two pages suggest that medieval kings were concerned about the problem of crime?
3. Make a list of anything you would like to know about or don't understand about crime and punishment in the Middle Ages. As you work through this chapter see if you can find the answers.

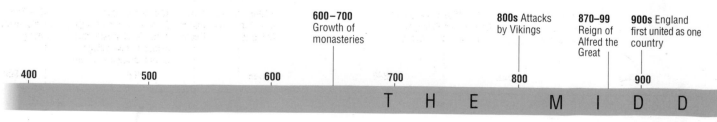

600–700 Growth of monasteries

800s Attacks by Vikings

870–99 Reign of Alfred the Great

900s England first united as one country

400 500 600 700 800 900

T H E   M I D D

SOURCE 3 From the *Flowers of History*, a fourteenth-century chronicle written in the south of England. This extract describes the execution of William Wallace in August 1305. Wallace fought for ten years against Edward I of England, winning the Battle of Stirling and inspiring widespread Scottish resistance to Edward's conquest

" ... William Wallace was condemned to a most cruel but justly deserved death. He was drawn through the streets of London at the tails of horses until he reached a gallows of unusual height, especially prepared for him. There he was hung, taken down while still alive and then mutilated, his bowels torn out and burned in a fire. His head was then cut off, his body divided into four and sent to four parts of Scotland. Behold the end of the merciless man who himself perishes without mercy. "

1. a) What different methods of execution were used in Sources 1 and 2?
b) Why do you think different methods were used in Sources 1 and 2?
2. Why do you think Wallace was punished so cruelly?
3. Why was the method of execution in Source 4 different from the others?

SOURCE 4 The execution of a HERETIC in the fifteenth century. Heretics refused to believe in the official beliefs of the Catholic Church, the only Christian religion at the time. Heretics were burned so that their bodies would be utterly destroyed, leaving nothing for the day when God would resurrect Christian believers

The later Middle Ages 1100–1500

Crime

Most crime was theft of money, food and belongings, usually of low value. Violent crimes were a small minority of cases.

Policing

The hue and cry and tithings were still used. Other government officials such as the county CORONER and SHERIFF played a leading role in investigating some crimes. Leading villagers were appointed as CONSTABLES to help keep order.

Punishments
Executions and other physical punishments were still the most common punishments, along with fines in the manor courts. There were local prisons but only for holding prisoners awaiting trial. Prison sentences were not used as a punishment.

Trials
Juries still decided cases. Trial by ordeal was no longer used after around 1200. The system of courts developed further. From the 1100s royal judges travelled around the country dealing with serious cases. County courts were held by Justices of the Peace who were the leading local landowners. Each manor still had its own court held by the local lord, often once a week.

1066 The Norman Conquest	**1100–1200s** The age of Cathedral building and growth of universities		**1300s** Stories of Robin Hood being told	**1349** Black Death	**1381** Great Revolt. Combined with the effects of the Black Death, this helped to give village labourers their freedom	**1470s** The development of printing

1000	1100	1200	1300	1400	1500

L E   A G E S

Was Saxon justice harsh and superstitious?

Who made the laws in Saxon England?

Between AD500 and 1100 England changed from being a mass of small kingdoms into one united country, as you can see in Source 1. During these centuries, kings played a vital part in every aspect of government and especially in crime and punishment. The main roles of the king are summarised in the notes around Source 2.

1. According to the notes around Source 2:
a) Who made the laws in Saxon England?
b) Were the same laws used throughout the country?
c) Did Saxon laws try to prevent violence?
2. What did the illustrator of Source 2 think was an important part of the king's work?

SOURCE 1 Maps of the Anglo-Saxon kingdoms, c. 600 and Norman England, c. 1100

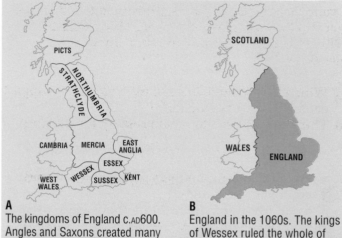

A
The kingdoms of England c.AD600. Angles and Saxons created many small kingdoms, but gradually strong warrior kings created the large kingdoms you can see here. Each kingdom had its own laws and so did the many kingdoms that made up Scotland and Wales.

B
England in the 1060s. The kings of Wessex ruled the whole of England, making the country united for the first time since the Romans had left. When the Normans conquered England in 1066 they took over a united country with one set of laws for the whole country.

1. A king's most important tasks were to defend his country from attacks and to make sure his laws were obeyed.

2. Laws were made by kings after consulting nobles and bishops. At first, laws were learned and remembered but soon they were written down which made them more official and powerful.

3. The king's laws had two main aims:
a) to protect landowners' property from damage or theft
b) to protect people from violence, although FREEMEN got more protection than slaves.

SOURCE 2 A Saxon king and his advisers. The advisers may be his councillors or it may be a court of justice. This illustration is from an eleventh-century manuscript

Saxon laws

■ TASK

Sources 3 and 4 are extracts from laws made by two Saxon kings, Ethelbert and Alfred the Great.

One important word used in the sources is *wergild*, which means blood price. A wergild was the price that a guilty person had to pay as punishment for a crime. You will find out more about wergilds on page 28.

Read through the laws and then answer these questions.

1. Which laws would you use as evidence to support each of these statements?
a) The law was used to create respect for the king.
b) An important part of the king's work was to keep the peace.
c) Religion played an important part in Saxon England.
2. Can you learn anything else from the laws in Sources 3 and 4?
3. Which of these statements fits your conclusions best? Explain why.
a) Saxon laws were harsher and more primitive than I expected.
b) Saxon laws were fairer and more complex than I expected.

SOURCE 3 The Laws of Ethelbert, King of Kent, c. 603

❝ 1. *If anyone steals the property of God and the Church he is to pay twelve-fold compensation.*
4. *If a freeman steals from the king he is to repay nine-fold.*
9. *If a freeman steals from a freeman he is to pay three-fold.*
17. *If a man is the first to force his way into another man's homestead he is to pay 6 shillings compensation; he who enters next is to pay 3 shillings; each afterwards is to pay a shilling.*
18. *If anyone provides a man with weapons, when a quarrel has arisen, and yet no injury results he is to pay 6 shillings compensation.*
20. *If however a man is killed, the lender of the weapon is to pay 20 shillings compensation.*
21. *If anyone kills a man, he is to pay as an ordinary wergild 100 shillings.*
22. *If anyone kills a man he is to pay 20 shillings at the open grave and the whole wergild within 40 days.*
23. *If the slayer departs from the land, his kinsmen are to pay half the wergild.*
39. *If the hearing of either ear is destroyed by violence, 25 shillings shall be paid as compensation.*
40. *If an ear is struck off, 12 shillings shall be paid as compensation.*
41. *If an ear is pierced, 3 shillings shall be paid as compensation.*
42. *If an ear is lacerated, 6 shillings shall be paid as compensation.* ❞

SOURCE 4 The Laws of King Alfred the Great, 871–899

❝ 6. *If anyone steals anything in church he is to pay the normal fine and then have his hand struck off.*
9. *If a pregnant woman is murdered, the killer is to pay the full wergild for the woman and half for the child.*
13. *If at work one man accidentally kills another by letting a tree fall on him, the tree is to be given to the dead man's kinsmen.*
14. *If anyone is born dumb or deaf so that he cannot deny or confess sins then his father is to pay compensation for his crimes.*
19. *If anyone lends his weapon to another so that he may kill a man he is to pay a third of the wergild.*
23. *If a dog bites or tears a man to death the owner is to pay 6 shillings for the first offence, on a second occasion 12 shillings.*
38. *If anyone fights in the presence of the king's officials he is to pay wergild and also 120 shillings to the official as a fine.*
40. *If anyone neglects the rules of the Church in Lent he is to pay 120 shillings.*
43. *These days are to be given to all free men, but not to slaves or unfree labourers: 12 days at Christmas, and the day on which Christ overcame the Devil [15 February] and the anniversary of St Gregory and seven days at Easter and seven days after, one day at the feast of St Peter, St Paul and in harvest time the whole week before the feast of St Mary and one day at the feast of All Saints.* ❞

Saxon punishments

The blood feud

Early Saxon kings allowed the victims of crimes to punish the criminals themselves. If someone was murdered, the family had the right to track down and kill the murderer. This right was known as the BLOOD FEUD. There were two problems about this legal violence. Firstly, it often led to even more violence as families and their friends banded together to take revenge for an attack and then this led to another attack. Secondly, it did not protect people who did not want to use violence against those who had harmed them.

Wergilds or blood price

Later kings abolished the blood feud and introduced money fines called wergilds for many crimes including some murders. The victims received compensation in money. The level of punishment was decided by the king, through his laws. This made further violence much less likely. Saxon laws were extremely detailed about the fines that criminals had to pay (see Source 5). The wergild for killing a nobleman was 300 shillings and the wergild for killing a freeman was 100 shillings. If the criminal could not afford to pay the fine, then he or she was sent into slavery.

Capital punishment and physical punishment

However, not all crimes were punished by fines. Some serious crimes carried the death penalty – treason against the king, arson and betraying your lord. Reoffenders were also punished harshly if they were caught. Punishments for regular offenders included mutilation, for example cutting off a hand, ear or nose or 'putting out' the eyes.

Outlaws

An accused person who did not come to court was OUTLAWED. This meant he no longer had the protection of the law and could be killed by anyone as punishment.

Custody

SOURCE 6 This prison at Bradford-on-Avon in Wiltshire is one of the earliest surviving in Britain. Prisons such as this were only used for holding accused people before trial. Imprisonment was rarely used as a punishment because it was expensive. Gaolers would have to be paid and criminals would have to be fed. This was impossible at a time when kings only collected taxes for wars or to pay for other out of the ordinary events

3. Why were many crimes punished by fines?
4. Which crimes and criminals were punished with violence?
5. Why was imprisonment rarely used?
6. Look at Source 5. What fines should be paid for the other wounds?
7. Would you describe Saxon punishments as harsh or lenient? Explain the reasons for your answer.

mouth or eye disfigured – ?

hearing of either ear destroyed – 25 shillings

chin bone smashed – ?

teeth – ?

belly wounded – 12 shillings

rib broken – ?

broken arm – 6 shillings

fingers – ?

thigh broken – 12 shillings

foot struck off – 50 shillings

big toe struck off – ?

eye knocked out – 50 shillings

ear struck off – ?

nose lacerated – 6 shillings

disabled shoulder – ?

thumb struck off – 20 shillings

SOURCE 5 Wergild or blood price for a variety of wounds, taken from the laws of King Ethelbert of Kent in 603

Law enforcement: keeping the peace and catching criminals

There was no police force in Saxon England. In the early Saxon kingdoms people relied on their friends and families to help them catch thieves or other wrongdoers.

Tithings

By the tenth century, kings had set up a different kind of self-help system – known as a tithing. A tithing was a group of ten people. All males over the age of twelve had to belong to a tithing. This meant that they were responsible for each other's behaviour. If a member of the tithing broke the law, the others had to bring him to court or pay the compensation fine to the victim.

8. Who belonged to tithings?

9. How were tithings supposed to stop crimes?

10. Tithings were used to stop crimes or catch criminals. What do you think were:
a) the strengths
b) the weaknesses
   of the tithing system?

Trial by jury

In a modern trial there are lawyers to prosecute and defend, and jury members must have no prior knowledge of the accused.

By contrast, at a Saxon trial there were no lawyers to prosecute or defend the accused person. The accuser was the person who claimed to be the victim of the crime. The jury was also different. It was made up of men from the area who probably knew both the accuser and the accused.

Both the accused and the accuser told their version of events to the jury. It was then up to the jury to decide who was telling the truth. If there was no clear evidence (such as a witness having seen the crime take place) they used their experience of the people concerned. If the jury felt the accuser was more honest in general than the accused, they swore an oath that the accused was guilty. The jury's oath-taking was called COMPURGATION.

11. List two differences between a Saxon trial and a trial today.

12. Look at Source 8. Which courts:
a) did villagers attend most frequently?
b) dealt with the most serious crimes?
c) organised the local system of peace-keeping?

Now you are twelve you must take on your responsibilities to protect the peace of our village.

He looks like a good lad. We should be able to rely on him.

Yes, unlike someone else I could name. He's going to cause trouble soon if we don't keep a close eye on him.

SOURCE 7 Key features of a tithing: all members could be held responsible if one of them committed a crime

SOURCE 8 Saxon courts. As Saxon kings built up stronger control over the whole country they developed a series of courts which dealt with different kinds of case.

The royal courts – *here the king decided cases involving his lords and other serious crimes.*

Shire courts – *these were held in every shire or county and met twice a year to deal with serious cases such as murder. All landowners and a representative from each village had to attend the shire court. Local noblemen acted as the judges.*

Hundred courts – *all freemen had to attend these local courts which met every month. This was where they joined tithings and swore to keep the peace. The hundred courts dealt with less serious cases.*

Private courts – *were held by all landowners in their own villages or manors. The landowner was the judge. These courts dealt with people who had broken local rules, such as workers who had not done enough work on the lord's land or slaves who had tried to run away.*

Trial by ordeal

There were times when the jury members could not agree with each other. This was usually in cases of theft or murder when there was no witness.

Trial by ordeal was the solution to this problem. A twelfth-century law said that 'the ordeal of hot iron is not to be permitted except where the naked truth cannot otherwise be explored.' Then God was asked to decide whether the accused person was guilty and the accused had to undergo trial by ordeal. Human beings might not know the truth but God certainly would!

There were different kinds of trial by ordeal but, whichever one was used, a careful religious ritual was followed.

The person taking the ordeal had to fast for three days beforehand and hear mass in the church.

The ordeals, except trial by cold water, took place *inside* the church.

As the ordeal by hot iron began the priest said these words: 'If you are innocent of this charge you may confidently receive this iron in your hand and the Lord, the just judge, will free you, just as he snatched the three children from the burning fire.'

Trial by hot iron

This was usually taken by women. The accused had to carry a piece of red-hot iron for three metres. Her hand was then bandaged and unwrapped three days later. If the wound was healing cleanly without festering everyone would know that God was saying she was innocent. But if the wound was not healing cleanly God was saying she was guilty.

Trial by hot water

This was usually taken by men. The accused put his hand into boiling water to pick up an object and lift it out. This might not be easy. One of the earliest accounts of this ordeal describes how the accused 'plunged his right hand into the cauldron. In the bubbling it was not easy for him to grasp the little ring but at last he drew it out.'

The arm was then bandaged. Three days later the bandage was taken off. Again, the person was innocent if the wound was healing cleanly.

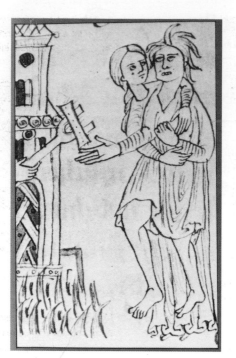

SOURCE 9 *Two medieval illustrations of trial by ordeal*

Trial by cold water

This was also usually taken by men. People believed that water was pure and so would reveal the truth. The accused was lowered into the water (a river or pond as close to the church as possible) on the end of a rope. The rope was knotted above the waist. If the person sank and the knot went below the surface then he was innocent because the 'pure' water had been willing to let this innocent person beneath its surface. However, if he and the knot floated then they believed the water was rejecting him because he was guilty.

Trial by consecrated bread

This was taken by priests. The priest first had to pray, asking that he be choked by the bread if he lied. Then he had to eat a piece of consecrated bread. If he choked then he was guilty because God would not let a sinner eat consecrated bread. This might seem a much more lenient ordeal but people believed that God was sure to punish a priest who lied and so it was seen as the most effective of all ordeals.

13. What ordeals are shown in Source 9?
14. When was trial by ordeal used?
15. Trial by ordeal could not have decided for certain whether the accused was guilty. Why do you think the Saxons used trial by ordeal?
16. Do you think Saxon trials were based on logic or superstition? Give reasons for your answer.

1. If a member of a tithing committed a crime, the others had to deliver him to court to be tried or pay compensation for his crimes.

2. The jury in a Saxon court was made up of local people who knew the accuser and the accused. Both put their side of the story before the jury.

3. Any witnesses also had to appear before the jury. If there were no witnesses, the jury had to decide guilt or innocence based on their own knowledge of the people involved. If the jury could not decide, the accused had to undergo trial by ordeal.

SOURCE 10 Saxon justice: the process leading to trial by **S**ordeal

4. Most trials by ordeal took place inside a church. The local priest had to supervise each trial. In our example the accused had to plunge his hand into boiling water to lift out an object.

5. The hand of the accused was bandaged and left for three days. Then the bandages were taken off. If the wound was healing cleanly it was taken as a sign from God that the person was innocent. If the wound was festering, the person was found guilty and sentenced to an appropriate punishment.

■ TASK

Imagine you have been asked to select items for a Saxon time capsule which will show future centuries what Saxon justice was really like. You may choose items of evidence which show that Saxon justice was harsh and superstitious. You might choose items which show the opposite.

You can only select three items. What will you select and why?

List your items and for each one, explain what it tells you about Saxon justice. You could choose documents, illustrations or any other piece of information.

Did the Norman Conquest make the laws harsher?

IN 1066 SAXON England was conquered by William of Normandy. Over the next ten years English lords lost their lands to Normans. Castles were built to terrorise the English. When William died in 1087 an English monk wrote his assessment of William, in the *Anglo-Saxon Chronicle*. He began:

'A hard man he was, and fierce; no man dared go against his will ... '

This page gives you the rest of that monk's assessment of William but it has been turned into the form of an interview, as if the monk had been giving his views to a newspaper reporter.

How did William treat the English?

He destroyed people's homes to make way for new castles to be built. Many people have suffered. The English naturally tried to fight back against the conquerors. They laid ambushes and sometimes killed Normans. William ordered that if any Norman was murdered all the people in the region must join together to pay a fine. It was called the murdrum fine.

Did he introduce new laws?

William decided to keep the laws of the English kings. After all, he wished to be seen as the true heir of Edward the Confessor and so he wanted to show that he respected the old laws. He also made new laws including the hated forest laws. Trees could not be cut down for fuel or for building. People in the forests were forbidden to own dogs or bows and arrows. Even if deer ate their crops, they could not do anything because the punishment for killing a deer was to be blinded. This King William loved the stags as if he were their father.

How did he treat rebels?

Rebels were executed without mercy. William even put his own brother, Bishop Odo of Bayeux, in prison. In the north, corpses were left rotting in the houses and fields after William's army had devastated the region. Refugees called at our monasteries as far south as Worcester. The land in the north was eerily silent because so many people had been killed or were in hiding.

Did William make the English more law-abiding?

In some ways he did. It is said that a man with a chest full of gold could travel through the kingdom untroubled by thieves or outlaws. No man dared kill another, even if he had done much evil to him. William was such a harsh, efficient ruler that no one dared to go against his orders or laws. The country is probably more peaceful but it is not because the English loved William. They feared him.

SOURCE 1 William faced many rebellions, especially in 1069–70 when there were risings in the south-west, on the Welsh border, in East Anglia and in the north. William responded by destroying houses and livestock throughout the north, a punishment meant to stop any further rebellions

Burglary

Constable

Court

Fines

Evidence

Gaols

Justice

Prison

Police

Arrest

SOURCE 2 One change resulting from the Norman Conquest was the introduction of many French words and others from Latin into the English language. These words included many to do with the law

How did he punish law-breakers?

Harshly. William believed that crimes were committed against the king's peace rather than against other people. So he punished people for daring to break his peace. He used the death penalty for serious crimes and fines for lesser crimes. William ordered that the fines should be paid to the king's officials instead of to the victims as compensation.

Did he change the trial by ordeal?

No, he was a religious man and believed that God decides who is guilty. He introduced trial by combat – the accused fights his accuser until one is killed or beaten. God has decided that the loser is guilty and then he is hanged.

1. Complete a table like the one below.
a) Decide whether laws changed, stayed the same or had some changes and some continuities. Then tick column A, B or C.
b) In column D write down the evidence from the interview which supports your answer.
c) Repeat this for the other three topics.

	A Change after 1066	B Continuity after 1066	C Change & continuity	D Evidence for choice
Laws				
Amount of crime				
Punishment				
Trials				

2. Why do you think that William did not change the laws or punishments completely?

Summary: The early Middle Ages

Laws

- Saxon kings made laws on a wide range of issues.
- The Normans kept the Saxon laws but added new laws such as the forest laws.
- The Normans enforced laws more harshly than the Saxons to prevent or punish rebellions.

Policing

- There was no police force paid for by the king.
- Tithings were organised. Members had to bring to court any other member of the tithing who was accused of a crime. If they failed to do so all members of the tithing had to pay compensation.

Trials

- Juries decided whether the accused was guilty.
- Trial by ordeal was used when the jury could not reach a decision. God decided if the accused was guilty.
- There was a variety of types of ordeal. The Normans kept trial by ordeal, but also introduced trial by combat.
- By 1100 a series of courts had developed. Royal courts and shire courts met twice a year to deal with serious cases. Village or manor courts were held weekly by every landowner.

Punishments

- In the early Saxon period a wergild (blood price) was paid to the victim of crime.
- Serious crimes were punished by death and frequent reoffenders were mutilated or executed.
- Anyone who refused to attend court was outlawed.
- Norman kings believed that any crime was an insult to the king's peace. Therefore, the system of wergild ended and was replaced by punishments that were designed to emphasise the power of the king, rather than to give compensation to the victim. The Normans executed rebels, and destroyed crops, animals and villages to prevent rebellion.

REVIEW TASK

Was Saxon and Norman justice harsh and superstitious?

These tasks will help you summarise your work on pages 26–33.

1. a) Make a list of the evidence showing that kings tried to protect their people from crime.
   b) 'One of the main duties of a king was to protect his people from law-breakers.' Does your list prove that this statement is true or untrue?
2. Copy and complete a table like the one opposite. Use the summary on this page or go back to the details on pages 24–33. Fill in the empty column with evidence to support each of the descriptions of Saxon and Norman justice.

Saxon and Norman justice was:	Evidence
Harsh	
Fair	
Superstitious	
Intelligent	

3. Use your completed table to write an essay with the title: 'Was Saxon and Norman justice harsh and superstitious?'. You can get a sheet from your teacher to help you.

THROUGHOUT THE MIDDLE AGES a king's main duties were to defend his country from enemies and to defend his people from law-breakers. Between 1100 and 1500 kings took an even closer interest in laws, crimes and punishments. They made important changes to the legal system which were meant to make people more law-abiding and to make the system of catching and punishing criminals more effective. Over the next four pages you will examine those changes through a real murder from the period. So let's start with the crime.

Murder in a medieval village

JOHN THE SHEPHERD'S house looked empty. Roger Ryet had already walked past it once, glancing in through the open shutter, just out of curiosity. There wasn't much to see – a well-swept floor, a couple of benches, a table. Hanging over one of the benches was a piece of cloth. 'Nice piece of cloth,' thought Roger, 'it'll make a good tunic.' He carried on, hopeful that today he would get work on the lord's land and be able to buy a new tunic.

Thief!

the street. The cloth was in arm's reach through the shutter. Roger reached in, grabbed the cloth and started to run away.

'Thief!' shouted a man's voice. Roger reeled with shock. Where had the man come from? He'd been sure there was no one about.

The man blocked Roger's path; a woman was running up behind him. Roger hesitated, gripping the cloth tightly. He had to move. He had to get away. In his other hand he held his knife. He moved forwards, desperate to escape. Seconds later, John the Shepherd lay dead. His wife, Isabel, knelt screaming by his side.

Roger did not find work. In this village and those all around, there were many men clamouring for work. By the time he arrived, others were already turning away disappointed. Roger cursed, knowing how desperately he needed money. His own scrap of land did not produce enough food to live on.

Now Roger was walking back past John the Shepherd's house again. The shutter still stood open, the cloth still lay on the bench. There was no one in

■ TASK

This is a true story from Norfolk in the early 1300s. Your first task is to decide 'what happened next', after John the Shepherd was killed.

In the box opposite you can see the possible ways Roger Ryet might have been caught, put on trial and punished. Only some of them are correct. Use some of these phrases to write a short paragraph saying what you think happened to Roger next. Pages 36–38 will tell you whether you were right.

What happened next?

When the King's judges arrived in Norfolk, Roger went before the court.

Roger had to face trial by ordeal, plunging his arm into boiling water.

Roger was hanged by order of the judges.

The local men chased Roger in the hue and cry, led by the local constable.

A message was sent to the local sheriff who took Roger off to prison.

The Norfolk coroner held an enquiry into the death and his jury decided that there was enough evidence to accuse Roger in court.

Roger paid Isabel the wergild (blood price) of 200 shillings for her man.

Catching Roger Ryet

The hue and cry

Roger had stolen a piece of cloth and stabbed John the Shepherd in front of John's wife, Isabel. Roger ran away. Isabel's shouts would have raised the hue and cry. Every villager would join the hunt for the murderer. If the villagers ignored the hue and cry, then the whole village would be fined a large sum of money by a court.

Since Roger was well known in the village and there were witnesses to the crime Roger was likely to be caught, especially if the villagers joined the hue quickly. However, if he could run fast or knew somewhere good to hide he might get away.

The constable

The hue and cry would be led by the local constable. Constables were first appointed in the 1250s. They were not regular police. They were local people who by day did their usual jobs, but who tried to keep the peace in their spare hours. They were not paid and held the job for only a year at a time.

In towns they were helped by the WATCH: citizens who kept watch for crime during the night and handed over any suspected wrongdoers to the constable in the morning.

The coroner

John's death would also be reported to the county coroner. Coroners were first appointed by the king in the 1190s. Their task was to enquire into all unnatural deaths with the help of a local jury. The jurors would swear that John had been murdered and that Roger was the suspect. Then the coroner informed another royal official, the sheriff of the county.

SOURCE 1 Sanctuary knocker, Durham cathedral

The sheriff and the posse

The sheriff's job was to track down and imprison criminals. If the villagers did not catch the criminal in the hue and cry, then the sheriff and his POSSE would have to take up the pursuit.

The full name of the posse was *posse comitatus* meaning 'the force of the county'. Any male over the age of fifteen could be summoned by the sheriff to join his posse to catch criminals or stop riots.

The sheriff also investigated all other major crimes such as robberies. Again a local jury swore on oath, identifying the person they thought had committed the crime and the sheriff had to try to track down the suspect.

Sanctuary

Roger might have tried to run for SANCTUARY. This would have been his best means of escape. Sanctuaries were safe areas in churches and cathedrals. Once a criminal reached sanctuary even the county sheriff could not take him out by force. A careful ritual was followed when someone claimed sanctuary. For example: one day in 1497 a thief called Coulson who had escaped from prison, hammered on the Durham sanctuary knocker (see Source 1). Two watchmen, who were stationed over the cathedral porch, let Coulson in. Then they tolled the bell to let the townspeople know that someone had claimed sanctuary. Coulson had to decide whether to stand trial or to leave the country within 40 days. While in the cathedral he wore a black gown with a yellow cross on the shoulder. He chose exile, and, on his way to the coast, had to carry a white cross, the mark of a sanctuary man.

Why did they use these methods?

Medieval society was an extremely HIERARCHICAL society. Medieval kings relied on their nobles to keep order. Lords had great control over the peasants. They tried to impose law and order. They did not think they needed a police force although constables were a move in that direction.

This worked fairly well for the stable village society, but not as well for the mobile society that England was gradually becoming.

Roger's trial

We don't know how Roger was captured, but he was. Once he was caught Roger would have been held by the sheriff, probably in the local gaol. As Roger was charged with murder, his trial would take place in a royal court (see Source 2).

The royal courts

In this court Roger faced a local jury, representatives of the villages in the area. Just as in Saxon times, their task was to swear on oath whether they believed Roger was guilty or innocent.

In Roger's case the jury found him guilty because John's wife was an eyewitness and she was trusted to tell the truth. If there had been no witness, Roger would have been judged on what the jurors knew of his character. Was he generally trustworthy?

Roger's trial would have been very quick. There were no lawyers to defend him and no opportunity for him to question witnesses. His trial could have taken just ten or fifteen minutes before the judge declared his sentence.

Trial by ordeal abolished

Even if the jury had been unable to decide whether Roger was guilty he would not have faced trial by ordeal. Trial by ordeal had been abolished around 1215 because the Church was against it.

SOURCE 2 A medieval illustration of the King's Bench, one of the most important royal courts in the country, which was based at Westminster. The court Roger attended would have had a lot in common with this because he went before one of the king's judges. The judges sit above everyone, beneath the king's coats of arms. Clerks keep records of each case. The jurors sit on the left and the accused stands looking towards the judges while a line of prisoners await their turn

SOURCE 3 Courts in the late Middle Ages

> ❝ **Royal courts:** *royal judges visited each county two or three times a year to hear the most serious cases. This system was begun by Henry II from the 1160s (see Source 2).*
>
> **Quarter sessions:** *the royal courts could not hear all cases – there were too many. From 1363 local gentry and noblemen acted as judges in their own counties. They were known as Justices of the Peace (JPs). They held courts four times a year which therefore became known as QUARTER SESSIONS. These quarter sessions were a vital part of the legal system. They took over some of the work of the royal judges so that cases did not have to wait so long before a trial took place. JPs dealt with all kinds of cases, from murder to whether local landowners were paying their workers too highly.*
>
> **Private courts and manor courts** *were held by all landowners in their own villages or manors. The landowner was the judge. These courts dealt with workers who had not done enough work on the lord's land or people who had broken other local rules. They also ordered that people who had committed serious crimes should be held in prison until they could be tried at one of the royal courts or quarter sessions.*
>
> **Church courts:** *the Church had its own courts to try priests and other churchmen.* ❞

Punishing Roger

Roger was found guilty and so the punishment was execution. The Saxon system of wergilds had been replaced by violent methods of execution or mutilation. Execution was not only the normal punishment for murder and other serious crimes, but it was also used for minor offences such as for stealing goods worth more than a shilling. There were ways of avoiding the death penalty (see opposite panel).

Unfortunately for Roger, he was illiterate and had not learned the NECK-VERSE (see the column opposite). He wasn't needed in the army and he wasn't rich enough to buy a pardon. He could not become pregnant, and he didn't become a KING'S APPROVER.

There was no way to save himself. Roger was taken to the public GALLOWS where he was hanged.

SOURCE 4 In 1249 Walter Bloweberme was convicted of a theft that carried the death penalty. To save his life he agreed to become an approver – his life would be spared if ten people he accused of crimes were found guilty. Walter accused six people in Guildford and seven in Hampshire. The six in Guildford were declared guilty. In Hampshire three men were declared innocent by the jury, three fled and so were found guilty. One man called Hamo Stare took up his right to fight Walter to prove his innocence. Source 4 shows this 'combat of approvers'. Walter Bloweberme is on the left. Hamo is on the right. Source 4 also shows Hamo on the gallows because he lost the fight.

As a result of his ten successful convictions Walter was allowed to go abroad into exile but in 1250 he was again accused at Westminster of robbery. The court looked up its past cases and found Walter's record. He was hanged

Five ways to avoid the death penalty in the late Middle Ages

1. Claim benefit of clergy

The most common way out was to claim 'benefit of clergy' because clergy (churchmen or priests) could not be punished in the king's courts. They were handed over to the local bishop for punishment and the church did not execute people for crimes.

To prove you were a churchman you had to read aloud this passage from the Bible:

'Oh loving and kind God, have mercy. Have pity upon my transgressions.' (Psalm 51, verse 1.)

This verse from the Bible became known as 'the neck-verse' because reading it saved the necks of many criminals who avoided being hanged. The theory behind this law was that in general the only people who could read were churchmen. However, clever criminals learned the verse by heart even if they could not read – although holding the Bible upside down while reading was a give-away! Only men could take advantage of 'benefit of clergy' as a legal loophole because women could not become priests.

Benefit of clergy did not get you off punishment altogether. The Church preferred mutilation to execution since it wanted to give the convict a chance to repent!

2. Join the army

Sometimes during times of war, criminals were spared execution on condition that they joined the army.

3. Buy a pardon

Richer people could buy pardons because kings were usually desperate for money.

4. Get pregnant

Women who were pregnant could not be hanged. If they claimed they were pregnant they were examined and if found to be pregnant, their punishment was postponed and often COMMUTED.

5. Become a king's approver

The final method of escaping punishment was to become a king's approver by giving evidence that would convict other criminals (see Source 4).

Summary: The late Middle Ages

Laws
■ Kings made laws on a wide range of issues.

Trials
■ Juries decided whether the accused was guilty.
■ Trial by ordeal was used until 1215 when it was abandoned by the Church.
■ The system of courts was reorganised to make it more efficient. Royal judges travelled round the country to hear cases and local landowners acted as JPs. They played an important part in keeping the peace in each county.

Policing
■ There was no police force. Villagers had to raise the hue and cry to chase criminals. Constables were chosen from the leading villagers.
■ Tithings were still used. If a member of a tithing was accused of a crime the others had to bring him to court or they would all have to pay compensation.
■ Coroners and sheriffs had to investigate all major crimes and bring the accused before the royal judges.

I'm taking you to the sheriff!

Punishments
■ Wergilds were no longer used. Serious crimes were punished by death and mutilation.
■ Anyone who refused to attend court was outlawed.
■ Anyone who could read a verse from the Bible could claim 'benefit of clergy' and therefore had the right to be tried and punished in the church courts which often imposed lighter sentences such as mutilation instead of execution.
■ Executions took place in public as a warning to others.
■ The STOCKS and fines were used as punishments in local manor courts.

■ REVIEW TASK

Changes to the legal system in the later Middle Ages

1. Draw up a table like the one below to show the changes in the legal system.

	Situation in 1100	Changes made by kings	Continuities
Policing			
Trials and courts			
Punishments			

2. Complete the table by comparing the summary diagram above with the diagram on page 34. Add as much detail as you can from pages 35–38.
3. You are one of the King's judges. The King has asked you to write a report on the effectiveness of the legal system for catching and punishing criminals. Make sure you list:
a) the improvements that have been made since the 1100s. Explain which changes helped the fight against crime most effectively and why.
b) your recommendations for changes that are still needed. Think about what has **not** been done.

Were the Middle Ages lawless and violent?

BY THE LATE Middle Ages there is a lot of evidence about crime and punishment for historians to work with. The courts kept detailed records of each crime they tried and each punishment given, such as the case of Roger Ryet. Many of these records have survived to the present day. They help us to work out whether the Middle Ages was really a lawless and violent period.

Case studies from the royal courts

Serious crimes were tried by the royal courts. You read on page 37 how royal judges visited each county two or three times a year. Every case was briefly recorded. Cases 1–9 were all tried in the royal courts in Norfolk between 1307 and 1316. Look at how these real individuals were treated by the judges and juries.

Case 1

Margaret, wife of William Calbot, was taken [captured] for killing Agnes and Matilda, her daughters. The jurors say on their oath that Margaret killed Agnes, aged two, with a staff as she lay in her cradle and forced Matilda, aged four, to sit in the fire. The jurors say that at the time she killed the children and for a long time before she was insane. After the crime she went and brought the neighbours to show them Agnes and Matilda. On this evidence they say that she was insane at the time of the murders. She is returned to prison until the king's will is known.

Case 2

John Walsh is taken for the death of Richard Cous. The jurors say on their oath that there was an argument between John and Richard and that they were using insulting language when Richard drew a knife and threatened to wound John. John fled into an angle between two walls. Seeing no escape John drew his sword in self-defence. Richard ran towards John with his knife outstretched in order to kill John but he ran into John's sword which entered his body. He died of the wound at once. The jurors say that John could not have avoided death in any other way than by drawing his sword. He is returned to prison to await the king's pardon.

Case 4

Walter Asketel, his wife Catherine and Catherine's mother, Joan, were taken on suspicion of possession of stolen goods – one blue tunic and one surcoat worth 2s [s = shillings]. Walter and Joan are acquitted but the jury says that Catherine is guilty. She is to be hanged. Catherine says that she is pregnant. Six matrons examine her and confirm that she is pregnant. She is returned to prison.

Case 3

Peter le Synekere was taken for the burglary of the house of Godfrey of Gayton and for stealing half a bushel of wheat worth 14d [d = pence], one tunic worth 10d and 3 hoods worth 8d. The jurors say that Peter stole the grain and other goods but they say that he did this because of hunger and destitution. He is returned to prison until consultations are made.

Case 5

Roger of Lynford was taken for stealing three chickens worth 4d from Roger of Thorpe. The jurors say that Roger did steal one chicken and one hen worth 2d but the value of the stolen goods was not high enough to warrant conviction. Therefore he is acquitted.

Case 6

Alice of Rainham was taken with one tunic worth 2s and because she is a common cutter of purses. She is returned to prison because the jury did not appear.

Case 7

Hamon, son of John in the Corner, was taken for stealing at night, one mare worth 10s and for stealing one horse worth 13s 4d and for robbing Thomas le Neve of goods worth 40s. He stands trial and is convicted. He is to be hanged.

Case 8

Ellen Attehole was accused because she is a common thief and receiver of thieves. She stands trial. The jurors enquire if any evil deeds are known of her. They say they do not believe any of the evil rumours about her. She is acquitted.

Case 9

William Bithewater was taken for stealing seven pairs of hose from Edward of Barking. He stands trial and is convicted. He is to be hanged.

■ TASK

1. Draw up and complete a table like this one:

Case	1	2	3	4	5	6	7	8	9
Person									
Crime									
Verdict and sentence									

2. Some of the statements below are true and some are not. Take each statement in turn and look at the cases. Which cases provide evidence to help you decide whether the statement is true? If the statement is not true rewrite it so that it becomes accurate. Your teacher can give you a table to complete to help with this Task.

a) Punishments for minor theft were harsh.

b) Jurors showed sympathy to some criminals accused of minor crimes.

c) Pregnant women could escape punishment.

d) The accused were shown no mercy whatever the reasons for their crimes.

e) Jurors made decisions based on the general trustworthiness of the accused.

3. Although this is a very small sample of cases, what do they tell you about:

a) whether most crimes were violent crimes

b) whether jurors and courts took great care over the law?

Case studies from the manor courts: how did manor courts punish minor offences?

Most crimes were tried at the manor courts, held weekly in local manors. These courts also kept detailed records.

The following cases come from the manor of Wakefield which covered a wide area of the west of Yorkshire. It was the land of John de Warenne, Earl of Surrey. Every court record was headed by a list of jurors.

Court 1: Wakefield, 10 October 1315

a) Thomas Clerk of Waddesworth for the escape of a cow 3d.
b) Henry of the Holgate for the escape of horses 3d. The same man for the escape of an ox 6d.
c) Robert Gunne for a trespass made 12d.
d) John Odam for breaking the hedge of a coppice 3d.

Court 2: Halifax, 18 October 1315

a) Thomas of the Hirst drew blood from William, son of Hawe, repelling force with force. Therefore William is fined 12d.
b) The township of Stansfield did not raise the hue and cry on the thieves that burgled the house of Amery of Hertelay nor prosecuted them and is fined 40s.

Court 3: Rastrick, 19 October 1315

a) John, son of Thomas of Dalton, slew John of Witacres and fled. Therefore it is ordered that he be taken when found.
b) John, son of Henry of Fikkesby, burgled the dairy of Bradley and furtively carried away 17 cheeses, each worth 10d. It is ordered that he be taken.

Court 4: Wakefield, 20 October 1315

a) The townships of Emelay and Breton say that a footpath leading from the mill of Horbury has been blocked by John of the More. He is fined 2 shillings.
b) The township of Thornes says that Master Robert Carpenter of Wakefield enclosed a piece of meadow in the fields of Snaypethorp by a ditch and paling so that the men of Thornes and Snaypethorp are not able to have common there as they ought to have. Therefore he is to be taken.
c) The wife of Gilbert the Theker because she brewed weak beer is fined 6d.

1. List the different types of crime dealt with by the manor court.
2. List three people who would later appear at a royal court if they were captured. You may need to refer back to pages 40–41.
3. The statements below are true. Take each statement in turn and look at the cases. Which cases provide evidence to prove the statements are true?
a) Villagers were expected to play a part in catching criminals.
b) The manor court was used to uphold the power of the lord of the manor.
c) The manor court protected the goods of the villager against another's greed.
d) Women received the same punishments as men.
4. 'Village life was violent and lawless'. Does the evidence show that this statement is true or false?

Court 5: Wakefield, 21 October 1315

a) Adam of Dene because he does not grind his corn at the lord's mill is fined 6d.

b) It is found by the jurors that the cattle of Matthew of Schellay have trodden down and depastured the oats of Richard Passemer to the quantity of three sheaves. Therefore it is decided that he make satisfaction to him and that he be fined 6d.

c) Nicholas Smith of Crigeleston appeared against Alexander Shepherd and complains that Alexander took a certain cow belonging to Nicholas at grass in a pasture and chased it to the house of Thomas of the Holgate and in chasing it he so violently struck and beat it that it bled for three weeks and Nicholas lost the profits from the cow for six weeks. Alexander came and defended the case – which was to be decided later.

Court 7: Birton, 7 April 1316

a) William, son of Richard Wolvet, and Adam, son of John Typup, opened the cellar door of the parson of Birton with a false key and stole bread and a girdle of the value of 6d. Therefore let them be taken.

b) The wife of Adam Shepherd of Heppeworth drew blood from Emma the wife of Adam Smith, and is fined 12d.

c) John Vicar of Braythewell entered many times with force and arms the wood of the lord in Holnefryth and killed, took and carried away the wild animals of the said earl and assaulted, shot at and wounded the lord's men. Therefore let him be taken.

d) John of Amyas has turned the watercourse of his vineyard which used and ought to flow into a ditch behind his garden so that it now runs on the street. Therefore it is ordered that the watercourse be put back.

Court 6: Wakefield, 22 January 1316

a) The jurors say that Juliana, daughter of William and Isabel, is married without the lord's leave. She is fined 6d.

The stocks were used regularly to punish villagers for minor crimes. The main purpose was to humiliate offenders so that they would not break the law again and so that others would be more likely to keep the law. The pillory was used particularly for dishonest traders. London records give details of the offences that were punished by being put in the pillory. They included selling 'stinking eels', 'selling oats, good on the outside, the rest bad', 'selling rings made of brass, plated with gold and silver as if they were gold and silver', 'lies uttered against the Mayor' and 'selling a stinking partridge'

■ TASK

Work with a partner to look through the royal and manor court records on pages 40–43.

1. What was the most common form of punishment
   a) from the royal courts?
   b) from the manor courts?
2. Of the cases judged by the manor court, what was considered the most serious crime? (Think about the level of the fine.)
3. List three different crimes from the royal court and three from the manor court which would still be regarded as crimes today. For each one explain whether you think it is regarded as:
   a) more serious
   b) less serious
   c) much the same
   today as in the Middle Ages.

An overview of medieval crime

You have seen how court records from this period give useful evidence about crime and punishment. We have much more evidence about this period than about Ancient Rome. Reading through such records gives the impression that there was a lot of crime. That is because the records don't tell us about the vast majority of law-abiding citizens leading peaceful lives.

Historians have used court records such as those on pages 40–43 to build up a detailed picture of medieval crime and punishment.

'The dark figure' (see left) is a phrase historians use about the number of unrecorded crimes that took place. Although some statistics of medieval crimes look neat they only tell us about the crimes that came to court. We don't know how many crimes were never reported and therefore we do not know what the true crime rate was. That number of unrecorded crimes is called 'the dark figure' and here he is! You will meet him again in later chapters. Sources 1–6 and the information below summarise historians' findings about:

- the main types of crime
- the amount of crime
- the reasons for crime.

5. Which crimes were most common in the Middle Ages?
6. Why did most murders occur?
7. Which goods were most commonly stolen?
8. Study Source 6. What does it suggest about the relationship between poverty and crime?

SOURCE 2 This table compares figures from England in the 1300s with 1995–97 statistics

Place	Murders per 100,000 people
14th-century England	*12.0*
London	*2.1*
Washington DC (USA)	*69.3*
Moscow	*18.1*

	Number of murders	% of all murders
Argument	178	51.3
Domestic dispute	3	0.9
Revenge	2	0.6
Dispute over property	13	3.7
Drinking	15	4.3
Self-defence	25	7.2
Jealousy	2	0.6
Accident	6	1.7
Robbery	85	24.5
Insanity	1	0.3
Others	17	4.9
Total	347	

SOURCE 3 These statistics deal with murders in Northamptonshire between 1300 and 1415. Most murders were committed in spring and summer when villagers were working together in the fields and arguments flared up over sharing work or straying animals. Most involved neighbours and family, and were crude and impulsive rather than carefully plotted. Violent crimes were as likely to be committed by knights and members of noblemen's households as by villagers

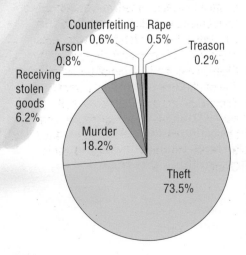

Counterfeiting 0.6%
Rape 0.5%
Arson 0.8%
Treason 0.2%
Receiving stolen goods 6.2%
Murder 18.2%
Theft 73.5%

SOURCE 1 Pie chart showing the major crimes committed in eight counties between 1300 and 1348. Although theft was the most common crime the number of thefts per head of population was much lower than today

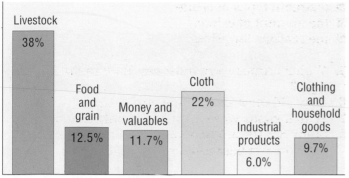

SOURCE 4 This graph shows the kinds of goods stolen in Norfolk between 1300 and 1348. Thefts were more common in the spring and summer when livestock was grazing or goods were lying around openly whereas in winter animals were slaughtered and property was locked away. Three-quarters of crimes were committed by people known to the victim many of whom were respectable villagers. There were few professional criminals

SOURCE 5 This graph shows the percentages of men and women accused of major crime. Women rarely committed crimes alone and were more likely to be involved in thefts of food and clothing

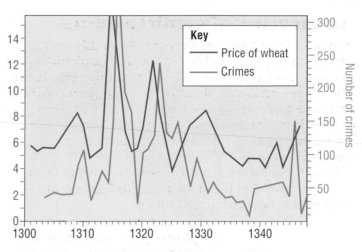

SOURCE 6 This graph shows the changing price of wheat in Norfolk (in shillings) from 1300 to 1348 and the changing numbers of crimes heard in the royal courts. The early 1300s were particularly difficult years for many peasants because a growing population meant more people were competing for work and wages were low. At the same time a series of bad harvests pushed up the price of food. The lines of the graph do not coincide exactly because most crimes were dealt with by the courts at least six months or a year after they had been committed

■ **TASK**

Were the Middle Ages lawless and violent? Write a short essay with this title. You can get a sheet from your teacher to help you. Use examples from the last six pages to support your argument.

SOURCE 7 Some causes of crimes are very familiar. In 1222 there was a contest between wrestlers from the city of London and wrestlers from outside the city. When the London team won, riots broke out and were only stopped by the Chief Justice and a band of armed men. The ringleaders of the rioters were hanged. There were many casualties of ball competitions, such as that shown here. A student called Adam was killed in 1303 while playing ball in the High Street in Oxford

What can the legend of Robin Hood tell us about medieval crime and punishment?

The legend of Robin Hood

1. Robin was the son of a nobleman. He went to the Crusades with King Richard I.

2. Robin returned to find he had lost his lands to the evil Sheriff of Nottingham and Richard's brother, John, was trying to take over the throne.

3. Robin joined a band of outlaws living in Sherwood Forest. The other outlaws were a mix of townspeople, peasants and priests. They had become outlaws because they had been unjustly accused of crimes.

4. Robin was a brilliant archer. He became leader of the outlaws.

5. Together they fought against the Sheriff of Nottingham and Prince John, and anyone else who harmed the poor and defenceless.

God bless you, Robin.

6. If the outlaws stole anything they gave it to the poor. They attacked rich bishops and priests who did not lead the simple life expected of churchmen.

7. The outlaws were good friends who stayed together for years, sharing everything. They did not suffer hardships from living in the forest.

It is good to be back in England.

8. Eventually King Richard returned from the Crusades and rewarded Robin for supporting him against Prince John.

Arise, Sir Robin. All your lands are returned to you.

9. The King gave Robin his lands back.

The story-strip opposite tells the version of the Robin Hood legend that we see and hear most often in films such as Source 2. However, the story has been constantly changing over the centuries since it was first told. At least six different stories are known to have been told regularly in the 1400s. They include familiar characters such as Little John and the Sheriff of Nottingham. But they also include many elements that are not in our modern story.

Stories such as Robin Hood play a big part in building up our own images of life in the Middle Ages and especially of crime, punishment and law enforcement.

The stories about Robin Hood give the impression:

■ that the life of an outlaw was romantic and outlaws were honourable
■ that the medieval system of trials and punishments was unfair and unreliable and biased against the poor
■ that the rich and powerful were a law unto themselves and the poor had no real defence against a rich noble.

1. Look at each of the points in the list above.
a) Which of these impressions do you agree with?
b) Which do you disagree with?
c) Which do you need more evidence about before you decide? In each case explain your answer carefully.

Was there really a Robin Hood?

The irritating answer to this question is that we don't know. Court records from the Middle Ages show that there certainly were people called Robin Hood or Robert Hood who were accused of crimes, but not the daring deeds committed by the legendary Robin Hood or at the time of King John or King Richard.

The stories were well known in the late 1300s and may well have been known a century earlier in the 1260s. Other countries had similar legends.

The stories would originally have been told by minstrels or by village story-tellers. They were popular because they were exciting and peasants enjoyed hearing about ruthless sheriffs, rich bishops and corrupt tax-collectors suffering for once. The listeners forgot for a moment the real world where people like themselves were usually the victims of outlaws. The Robin Hood stories let them escape from everyday problems into a dream world where they lived, free of other people's authority, with plenty of food, adventure and good friends.

SOURCE 1 Adapted from *Bandits* by E.J. Hobsbawm, 1969

66 *Robin Hood, the noble robber, is the most famous and popular type of bandit, and the most common hero of ballad and song. There is a need for such heroes and champions … Robin Hoods are to be found in most countries in the world. In nineteenth-century America Billy the Kid was a Robin Hood stealing from white people to give to poor Mexicans. That is why Robin Hood cannot die, and why he is invented when he does not really exist. Poor men have need of him for he represents justice.* 99

WARNER BROS. *present* "THE ADVENTURES OF **ROBIN HOOD**" with **ERROL FLYNN** OLIVIA De HAVILLAND BASIL RATHBONE CLAUDE RAINS A WARNER BROS. PICTURE COLOUR BY TECHNICOLOR

SOURCE 2 This still from a film made in the 1930s shows Robin Hood (right) fighting against Prince John's supporters

What were outlaws really like?

■ TASK

The text and sources on this page are about real outlaws. Use these to test the accuracy of four features of the Robin Hood legend listed below.

a) Outlaws only stole from the rich and churchmen.
b) Outlaws helped the poor.
c) Outlaws were loyal to each other.
d) Outlaws had been wrongly accused of crimes.

Read the text and sources on these two pages and decide whether each of the features above is true.

Victims

Gangs of outlaws were feared. They stole from anyone, including villagers, frequently stealing food, clothing, pots and pans. Poor villagers were easier targets than well-protected knights and noblemen.

They kept the money rather than giving it to the poor, and they did not necessarily share it equally among themselves. In one case a gang member, John Drestes, testified in court that he and nine other men had robbed Robin Wyot, a fisherman, of cloth and money, valued at 50 shillings. John Drestes did exceptionally well, getting 17 shillings for his part. In a three-way split of 18 shillings, one man told the justices that he got only 1s 6d.

Churches were favourite targets for gangs because they contained valuable ornaments made of gold and silver and money which had been given for the care of the poor. Court rolls record that a gang 'armed as for war' wounded the vicar at Stanford and stole goods worth £10.

Methods

Outlaws threatened their victims with arson, extorting money or goods in return for not burning homes down. This was a serious threat from the 1300s onwards when many peasants were growing richer and employed carpenters and other craftsmen to build their homes.

Outlaws regularly used violence. They did not invite a traveller for a meal in the forest and gently take his money. They held a knife to the victim's throat and made him choose his money or his life. Sometimes they did not bother with the choice, simply killing their victim. Around ten per cent of murder victims were killed during robberies, usually by these roving bands. The typical victim was a shepherd going alone to the fields and later found dead or wounded, and often naked because his clothes had been stolen.

These crimes explain why juries found violent robbers guilty and were glad to see them hang. Juries did not find the excuses for them that they did for fellow-villagers, even those accused of murder. Ordinary people had little sympathy for outlaws.

> **S**OURCE 4 From the manor court records of Wakefield
>
> 66 *Richard de Windhill was taken as a suspected thief because he came with a message from several thieves to the wife of the late William de Stodlay begging food for the thieves. He threatened to burn her unless she gave him food and money and fled when the earl's foresters tried to capture him.* 99

SOURCE 5 This medieval illustration shows the hanging of a gang of thieves who stole from a church. In 1270 Henry III heard complaints that 'no religious person could pass through the counties of Nottingham, Leicester and Derby without being robbed'

Daring rescues

In the legends, Robin Hood and his men rescue each other from the gallows. There is real life evidence of such daring escapes.

Nicholas Tailor and his gang cut down from the gallows Nicholas's brother, Henry, who was being hanged for burglary. They took him to a church where he promised to go into exile, leaving the country within 40 days. In one case in Bedfordshire the gang got there too late to rescue their companion so they killed the hangman instead.

Gangs found other ways to avoid hanging. All 38 members of a gang captured in Yorkshire were handed over to the Church for punishment when they each read the 'neck-verse'. As professional criminals they had deliberately learned it to save their lives!

A typical gang?

Gangs often stayed together a long time, had strong leaders and a mix of members including knights and priests (who were useful for writing threatening letters).

One such gang was the Folville gang which rampaged around Leicestershire for twenty years, led by Eustace Folville and his brothers. Their father was a knight and lord of a manor in Leicestershire. They were never captured. Without a police force it was impossible to check every hiding place but, just as importantly, they may well have been protected from capture by wealthy friends. Local people warned them of danger when they murdered unpopular royal officials.

Source 6 shows the kind of robbery they carried out. As the sons of a knight they would have been well used to wearing armour and using weapons effectively so that merchants had no chance of escape.

SOURCE 6 A medieval illustration of a highway robbery

The career of the Folville gang

1326	Eustace Folville, two of his brothers and a gang of 50 men murdered Roger Bellers, a government official, in Leicestershire. They were declared outlaws but were not caught.
1327	The Folvilles' crimes and many others were pardoned as part of the celebrations when Edward III became king.
1327–29	The Folvilles were involved in at least three murders, a rape and three robberies.
1329	The Folvilles' crimes were pardoned for their part in fighting against the rebellious Earl of Lancaster.
1331	The monks of a local abbey paid the Folville gang £20 to destroy a watermill belonging to a rival.
1332	The Folville gang captured one of the King's judges and held him to ransom. Again they were outlawed.
1333	The Folvilles were pardoned 'in return for good services in the Scottish war'. After this Eustace was a soldier for several years but then became involved in more crime before dying peacefully in 1345. A monk recorded his death because of his bravery, daring and fame.

2. Compare the Folville gang and the Robin Hood legend. List the ways that the Folville gang:
a) were like Robin Hood's men
b) were different from Robin Hood's men.
3. Did outlaws really live like Robin Hood? Give reasons for your answer.
4. Why did the Folville gang escape punishment?

Were the rich really above the law?

The best-known character in the Robin Hood stories – after Robin himself – is the Sheriff of Nottingham. The sheriff is supposed to uphold the law but spends more time breaking it because there is no one to control him. In the Middle Ages powerful nobles and officials were sometimes seen as the main threat to law and order.

Is this an accurate impression? Here are two contrasting case studies from the later Middle Ages.

■ TASK

'The rich and powerful were a law unto themselves. There was little defence against nobles who broke the law.'
a) What evidence supports this view?
b) What evidence suggests this is not true?
c) Is this statement true or not? If you think it is untrue then rewrite it to make it more accurate.

Henry V

Henry V's intimidating and powerful personality was important in making his nobles obey him. He was also a good organiser who worked long hours to make sure the courts and other aspects of government were efficient.

Sometimes he sent his royal judges to sort out the trouble. Sometimes he took action personally. For example, he summoned two knights to his court because their feuding had led to private battles in Yorkshire and Lancashire. When they arrived Henry was beginning a meal of oysters. Henry told them they would be hanged if they did not end their quarrel before he finished his oysters. They settled their disagreement!

Henry showed that he was going to force even rich and powerful noblemen who supported him to obey the law. Some of his supporters had been terrorising Shropshire. They expected the King to turn a blind eye to their crimes, but instead Henry forced their leader to agree a bond of £3000 that his men would keep the peace. This meant that if any of them broke the law then not only they but their leader, Arundel, would be ruined. Shropshire became much more peaceful.

If I don't obey the King I will be ruined, and my followers must also obey him.

If we break the law we will be ruined and so will our Lord.

The courts have not been so busy for years.

■ TASK

'The Robin Hood legend is so inaccurate that we learn nothing useful from it about medieval crime and punishment.' Write an essay to explain whether you agree or disagree with this statement. Support your answer using plenty of examples from pages 46–48.

> **SOURCE 7** From a petition sent to King Henry VI by John Paston in 1450
>
> 66 *On 28 January Lord Moleyns sent a thousand riotous people to our mansion, arrayed in manner of war with body armour, helmets, knives, bows, arrows, guns, pans with fire in them, crowbars for pulling down houses, pickaxes to mine the walls and trees to break up gates and doors. My wife was in the house with twelve people. They were driven out and [the intruders] mined through the walls into my wife's room and carried her out of the gates and then they cut through the posts supporting the house and let them fall. They broke up all the rooms and chests, rifled them and carried off the goods, clothes and money that we and our servants had to the value of £200 and said openly that if they had found me there with some of my servants we would have been killed.* 99

Henry VI

By contrast, Henry VI was not as willing or able to tackle crime. In the 1400s John Paston of Norfolk was having trouble with his neighbour Lord Moleyns.

Henry VI took no notice of Paston's request for help. The King did not punish Moleyns. In fact he ordered the sheriff to choose a jury which would find Moleyns innocent.

A strong king would have punished nobles who broke the law but Henry VI was a weak king. He wanted the support of people like Moleyns so he let them get away with violence.

There were many other incidents like this because Henry VI could not keep the country peaceful. He was a weak character who was easily influenced by his advisers. Eventually he was deposed as king.

Moleyns

Moleyns supporter

Paston

$\mathcal{S}$ummary: Crime and punishment in the Middle Ages

Headline: Better trials

The big change in this period was the improved legal system. Medieval kings tried to deal more effectively with criminals who were caught. The system of trials steadily became more complex and was respected by the people. Juries, judges and sheriffs carried on doing their tasks for hundreds of years without major changes which suggests that people thought that the system was effective.

Crime

The majority of crimes were minor ones, such as letting animals stray. Theft was by far the most common crime to come before the royal judges and the JPs. Violent crimes made up less than 20 per cent of serious crimes and a far smaller percentage of all crimes.

But although we have plenty of evidence about crimes that came to court, we do not know how many crimes were actually committed. The 'dark figure' of unrecorded crimes may have been very high. However, it is almost certain that this period does not deserve the title of the Murderous Middle Ages. The Middle Ages were not nearly as violent as we are led to believe by films and television.

This was partly because kings and landowners worked hard to improve the legal system. The system of trials became steadily more detailed and was respected by people. Juries, judges and sheriffs carried on doing their tasks for centuries without major changes which suggests that people thought that the system was effective.

Attitudes to crime

Medieval attitudes can be summarised like this:

- local communities were expected to police themselves using tithings, constables and the hue and cry
- people were expected to obey the king's law. Royal judges held courts to show the king's power
- kings could not afford the costs of police or prisons as punishments
- punishments were harsh and took place in public to frighten others away from committing crimes
- most people, from labourers to nobles, realised that breaking the law was a danger to everyone and the law had to be upheld.

Causes of crime

The illustrations below show some of the reasons why crime was a problem in medieval England.

1. Which of these reasons still cause crime today?
2. Which of these reasons were a particular problem for medieval kings?

Human Nature Rules O.K.

Alcohol Greed Youth Hooliganism

For the baby's sake, give us food.

I can always read the neck-verse if I get caught – the church courts won't punish harshly.

I can't help the high price of bread – the harvest has been poor.

I'll get away with this. Who is there to catch me?

Obstacles to crime: What methods did they use to tackle crime in the Middle Ages?

Here is another obstacle course like the one on page 21. It focuses on: **How did people try to solve the problem of crime?**

Here you can see the methods in use during the Middle Ages. The barriers are the methods that kings and their advisers tried to use to prevent crime: methods of catching criminals, trials and punishments. As you can see, these methods were not successful – criminals were still able to steal through and commit their crimes.

3. Which method did kings rely on most to stop crime?
4. Why did medieval kings choose these methods rather than others?
5. How effective do you think these methods were?
6. Compare this picture with the Roman 'obstacle course'. In what ways are they:
a) the same
b) different?
7. Chapter 4 deals with the period from 1500 to 1750. During those years much harsher punishments were introduced known as THE BLOODY CODE. Do you expect this change to make the fight against crime more successful?

■ TASK

1. Fill in your own copy of the table below. Note down the main changes since the Roman period and main continuities.
2. Write an essay with the title: 'Did medieval kings really try to stop crime?'.
   You can get a sheet from your teacher to help you plan the essay.
3. Using all that you have found out from pages 24–53, list the punishments used in the Middle Ages.
a) Why were punishments harsh?
b) Did punishments become harsher during the Middle Ages?

The Middle Ages and the future

A series of important developments took place in the Middle Ages that were to influence the system of justice in England for centuries. These included:

■ the use of villagers and townspeople as unpaid constables to keep the peace
■ courts held by royal judges around the country and by local landowners – the JPs
■ the role of juries in deciding guilt or innocence
■ punishments in public that were meant to terrify onlookers into obeying the law.

	Roman Empire	Medieval England	Change or continuity?
Laws	Laws were made by the Emperor and the Senate. They were written down in detail, often updated and covered all aspects of crime.	Laws dealt with all levels of crime from treason against the king to selling under-weight bread in the market. Local laws were laid down by the lords of the manor.	
Policing	There was no effective police force in Rome but the Emperor's guard protected the Emperor and stopped riots. The army acted as a police force in the provinces of the Empire.	There was no police force. Tithings and the hue and cry were the main methods of catching offenders. The sheriff and posse chased criminals on the run. Leading villagers were appointed as constables. These methods were effective if there were witnesses to crimes, but were much less effective at solving crimes with no witnesses.	
Trials	Victims of crime had to collect evidence and bring the accused to court. They could hire trained lawyers if they could afford them. Juries decided serious cases; judges decided less serious ones.	Trial by jury was used for most offences. Trial by ordeal was abolished in 1215. From the 1100s royal judges travelled the country dealing with serious cases. Trials lasted about 15 minutes. County courts were held by JPs who were leading landowners. Each manor had a weekly court run by the local lord.	
Punishments	Punishments were harsh and often violent. Executions were common although noblemen were allowed to go into exile to escape execution. Prisons were not used, except for debtors.	Capital punishment was the most common punishment in royal courts and was used for many offences including theft. Hanging and other punishments were carried out in public to scare possible offenders. Fines were the most common punishments in manor courts. Prisons were only used for people awaiting trial. The stocks, pillory and whipping were also used for minor crimes.	

PROTEST 1300–1700

Why were protesters treated as rebels and traitors?

ON PAGES 23–54 you have been exploring how kings tried to prevent crimes such as theft or murder. The most serious crime of all was treason – rebelling against the monarch.

Throughout the Middle Ages rebellions by nobles were quite common, especially if a king was acting unfairly. Sometimes these rebellions led to a king being deposed.

Rebellions by ordinary people were much rarer. In this chapter you can study the greatest rebellion of all, the Great Revolt of 1381 which is also known as the Peasants' Revolt.

Rebels and traitors usually faced savage deaths in the late Middle Ages. Heretics were executed because they had rebelled against God. Noblemen were executed because they had broken their oaths of loyalty to the king. All executions were public to warn people that they must obey the king and the Church, and to frighten them away from crime. Traitors were dragged or carried through the streets to their deaths so they could be seen by as many people as possible.

Harsh treatment of rebels who had tried to depose the king may not be very surprising. What is more surprising is that ordinary people who were simply protesting were treated in the same way. However, in this period, as you will see, kings did not really make a distinction between rebellion and protest.

In this chapter you will investigate four case studies:

■ the Great Revolt or Peasants' Revolt of 1381
■ Kett's Rebellion of 1549
■ the Pilgrimage of Grace of 1536
■ the Gunpowder Plot of 1605.

Rebellion

We want change. We will have to rebel and replace the King with someone else.

We want change. We must protest so that the King will have to listen to us.

Protest

■ TASK

Record the main details about the four case studies in a table like the one below. In the final column give your opinion about whether each event was a rebellion or a protest.

Reasons for protest/ rebellion	Actions of rebels/ protesters	Punishment	Reasons for punishment	Protest or rebellion?
1.				
2.				
3.				
4.				

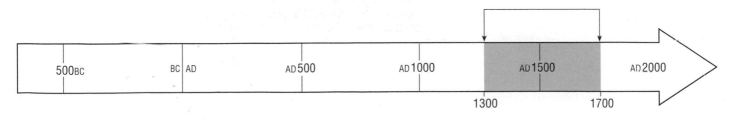

Case study 1: The Great Revolt of 1381 – a protest against poor government

IN 1381 GROUPS of villagers gathered in Kent and Essex before marching on London. They were demanding:

- fairer taxes
- better protection from French attacks on the coast
- freedom to work wherever they wished and to earn higher wages. As peasants, some were unable to marry or leave their villages to work elsewhere without permission from their lord of the manor. They also had to work on his land several days each week.

The rebels marched to London, attacked the Tower of London, murdered two of the King's leading advisers, including the Archbishop of Canterbury. The rebellion only ended when the fourteen-year-old king, Richard II, met the rebel leader, Wat Tyler. Tyler was killed by one of the King's men and the disheartened rebels disbanded.

How did the King and his advisers treat the rebels? You can find out from the information in the Source Investigation below and on page 57.

SOURCE 1 Two contrasting paintings of the murder of Wat Tyler in the Great Revolt of 1381

A is a fifteenth-century interpretation of the event. Richard II (wearing a crown) is shown once on the right addressing the gathered peasants (although the artist has shown them dressed as soldiers) and again on the left watching as Wat Tyler is killed. Do you think he is approving or trying to stop the murder?

B is a nineteenth-century interpretation. Richard II is shown on horseback, to the right, wearing a crown. How does B differ from A in its interpretation of the event?

■ SOURCE INVESTIGATION

1. What does Source 2 tell you about:
a) the severity of the punishments
b) the numbers of executions?
2. Read Sources 3 and 4. How far do these sources agree with Source 2?
3. List the questions you need to ask about Sources 2–4 to help you decide whether the sources provide reliable evidence about the punishments.
4. Read the Background Information panel about Sources 2–4. Does this provide answers to any of the questions you listed in answer to question 3?
5. Do you think Sources 2–4 provide reliable evidence about the punishment of the rebels? Explain your answer.
6. Read Sources 5 and 6. What do these historians say about the executions?
7. What evidence are the writers of Sources 5 and 6 using?
8. Do you think that chronicles (like Sources 2–4) provide better evidence about the numbers of executions than the records used in Source 5?
9. 'The rebels of 1381 were savagely punished.' Explain why you agree or disagree with this statement.

SOURCE 2 Thomas Walsingham, *The English History*

" The Mayor of London, acting as a judge, tried the rebels from the city and those who could be caught from Kent, Essex, Sussex, Norfolk, Suffolk and other counties. The Mayor had all those beheaded who were found to be involved in the revolt. "

SOURCE 3 An anonymous monk, the *Anonimalle Chronicle*

" Many rebels were taken and hanged in London and elsewhere. Numerous gallows were erected around London and other cities and towns of the south. "

SOURCE 4 Jean Froissart, *Chronicles*

" Now I will tell you about the King of England's vengeance on the ungrateful rebels. The King was advised to travel his country through every shire to punish all the evil-doers. The King did this at Canterbury, Sandwich, Yarmouth and all other places of his realm where any rebellion had been and there were hanged and beheaded more than 1500 people. "

SOURCE 5 Adapted from R.B. Dobson, *The Peasants' Revolt of 1381*, 1983

" According to most of the chroniclers the judges punished the rebels with harsh severity but the evidence of trial records suggests that the judges were less vindictive. Not many more than 100 persons can actually be proved to have been sentenced to death for their part in the rising. However, the question of how many rebels were executed is difficult because at least some of the more notorious rebels were executed without trial.

The records of Parliament show that lords and commons discussed the revolt and its aftermath in a spirit of reasonable moderation. They rejected the villeins' demand for freedom but there was no savage persecution of the rebels. An amnesty was available to everyone who asked for pardon except for 287 named people. "

SOURCE 6 Adapted from N. Saul, *Richard II*, 1997

" It seems that few executions were carried out without trials. In London the Mayor executed a number of leading rebels. Elsewhere only the Bishop of Norwich followed his example. One possible reason is that the statute [law] of Treason did not refer to rebellions by ordinary people. The government wanted the rebels to be treated as traitors but local judges did not often agree. Court records show that many leading rebels got off lightly with periods of imprisonment and many lesser rebels obtained pardons. "

Background information about the chroniclers

Thomas Walsingham (Source 2)

Walsingham was a monk at the abbey of St Albans from the 1370s until his death in 1422. He wrote a history of England, bringing it up to date by including the events of his own lifetime such as the revolt of 1381. St Albans abbey was badly affected by the revolt. The abbey owned large areas of farmland and peasants on that land were not free to work for themselves. In 1381 they demanded their freedom from the abbey. According to Walsingham they 'sought to better themselves by force and hoped to subject all things to their own stupidity.'

The *Anonimalle Chronicle* (Source 3)

This chronicle was compiled by a monk in Yorkshire soon after 1381. He seems to have based his chronicle closely upon another chronicle written in London by a government official.

Jean Froissart (Source 4)

Froissart was a court poet and writer who was born in Flanders in the 1330s and died in the early 1400s. He travelled throughout Europe, visiting England in the 1360s and again in 1395. His chronicle was written for the enjoyment of nobles, kings and queens and he got information from many English noblemen.

Case study 2: Kett's Rebellion of 1549 – a protest against economic change

DURING THE MIDDLE AGES widespread protests such as the Great Revolt of 1381 were rare, but during the 1500s protests became much more common.

Anger about rising food prices was particularly common. If bad weather caused poor harvests then food prices rose steeply, making it difficult for many people to afford enough food. Nothing can control the weather, but people who face hard times often protest against the other things that make the hard times worse. So, many protests about poverty became protests against economic changes taking place in society at the time. The protesters therefore included not only the poor, but also wealthier people who wanted to see the economic problems dealt with.

Kett's Rebellion is one example.

The background

In 1549, after a bad harvest, food prices were rising. To make matters worse there was a wave of enclosure – common land was being taken over by landowners for sheep farming to supply the blossoming wool trade. This was good for the landowners because sheep farming was very profitable, but it was a disaster for farm labourers since sheep farming employed fewer people.

Protesters blamed landlords for their desperate situation. They broke down fences and hedges that had been built by the landlords.

King Edward VI's main adviser, Somerset (who was virtually the ruler of England since the King was only a youth), set up a commission to investigate what should be done about the problem.

July 1549: Norfolk

The centre of these protests was Norfolk. In July 1549 a large group of protesters gathered to destroy the fences of a landowner called Flowerdew. They included prosperous townspeople and farmers as well as ordinary workers. They were led by a local landowner called Robert Kett who was one of Flowerdew's rivals.

Stage 1: peaceful protest
Kett led 16,000 protesters to Norwich. For six weeks the rebels camped outside the city walls. They prepared a list of 29 grievances including: high food prices; landowners raising rents, evicting tenants and taking over common land.

They went out of their way to proclaim their loyalty to the King. They held their own courts and church services using the latest Protestant rites. They wanted (and expected) the King to take action to stop the local landowners getting rich while the majority of the population suffered.

The King sent a local gentry leader to order them to disperse; they refused. The King's main adviser then offered them a pardon for disobeying the King's orders as long as they dispersed, but they still refused since they thought they were close to success.

Stage 2: armed protest
Possibly to force the King's hand, the protesters entered Norwich and tried to capture Yarmouth. Then the King took stronger action. The Earl of Warwick's army of 10,000 men put down the rebellion and killed 3000 rebels in battle.

Punishment

Kett himself was hanged in chains from the walls of Norwich castle. At least 50 others were executed.

SOURCE 1 This eighteenth-century painting shows Robert Kett, refusing the King's offer of a pardon

1. What were the reasons for this protest?
2. Would you describe this event as a protest, riot or a rebellion? Explain your answer.
3. Why did the government punish Kett so harshly?

Case study 3: The Pilgrimage of Grace, 1536 – a protest against religious change

The background

In 1534 Henry VIII left the Roman Catholic Church and set up the Protestant Church of England.

At the local level these changes had a great effect as you can see from Source 1. Almost everyone at this time went to church. Church was a central part of many people's lives. Now they saw changes taking place in their beloved churches. The customs and furnishings that people had known for many years had suddenly altered and they were shaken and frightened by this. They feared that they would be forced to change their religious beliefs. This might not seem important today, but at that time people were very afraid that if they did not worship God in the right way, they would be prevented from entering heaven when they died.

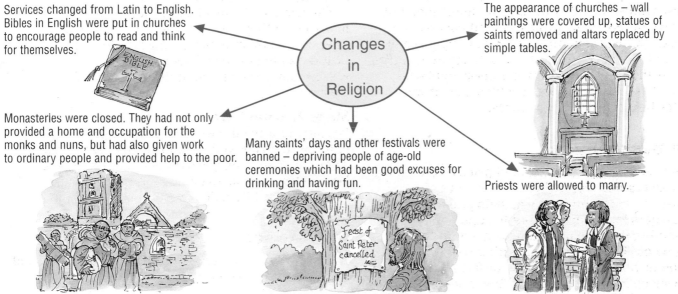

Services changed from Latin to English. Bibles in English were put in churches to encourage people to read and think for themselves.

The appearance of churches – wall paintings were covered up, statues of saints removed and altars replaced by simple tables.

Changes in Religion

Monasteries were closed. They had not only provided a home and occupation for the monks and nuns, but had also given work to ordinary people and provided help to the poor.

Many saints' days and other festivals were banned – depriving people of age-old ceremonies which had been good excuses for drinking and having fun.

Priests were allowed to marry.

SOURCE 1 For more than 100 years, conflict between Catholics and Protestants was an ever present part of English life and the cause of many protests

■ TASK

Below you can see the details of one of the earliest religious protests, the Pilgrimage of Grace, 1536.

	The Pilgrimage of Grace, 1536
Where?	The north, especially Yorkshire and Lincolnshire
How many rebels?	30,000
Who were they?	Ordinary people, led by Robert Aske, a lawyer and gentleman with support from some nobles
Aims?	For England to return to Catholic religious ceremonies, to reopen monasteries, to cut taxes. Some of the leaders wanted to see their rivals among the King's councillors dismissed.
What did they do?	They took control of York, Hull and Pontefract and assembled at Doncaster, ready to talk to the King's advisers. Only one person was killed during the Pilgrimage.

Henry VIII and his councillors faced a difficult decision about how to deal with this protest. They had three options. Which would you have chosen?

Option 1
Agree to meet the rebels' leaders and consider their complaints. Promise to reconsider your policies to reduce the fears and anxieties of the people. They say they are still loyal to the King. They have not tried to march south to attack the royal army.

Option 2
Pardon the majority of rebels but arrest the leaders. Imprison them for a short time but then release them as they have said all along that they are loyal to the King. Harsher action may only lead to further protests and rebellion.

Option 3
Pardon the majority of the rebels but arrest and execute the leaders for treason. Although they claimed they were loyal, they have opposed the King's policies and they must be punished as a warning to others.

Why did Henry VIII react so harshly to the Pilgrimage of Grace?

The King and his advisers took option 3. They pardoned the majority but arrested and tried the leaders for treason. They were condemned to death. Henry VIII ordered that they should be executed in their home counties as a stronger warning to other possible rebels. Aske was hanged, drawn and quartered in York. In total nearly 200 were executed for their protest.

Why were these protesters treated so harshly? Their protest was peaceful. Although the rebels criticised the King's advisers, they proclaimed their loyalty to him. So why were they treated as rebels and traitors?

Explanation 1: The Great Chain of Being

The picture in Source 2 tells us a great deal about sixteenth-century ideas. It comes from the front of the official Bible which was placed in every church at this time. At the top is God. Immediately below God is King Henry VIII. He is passing on God's orders (*verbum dei*) to his priests who then pass them on to the ordinary people – shown clustered at the bottom of the picture. This pattern was known as the Great Chain of Being. The message is that anyone who challenges or criticises Henry is also challenging God. God had created this pattern of society. If God's pattern was disrupted then there would be chaos for everyone – even if protests were peaceful.

That was the theory. Many believed it and you can see that the king and the nobles had their own reasons for wanting everyone to believe it. They did not want the Chain of Being turned upside down!

Explanation 2: Fear of Catholic invasion

There was another practical reason for treating rebels harshly. After Henry had created the Church of England, there was a danger of invasion by Catholic countries who wanted to restore Catholicism in England on behalf of the Pope. Any rebellion might encourage such enemies and give them the chance to succeed. As one writer said at the time: 'rebelling is like making a hole in the side of the ship you are sailing in.'

1. What were the aims of the people who joined the Pilgrimage of Grace?
2. Would you describe this event as a protest or a rebellion? Explain your choice.
3. Why were they treated as rebels?
4. Why do you think the leaders were punished so severely?

SOURCE 2 ▶
The title page of the Great Bible, first published in 1539 at Henry VIII's command

■ TASK

The leaders of the Pilgrimage of Grace were executed with great savagery. Put yourself in the expensive fur-lined boots of one of the King's advisers, a bishop or nobleman. Explain why these punishments are necessary.

Case study 4: 1605 – a conspiracy against the King

Background

Seventy years after the Pilgrimage of Grace there were still fears of religious protest.

■ ACTIVITY

Put yourself in the shoes of King James I. It is 1603 and you have just been crowned, following the long reign of Elizabeth I. One of the most important and difficult decisions you have to take is how to treat the Catholic people of England. There are laws banning Catholic services but they have not been strongly enforced. Your people, both Protestant and Catholic, are waiting to see what kind of policy you will take towards Catholics. These are your options:

Option 1
Maintain the same policy as in the 1590s. Keep the laws as they are but do little to enforce them.

Option 2
Repeal the anti-Catholic laws and allow people freedom to worship however they wish.

Option 3
Keep the laws but enforce them more strongly, PROSECUTING those who do not attend Church of England services and collecting fines.

The panels below and opposite give you information that you need to make your choice. Good luck!

Events in Elizabeth's reign

1559	Elizabeth created a moderate Protestant church.
1570	The Pope declared that Elizabeth was not legally queen, that English people need not obey Elizabeth and that anyone who assassinated her would be forgiven by the Catholic Church.
1571, 1583, 1586	Plots by Catholics to depose Elizabeth and put her Catholic cousin Mary, Queen of Scots, on the throne.
1574 onwards	Catholic priests sent to England to support Catholics and convert people to Catholicism.
1585	Beginning of war with Spain, the most powerful Catholic nation in Europe.
1587	Mary Queen of Scots executed after a plot to make her queen had failed.
1588	The Spanish Armada sent to invade England, depose Elizabeth and restore the Catholic Church.
1590s	Fifty-three Catholic priests executed for treason.
	By 1600 there was little sign of Catholic opposition to Elizabeth. The plots and risings had faded away.

Laws against Catholics
■ Heavy fines for not attending Church of England services.
■ Imprisonment and fines for taking part in Catholic services.
■ Catholic priests were accused of treason for trying to convert people to Catholicism.

But
No great efforts were made to investigate Catholics and fines were not collected. The government's aim was for the laws to frighten Catholics so that they did not try to rebel. Therefore Catholics were allowed to worship in their own way provided it was done in private.

What did people expect of James?
Catholics made up about five per cent of the people. They hoped for an end to anti-Catholic laws. James seemed to be tolerant and prepared to REPEAL these laws.

Protestants expected the anti-Catholic laws to be kept and some hoped that they would be strongly enforced. There was still great suspicion, hatred and fear of Catholics after the events of Elizabeth's reign. Many powerful members of James' council were strongly anti-Catholic and also believed that the country would be seriously weakened if it had more than one religion because this would produce arguments and disunity.

How would you react to James' decisions?

Time to put yourself in a different pair of shoes – a Catholic pair! King James has made his decisions.

■ He has ordered that Catholics who do not attend Church of England services should be fined and the fines should be collected promptly.
■ He has ordered that Catholics should be identified and convicted for holding private services.
■ James has declared his 'utter detestation of [Catholics'] superstitious religion'.
■ Finally, James has made peace with his Catholic enemy, ending a long and hugely expensive war. Spain will not be sending any further help to English Catholics.

This is not what you hoped for!
How are you going to react to this news?

Some old Catholic friends have suggested taking action against these new measures. Will you:

■ Join your friends in stirring up a protest, gathering together all the Catholics in the north and demanding a meeting with King James and his councillors. This should force him to rethink his policies.
■ Say 'no' to your old friends. The punishment for challenging the King is a horrifying death.
■ Join your friends in an attempt to kill James and topple his government. A meeting and protest will do no good.

What really happened in 1605?

The shoes you have been standing in – in case you haven't guessed – were those of Guy Fawkes. He was persuaded to join a Catholic plot to blow up James I and his ministers at the opening of Parliament.

The plot was discovered – some historians believe that the government knew about it right from the start. Fawkes was arrested, red-handed, in the cellar of the Parliament building which was already packed with gunpowder. The rest of the plotters were hunted down.

Source 1 shows the fate of the plotters. Having confessed under torture, they were tried and found guilty. They were dragged on hurdles to their execution through the crowds, hanged, but taken down while still alive, castrated, disembowelled and cut into quarters. Even the bodies of some of the plotters who had been killed in the Midlands were dug up and quartered. Then the quarters were sent to different towns for display on spikes above town gates.

One writer of the time explained that this display of human remains 'shows God's blessing upon the nation and the justice of the country that does punish them'. More practically, the humiliation and agony of the traitors was intended to put others off the idea of challenging the King. The government made sure that people celebrated 5 November by passing a law requiring celebrations and bell-ringing on that day every year.

■ TASK

1. Why did religious protests increase in the 1500s?
2. Why was there such fear of Catholics?
3. Which of the policies did you choose on page 62. Explain why.
4. Which of the options did you choose on page 63. Explain why.
5. Why did the plotters try to blow up James I?
6. Why was their execution so cruel?

In Chapter 6 you will return to this theme and see how the treatment of protesters began to change from 1700 onwards.

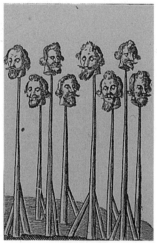
a

b   c

SOURCE 1 The execution of the plotters. Cheap prints of this kind sold well

4

CRIME AND PUNISHMENT IN EARLY MODERN BRITAIN 1500–1750

Execution mad! Why did punishments become so bloody between 1500 and 1750?

IN 1770 WAR with Spain seemed likely over some distant islands hardly anyone had heard of – the Falkland Islands. Sailors were desperately needed and so press-gangs scoured towns and villages, kidnapping any men they could find for the navy.

One of their victims was Mary Jones' husband. Eighteen-year-old Mary was left alone to look after two children. She was unable to pay for her lodgings so she was turned out into the street. Alone in London, confused and desperate, she took a piece of cloth off a shop counter, realised the shopkeeper had seen her and put it back.

She had not stolen anything but the shopkeeper insisted on prosecuting her because there had been a lot of shop-lifting in the area.

Mary was convicted of theft and hanged.

That terrible story provides just one example of the severe punishments being used in the eighteenth century. Punishments became harsher throughout the period. In 1688 50 crimes were punishable by death. By 1765 the number had risen to 160! So harsh were the punishments that the legal system in the 1700s became known as the 'Bloody Code'.

Nowadays it is difficult to read Mary Jones' story without shuddering. How could anyone condemn her to hanging? But they did. It's our job to find out why. One of the most important tasks facing a historian is to understand why people in the past behaved and thought as they did.

It is too simple to say that people in the 1700s were very cruel and hardened to the idea of executions. To really understand why Mary and hundreds like her were executed, and why punishments became so 'bloody', you will need to explore the influence of:

- changes in society
- changes in crime – what was happening to crime through this period, was it an increasing problem, did people think it was an increasing problem?
- changes in attitudes to punishment – were attitudes to punishment changing?
- changes in policing – how policing and law enforcement were changing.

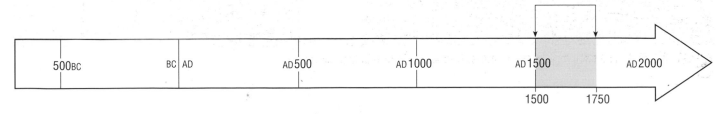

What was the Bloody Code?

SOURCE 1 A mass public execution in London, painted by a French revolutionary artist, Theodore Gericault

SOURCE 2 The number of crimes carrying the death penalty

1688	50
1765	160
1815	225

SOURCE 3 Some of the crimes that carried the death penalty in the 1700s

Stealing horses or sheep
Destroying turnpike roads
Cutting down growing trees
Pickpocketing goods worth one shilling or more
Shop-lifting goods worth five shillings
Being out at night with a blackened face
Sending threatening letters
Deliberately breaking tools used to manufacture wool
Stealing from a rabbit warren
Murder
(plus 150 or more others)

Execution

In the seventeenth century the death penalty was still used for major crimes such as murder, treason, COUNTERFEITING and arson just as it had been in the Middle Ages. Each year hundreds of people were hanged. Executions were always in public because it was thought this deterred the watchers from committing similar crimes themselves.

Execution was also used for theft of goods worth over one shilling – again as it had been in the Middle Ages.

All this shows **continuity**. The big **change** in this period was the number of (apparently minor) crimes punished by execution. Through the 1600s the number increased gradually, then from the late 1600s the number began to increase very rapidly as you can see in Source 2. In 1723 alone the Waltham Black Act added 50 new capital crimes. In fact the first reaction of the law-makers to any new crime which worried them was to make it a capital crime.

This was the 'Bloody Code'. Of course they didn't use the term 'Bloody Code' at the time. This was a name the critics of harsh punishment gave to it later on. To many people at the time, the Code was just common sense. If you want to stop crime you must punish it harshly.

1. Why did the legal system become known as the Bloody Code?
2. Describe two major changes in punishments in this period.
3. Why do you think imprisonment was still a rare punishment?
4. Most punishments still took place in public. Why do you think this was?

The big idea

Punishment should be as harsh as possible, and as public as possible to deter people from committing crime.

Punishment should get rid of the worst offenders, either by killing or transporting them.

Other punishments

As well as execution, there were many other punishments that could be used. Some of these you will know from earlier periods. A couple were brand new.

Old punishments

Pillory

The pillory was used to punish crimes such as cheating at cards, selling under-weight or rotten goods, and persistent swearing. Some criminals sentenced to the pillory did not suffer at all. A man who was pilloried for refusing to pay the tax on soap was cheered for an hour by the crowd! Two men who had won £4000 playing with loaded dice were not so fortunate – they were pelted with stones. Criminals convicted of sexual crimes, particularly involving children, were likely to be attacked and sometimes killed in the pillory.

Stocks

The stocks were used mainly for those who could not afford to pay fines, often imposed for drunkenness.

Ducking stool

The ducking stool was used to punish women who had been convicted of being SCOLDS, which meant swearing or arguing in public, trouble-making or disobeying their husbands.

Carting

Carting meant being paraded around the streets in a cart and was used to punish VAGRANCY, ADULTERY or running a brothel.

Whipping

Whipping usually took place on market day so it could be as public as possible. Whipping was ordered for a wide variety of offences. Vagrants were whipped before being turned out of the parish. Thieves who had stolen goods worth less than a shilling were whipped; so were regular drunkards and those who refused to attend church, or seriously misbehaved in church. On one occasion two men were whipped in London, one for stealing a radish, the other for child abuse. By the 1700s whipping was less common because transportation was used regularly as a punishment.

Fines

Many minor offences, such as swearing, gambling, drunkenness and failing to attend church were punished by fines.

Prisons

Prisons continued to be used largely for debtors. A sentence of imprisonment was rare, especially once TRANSPORTATION became such a routine punishment. Prisons were second-best. Far better to send the criminals overseas.

New punishments

Bridewell

Many towns built a house of correction in the late 1500s, to punish and reform offenders. The first of these was the Bridewell Palace in London and so all came to be known as Bridewells. Vagrants, unmarried mothers and runaway apprentices were sent to the Bridewell where they were whipped and set to hard work. They were also used as an extra punishment when other punishments or warnings had not worked. The authorities believed that crimes were usually a result of not working hard enough.

Transportation

The greatest change in punishments in this period was the introduction of transportation. From the 1660s criminals were sent to the American colonies. Between the Transportation Act of 1718 and 1769 70 per cent of the criminals convicted at the Old Bailey in London were transported. In all 36,000 people were transported. It became a routine sentence: seven years, fourteen years or life, depending on the crime. Charles Scoldwell was transported for seven years for stealing two ducks. Transportation for life was the most common punishment for murderers who escaped execution. Once in America, some prisoners suffered conditions that were close to slavery. Nevertheless, it was criticised in England by those who thought it was a soft option.

What factors affected crime and punishment 1500–1750?

■ TASK

How do you think each of the factors below might help explain the development of the Bloody Code? (Do not worry if you are not sure! You will be able to give a much fuller answer at the end of the chapter.)

1 Developments in crime

Most crime was theft of money, food and belongings, usually of low value. Violent crimes were a small minority of cases. This pattern of crime had not changed since the Middle Ages. The amount of crime seems to have gone up in the sixteenth and early seventeenth centuries but fell after that and was much lower in the early 1700s.

However, some crimes and criminals became well known, either because they were very common or because they got a lot of publicity in pamphlets and broadsheets (a type of early newspaper) that had not existed in the Middle Ages. These new types of criminals included:

- Vagabonds – poverty and unemployment in the sixteenth century led more people to wander the country in search of work and food. Some of these people were criminals already or turned to crime in desperation.
- Highwaymen – highway robbery by masked riders became a danger from the mid-seventeenth century onwards. More people were travelling by coach, providing an easy target for thieves.
- Smugglers – high taxes on many imports such as tea meant that there was a large market for smuggled goods sold at low prices. In some areas in the 1700s government revenue officers could not control the well-organised smugglers.
- Poachers – the laws against hunting were some of the harshest of all. Hunting deer or rabbits was punishable by death. In country areas poaching was part of many people's way of life.

Beware, hundreds of dangerous vagabonds at large in the county.

Stand and deliver! Your money or your life!

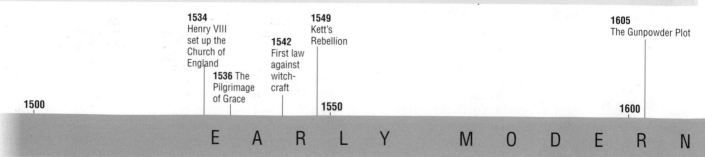

1534 Henry VIII set up the Church of England

1536 The Pilgrimage of Grace

1542 First law against witchcraft

1549 Kett's Rebellion

1605 The Gunpowder Plot

1500　　　　　　　　　1550　　　　　　　　　1600

E A R L Y   M O D E R N

2 The belief that crime was increasing

Despite the fall in crime in the late 1600s, most people believed that crime was increasing. There were several reasons for this belief.

Since the invention of printing in the late fifteenth century, more books and other printed material had appeared. By the late 1600s there was a market for broadsheets which attracted readers with tales of violent crimes. Earlier pamphlets had been published about particular crimes such as vagabondage and witchcraft.

Changes in religion in the 1530s under Henry VIII led to many religious protests and rebellions. Although these became fewer there was still a fear that rebellion for religious reasons could happen at any time. This period also saw the greatest rebellion of all – the English Civil War in which Parliament fought and beat the king – and this also made many people feel insecure for decades afterwards.

3 Methods of catching criminals

No police force had been created to catch criminals or collect evidence. Instead, the hue and cry was still used and the system of unpaid constables. In the early 1700s thief-takers – men who earned their living from the rewards they received for bringing criminals to justice – began to track down criminals, particularly in London.

As a result, criminals had little fear of being caught. The system of policing remained inefficient and did not deter people from crime.

I shall certainly vote in favour of the Transportation Act. We must protect our property from thieves.

4 The attitudes of the law-makers

The MPs who passed the laws that made up the Bloody Code were all wealthy landowners. Their motives for passing those laws were a mixture of wanting to do good for the people as a whole and wanting to defend their own rights and property from thieves and others who they regarded as criminals. Nearly everyone believed that the best way of deterring criminals was to have savage, terrifying punishments that would frighten people away from crime.

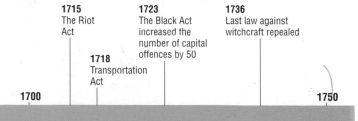

1642–49
The English Civil War

1650

1700

1715
The Riot Act

1718
Transportation Act

1723
The Black Act increased the number of capital offences by 50

1736
Last law against witchcraft repealed

1750

B R I T A I N

HOW DID CHANGES IN SOCIETY LEAD TO CHANGES IN CRIME?

Introduction: social change

LIFE IN ENGLAND was changing a great deal between 1500 and 1750. These changes affected crime and punishment in many different ways. Source 1 shows some of the main changes.

These changes:

■ created some new crimes
■ created some new opportunities for old crimes
■ created much anxiety about crime which helped lead to punishments becoming harsher.

Changes in society

1. Population growth
The population was steadily increasing. With more people it was harder for some to find work.

2. Increased wealth and increased poverty
England was becoming wealthier, so some people were getting richer. However, the majority remained very poor – particularly when bad harvests increased food prices or a fall in trade meant that people lost jobs.

3. Religious ideas
In the early 1600s the views of extreme Protestants began to influence more people. They believed in hard work. They were opposed to many traditional entertainments, especially on Sundays when people should be at church.

4. Increased travel
Better roads helped the development of coaches and so more people were travelling around the country. Horses became cheaper to buy.

5. Taxation
Governments were in greater need of money for wars and other expenses. As there were no income tax, many other taxes were increased including customs duties on imports.

6. Landowners' attitudes
Landowners were getting richer. They wanted to protect their property, rights and power against other classes. They wanted to keep the poor in their place.

7. Commerce
Business and trade were growing rapidly. London was becoming a major centre for commerce throughout England. Banks and banknotes were new developments.

8. Invention of printing
After the invention of printing in the fifteenth century, more books and other printed material such as broadsheets and pamphlets had appeared. Favourite topics for early pamphlets were alarming reports on crime.

9. Political change
In the 1600s England went through a political revolution and a bloody civil war which made many people feel insecure for decades afterwards.

SOURCE 1 Changes in society 1500–1750

■ TASK

Over the next nineteen pages you are going to investigate some changes in crime in detail, but before you plough into them think about the connections between these changes in society and some of the new developments in crime.

1. Here are seven types of crime that particularly worried people in this period. Which social change or changes from Source 1 do you think might have played a part in the development of each crime?
2. Are there any crimes that seem difficult to explain?
   Don't worry if you are not sure. These are just first ideas. You will have another go at this later.

Vagrancy

(wandering the country without a settled home or job)

Witchcraft

(using the Devil's power to harm your neighbour)

Poaching

(catching birds and animals on another person's land)

Drinking and not attending church

Highway robbery

(stopping a coach and robbing the passengers)

Smuggling

(bringing goods into the country without paying import tax on them)

Riot

(a group of people joining together to protest and sometimes damaging property or using violence)

71

What should we do with the vagabonds?

■ TASK

You have been asked to present a five-minute radio programme on vagabonds: 'Should we help them or punish them?'. You must present the programme as if you were in the early 1600s, showing the attitudes people had at that time. Use the material below and on pages 73–75 for your evidence.

Here is a suggested outline for your programme:

a) who the vagabonds are
b) why they are vagabonds
c) how great the problem of vagabonds really is
d) how they are punished and why they are punished this way
e) how they are helped and why they are helped in this way
f) your conclusions about whether the balance between helping and punishing is right.

Remember that you are trying to present this from the point of view of the people at the time.

Who were the vagabonds?

Vagabonds were beggars, tramps and vagrants who wandered the country without a settled job.

Some vagabonds were soldiers who had been demobbed, or criminals, but most were unemployed people moving to a new town or village looking for work. The records of the town of Warwick, for example, list among the vagabonds:

■ a girl from Cheltenham going to find work as a servant
■ a man from Henley-on-Thames who said that 'he had no trade to live on but is only a labourer and is come into the area to seek work but can find none'
■ a silk-weaver who had been to various places to seek work but was now heading for London
■ John Weaver of Stratford who had sold 'small-wares and was robbed of them and so was now forced to go abroad [elsewhere]'.

In the Middle Ages people had not been very free to move around from place to place. By the 1500s these restrictions had been removed and there was a lot of travel from town to town.

How were the poor helped?

Each village and town did try to help the genuine poor of their own parish. The aged, the sick and children of poor families received help to buy food, which was paid for out of the poor-rate, a local tax paid by the better-off residents.

Why did people think that vagabonds were a problem?

In the 1500s people became worried about vagabonds for three main reasons:

■ People felt that **idleness was wrong**. Puritan religion taught that everyone should work hard so they did not have time to be tempted to commit sins. In fact, not working was seen as a crime in its own right. Most people did not object to helping the genuine poor, who could not work because they were old or sick, but were suspicious of outsiders asking for help, especially if they appeared to be healthy and fit enough to work.
■ Vagrants were **blamed for many crimes** such as thefts, assaults and murders. It made sense to many people that vagrants were more likely to commit crime because that was the only way they could get money to buy food.
■ Many people **were worried about the cost**. Each village and town raised poor-rates to help the genuine poor of their own parish. Local people did not want to spend their hard-earned money supporting the poor or idle from another parish. They wanted them to return to their own towns or villages.

These worries were particularly acute at times of poverty when the number of unemployed and poor people, looking for work, naturally increased. And they were further stoked by alarming pamphlets and books such as Sources 1–3.

■ SOURCE INVESTIGATION

1. Look at Sources 1 and 2. Do these sources give the same impression of vagabonds?
2. Explain how Sources 1 and 2 could increase fear of vagabonds.
3. Compare Sources 3 and 4. Do William Harrison and Edward Hext agree about how serious a problem vagabonds were?
4. For each source explain how far it is
   a) useful
   b) reliable
   for the study of vagabonds in the 1500s.

SOURCE 1 The title page of Thomas Harman's book, warning against the dangers of vagabonds, published around 1567. Harman described 23 different types of vagabonds, including London gangs who were said to prey on wealthy visitors to the city

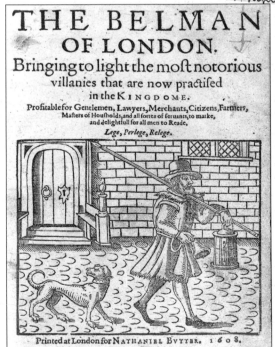

SOURCE 2 The title page of *The Belman* by Thomas Dekker, published in 1608. A Belman was a watchman and this book claimed to tell the secrets 'of all the idle vagabonds in England: their conditions, their laws among themselves, their degrees and orders, their meetings and their manners of living'

SOURCE 3 From William Harrison's *Description of England*, published in 1577

66 *With us the poor is commonly divided into three sorts. The third consists of the thriftless poor, the vagabond that will abide nowhere but runneth up and down from place to place.*

Idle beggars make corrosives and apply them to the fleshy parts of their bodies and lay ratsbane, spearwort, crowfoot and suchlike unto their healthy limbs to raise pitiful sores and move the hearts of passers-by so they will bestow large gifts upon them. How liberally they beg, what forcible speech which makes me think that punishment is more suitable for them than generosity or gifts.

They are all thieves and extortioners. They lick the sweat from the true labourer's brows and take from the godly poor what is due to them. It is not yet sixty years since this trade began but how it has prospered since that time is easy to judge for they are now supposed to amount to above 10,000 persons as I have heard reported. Moreover they have devised a language among themselves which they name canting such as none but themselves are able to understand. 99

SOURCE 4 From a letter sent by Edward Hext, a JP in Somerset, to Lord Burghley, Queen Elizabeth's chief minister, in 1596. Hext was warning Burghley about the 'daily multiplying' of thefts and other crimes

66 *I may justly say that the infinite numbers of idle, wandering people and robbers of the land are the chief cause of the problem because they labour not and yet they spend doubly much as the labourer does for they lie idly in the alehouses day and night eating and drinking excessively. The most dangerous are the wandering soldiers and other stout rogues. Of these wandering idle people there are three or four hundred in a shire and though they go two and three in a company yet all or the most part in a shire do meet either at a fair or market or in some alehouse once a week.* 99

How did they treat vagabonds?

Through the century government took different measures against vagabonds. The chart below summarises the main ones.

1530   **1540**   **1550**   **1560**

1531
Unemployed men and women found begging, or vagrants, should be whipped until their bodies 'be bloody' and returned to their birthplace or previous residence.

1547
First offence – two years slavery.
Second offence – slavery for life or execution.

1550
The 1547 Act was repealed as too severe. The 1531 Act was revived.

Were the vagabonds really such a problem?

Many ordinary citizens did live 'in terror of the tramp' as they put it. The harshness of the laws against vagabonds tells us that landowners and the government believed that vagabonds were behind many crimes and were a serious danger to peace. Some vagabonds **were** undoubtedly criminals – CUT-PURSES, petty thieves and fraudulent beggars – as described by Harrison. There were also some gangs although nothing like as organised as Harrison and others feared.

However, the real picture was not so alarming.

Most vagabonds were not a threat to law and order

Most vagabonds were not criminals or the devious beggars described by Harrison in Source 3. They were genuinely poor and unemployed people looking for work. As the population was increasing there simply was not enough work for everyone. In some areas, changed work patterns increased the problem (see page 72).

Even in years of good harvests many people could only just 'get by'. When the harvest failed, bread prices went up rapidly and the poor became desperate. Then they would travel in search of any kind of work, hoping against hope that something would turn up.

In the same way, workers in trades might suddenly hit a bad time when their trade went through a recession. They would then have to get on the road and look for work. For example, in 1528 the cloth trade with the Netherlands was disrupted by political disputes which caused poverty among the weavers.

SOURCE 5 A beggar being whipped. This was the normal punishment for vagabonds. For example, in April 1575 in Middlesex, 'John Allen, Elizabeth Turner, Humphry Fox, Henry Rower and Agnes Wort, being over 14 years old and having no lawful means of livelihood were vagrants and had been vagrants in other parts of the country. Sentenced to be flogged severely and burnt on the right ear'

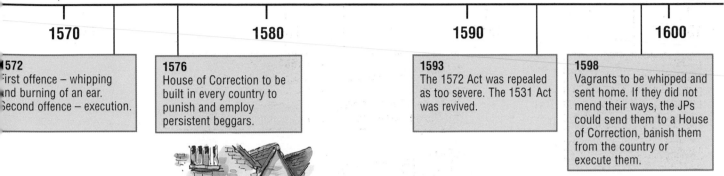

1570	1580	1590	1600

1572
First offence – whipping and burning of an ear. Second offence – execution.

1576
House of Correction to be built in every country to punish and employ persistent beggars.

1593
The 1572 Act was repealed as too severe. The 1531 Act was revived.

1598
Vagrants to be whipped and sent home. If they did not mend their ways, the JPs could send them to a House of Correction, banish them from the country or execute them.

In normal years vagrancy was not a big problem

The city with the greatest number of vagrants was London. It was the only large town in England in this period. Many people went there thinking that they would be bound to find work or that it offered good opportunities for crime. Even so, in 1560 the London Bridewell dealt with only 69 vagabonds.

However, following the bad harvests of the 1570s the number of vagrants had grown to 209 per year. The late 1590s were years of even greater poverty. Wages were at their lowest point since the year 1200. In 1600 the number of vagrants in London was up to 555.

In normal years Oxford JPs dealt with twelve vagrants per year. In 1598 they dealt with 67. It was the same story in Salisbury where there were 96 vagrants in 1598 instead of the usual 20 or fewer.

1. Study the timeline above. How would you describe the pattern of punishment through the century:
   a) increasingly severe
   b) increasingly lenient
   c) alternating between severe and lenient?
   Explain your choice carefully.
2. Why was there such an increase in vagrancy in some periods?
3. Why might problems of vagrancy in London have had an impact on the attitudes of law-makers?
4. What impact might the problem of vagrancy have on making punishments bloodier?

SOURCE 6 A beggar being hanged. For example, Thomas Maynard, Oswald Thompson and John Barres were tried in London in March 1576 for vagrancy and were found guilty. They were severely flogged and burnt through the right ear. In June they were again wandering at St Giles in the Fields and elsewhere. They were arrested as incorrigible [unreformable, incurable] vagrants, tried and hanged

Why did singing, drinking and celebrating Christmas become crimes in the seventeenth century?

THERE WERE RAPID changes in religion in the middle of the sixteenth century (see page 59). Those rapid changes seemed to come to an end in 1558 when Queen Elizabeth I decided that the Church of England should be a moderate church. This pleased the great majority of people but angered the Puritans (extreme Protestants) who believed that the Church under Elizabeth was too Catholic.

The Puritans

The Puritans wanted everyone to live strictly according to the word of the Bible. They believed that Sundays should be used only for religious worship. They were anxious to control and improve people's behaviour to save them from Hell.

After Elizabeth I died in 1603, the Puritans became increasingly powerful. By the 1640s and 1650s they controlled Parliament.

During this period they changed the laws to force people to follow a strict Puritan lifestyle.

- They strictly enforced existing laws against drunkenness and swearing.
- They introduced new laws to suppress horse-racing, cock-fighting, bear-baiting.
- They closed brothels and reduced the number of alehouses.
- They banned sport and games on Sundays. Even going for a walk was not allowed, unless it was walking to church.

Puritan laws of the 1640s and 1650s

1642	London theatres were closed.
1644	May Day celebrations were forbidden.
1650	Adultery was punishable by death.
	A law was introduced to punish anyone caught swearing.
1653	Weddings in churches were banned although this law was repealed in 1657.
1657	Betting and music in taverns and alehouses were made illegal.

What was wrong with Christmas?

The Puritans made unlawful many traditional customs that they believed were against the word of the Bible. In 1647 it became illegal to celebrate Christmas, Easter and Whitsun. A new non-religious holiday was introduced on the second Tuesday of every month.

Christmas and Easter celebrations were banned because Puritans believed that they were not true Christian festivals. They said they had originally been pagan festivals before the time of Christ and had simply been taken over by the Church. They therefore believed that people would go to Hell for celebrating a pagan festival.

These laws had a mixed impact. It was relatively easy for the Puritans to use soldiers to keep churches closed. However, it was harder to stop people singing carols, feasting or having private services in their own homes. In 1654 the Venetian ambassador noted that the Christmas festivities lasted almost a week even though they were against the law. Shopkeepers also marked Christmas by refusing to open their shops which were supposed to stay open as Christmas Day was an ordinary day.

1. Draw up a table with two columns. In the first column list things which the Puritans banned. In the second column explain why the Puritans banned each thing.
2. 'Governments can create a crime from something which appears to other people to be quite reasonable behaviour.'
a) Choose one example from this page to support this statement.
b) Choose one present-day example to support this statement.

SOURCE 1 The works of light (left-hand side) and the works of darkness (right-hand side): a Puritan engraving produced in 1639 to show what Puritans thought people should and shouldn't do on a Sunday

■ TASK

Source 1 shows some of the things that the Puritans approved of and the things they disapproved of. You are a member of a group of Puritans trying to draw up laws to encourage the works of light and ban the works of darkness. In groups of three discuss:
a) why these laws are needed
b) what problems you might have enforcing these laws.

You can get a sheet from your teacher to help you get started.

The streets of Dorchester in the 1620s

Here you can see some of the people who lived in Dorchester in Dorset in the 1620s at the time when the Puritans had control of the town. You can also see the crimes they committed. You have to decide how to punish them.

The information about the people shown in the picture is taken from a carefully researched book about this period by D. Underdown.

TASK 1

Work in groups.

You are Puritan judges in Dorchester in the 1620s. The people before you have been found guilty of a crime. You have to decide how to punish them. These are the punishments you can choose from:

pillory
stocks
ducking stool
carting
whipping
hanging
fines
the Bridewell.

For more information about these punishments see pages 66–67.

1. Choose one category of crime.
2. Decide how to punish each of the people in that category.
3. Write notes to explain why you chose that punishment.
4. If you have time, repeat steps 1–3 for another category of crime.
5. When you have finished, your teacher can tell you what the actual punishments were.

1. Missing church

a) John Facy and his wife. Baking bread instead of going to church.

b) Gabriel Butler, barber surgeon. Did not attend church because he was visiting a patient.

c) Mary Lovelace. Fined for missing church but she could not pay the fine.

d) Andrew Fooke and Katherine Goodfellow. They went off to Bockington to drink milk and cream instead of going to church.

e) John Colliford. Repeatedly missing church.

f) Henry Hobbes and Hugh Haggard. Talking in the street during the church service.

2. Swearing

a) Henry Gollop. Swearing 40 times.

b) Humphrey Perry. Swearing at his wife.

c) Agnes Keate and the widow Benfield. Screaming and swearing at each other in the street.

3. Alcohol related

a) Margaret Barter. Unlicensed ale-selling.

b) Matthew North. Drunkenness.

c) Mary Savage. Drunkenness and 'having lived a long time idly and disordered out of service.'

4. Disrespect and disobedience

a) Elizabeth Bull. Refusing to obey her husband despite warnings from the constable.

b) Joseph Dare. Singing rude songs about the constable.

c) George Jenkins. Begging after he had been forbidden to beg.

d) John King and Nicholas Symes. Men playing and laughing a second time during a church service after being warned.

5. Violence

a) John Hoskins and Richard Butler. Youths fighting in church.

b) Anne Samways and Em Gawler. Quarrelling in the street. Anne struck Em with a wash kettle.

c) Eleanor Galpin. She killed her ten-day-old baby when her husband fell ill and they faced severe poverty.

■ TASK 2

Work on your own.

1. Make a list of the crimes shown here that are no longer crimes today.

2. Why were they crimes in the 1620s when they are not crimes today?

W*itchhunt*

1645: the year of the witchfinder

One day in 1645, a cloaked figure rode into the small town of Manningtree in Essex. His name was Matthew Hopkins. Hopkins was about 25. He had failed to make a success of being a lawyer but he was about to become famous throughout England – as the witchfinder!

For reasons we do not know, Hopkins had begun scouring East Anglia for witches. At Manningtree he named 36 women as witches and began to gather evidence against them. He tortured his suspects, although torture was illegal and was not used in other enquiries into witchcraft. He kept his suspects standing up and forced them to walk until their feet blistered. He made sure they got no sleep, a very effective way of weakening their resistance. He humiliated the suspects by stripping them naked. Both methods were especially effective with old people. Worn down by Hopkins' torture, many suspects confessed.

Hopkins swore that he had seen their 'familiars'. If a mouse, fly or spider found its way into a cell Hopkins claimed it was the witch's familiar, created by the Devil to do the witch's bidding. His helpers found 'the Devil's marks' on the witches' bodies. Any scar, boil or spot was pounced on as the mark of the Devil. They were not difficult to find, as a lifetime of hardship and poor diet inevitably left marks or scars on most people's bodies.

Of the 36 suspects, nineteen were hanged and another nine died of fever in gaol. Six were still being held in prison three years later but their fate is unknown. Just one was acquitted and released – for providing evidence against her fellow suspects.

Success led to success – or fear led to fear. News of so many witches led other towns and villages to summon Hopkins to rid them of witches. At Brandeston, Hopkins accused the 80-year-old vicar, John Lowes, of witchcraft. Lowes was unpopular and had been accused of witchcraft before.

Hopkins made sure he was found guilty this time. He was tortured, 'swum' in a castle moat (see Source 3, page 83) and the Devil's marks were found in his mouth, quite possibly the mouth ulcers that would have been very common in an age of poor nutrition and even poorer dentistry. Lowes was hanged.

Hopkins disappears from the records in 1647. He probably fell ill and died. Why had he launched his witchhunts? Perhaps it was for the money. Witchhunters were paid 'per witch'. In one year Hopkins earned more than most people earned in a lifetime. Perhaps he wanted to make a name for himself. Perhaps he genuinely believed in and hated witches. No one knows for sure.

1. What kinds of people were accused of witchcraft?
2. Why did some confess to being witches?
3. What evidence did Matthew Hopkins use to show that the accused were witches?

Key dates in the history of witchcraft

1542 The first law was passed saying that witchcraft was a crime.
1590 The future King James I wrote an important book on witchcraft.
1645 The year when Matthew Hopkins, witchfinder, accused record numbers of people of witchcraft in Essex.
1717 The last trial for witchcraft.
1736 The last law saying that witchcraft was a crime was repealed.

The real story of witches

In the Middle Ages accusations of witchcraft had been dealt with by church courts. In the 1500s, in the middle of all the religious changes you read about on page 59, it was made a criminal offence, punishable by death and was to be tried by ordinary courts. No one knows for sure why this happened although some said that witches were involved in plots to topple the King by using their supernatural powers.

There was no sudden flood of witchcraft cases but over the next 200 years up to 1000 people (mainly women) were executed as witches.

The story of Matthew Hopkins is the most dramatic in the history of witchcraft in England but it is not typical.

- Such witchhunts were rare. The more common pattern was a steady, but low, number of accusations that someone was a witch and had used supernatural powers to harm another person (see Source 1).
- Most accusations were not the work of witchfinders like Hopkins, but of ordinary villagers accusing another person in their village of witchcraft.

The accusations were recorded and historians have been able to discover a typical pattern.

A typical case

1. A villager, usually an old widow, asks for help from a better-off neighbour, but is refused. Often this followed years of suspicion and tension between the widow and the neighbour.

2. The widow walks away muttering and cursing quietly, maybe even uttering a threat. Both feel angry. The neighbour feels guilty.

3. Some time afterwards, something terrible happens to the neighbour or her family – an illness to her children or animals. Perhaps even a death.

I suspect witchcraft – what else could have caused this sudden illness?

If she is a witch, we must stop her before she can do any more harm.

County	No. of accusations 1560–1700	No. of executions 1560–1700
Sussex	33	1
Surrey	71	5
Hertfordshire	81	8
Kent	132	16
Essex	473 (50 of these were the work of Matthew Hopkins in 1645)	82
Total	790	112 (Altogeth witch ir

SOURCE 1 Accusations of witch between 1560 and 1700 in five co more accusations that never came to accusations was 1558–1603. In Ess accusations took place between 15

Four cases of witchcraft

Case 1: Alice Samuel, 1593

Alice Samuel, a woman of 76, her husband and daughter were accused of making a ten-year-old girl ill. Then the girl's sisters said they too had been bewitched. At the trial the girls had fits when Alice denied witchcraft, but 'recovered' when Alice admitted the charge. Alice, her husband and daughter were all executed.

Case 2: Joan Cooke, Essex, 1567

Joan asked her neighbour for some butter but the neighbour refused. She was accused of bewitching the neighbour's cows, killing one and making the others give multi-coloured milk.

Case 3: George and Jennet Benton, Yorkshire, 1656

The Bentons tried to use a path across land belonging to Richard Jackson. When Jackson sent a servant to stop them George Benton threw a stone that broke two of the servant's teeth. Jackson took Benton to court, after which Benton was heard to say 'it should be a dear day's work to Richard Jackson or his [family] before the year went about'. After that, Jackson said that his wife went deaf, one of their children started having fits and Jackson himself felt strange and ill, feeling he was being pulled about and hearing music, singing and dancing when there was none.

Case 4: Alice Huson and Doll Bilby, Yorkshire in the 1660s

The daughter of the Corbet family fell seriously ill. She believed that Alice and Doll had bewitched her but her parents refused to believe her. They called in doctors from three different towns and sent the girl to a relative's house for a change of air but she did not recover. The girl still insisted that she was bewitched. After four years with no improvement in her health her parents accused the women of witchcraft. They were found guilty.

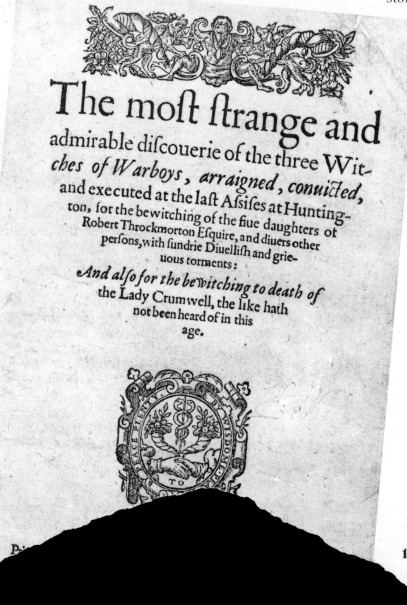

The most strange and admirable discouerie of the three Witches of Warboys, arraigned, conuicted, and executed at the last Assises at Huntington, for the bewitching of the fiue daughters of Robert Throckmorton Esquire, and diuers other persons, with sundrie Diuellish and grieuous torments:

And also for the bewitching to death of the Lady Crumwell, the like hath not been heard of in this age.

1. Look at cases 1–4. For each one explain which show the 'typical features' as described in the case on page 81 and which show [a]typical features'.

   [What] can you learn from case 4 [about] attitudes to witches?

   [pamphl]ets such as Source 2 have [spread belief in w]itchcraft?

SOURCE 3 This woodcut is from a pamphlet about the trial of Mother Sutton, who was accused of being a witch. Swimming as a way of identifying witches was first introduced in 1612 and was a reminder of the medieval trial by ordeal. The accused person's hands were bound and a rope tied around the waist. It was believed that the innocent would sink. If the accused did not sink, this was taken as evidence that he or she was probably a witch. The accused was then examined for the Devil's marks which were taken as the final proof of witchcraft

Were witchcraft trials fair?

A witchcraft trial was a bizarre mix of different ingredients.

Some aspects were like a normal trial. The accusers would present their charge. They would bring witnesses to support it. The accused would be asked to defend themselves. However, 90 per cent of those accused were women and most were elderly widows or spinsters who had no man to speak for them or defend them.

Other aspects were nothing like a normal trial. For example, 'swimming' (see Source 3) was a throw-back to trial by ordeal (see pages 30–31).

Many of the accused were found not guilty and only a small proportion of the accused were executed (see Source 1). Witches were usually only hanged if the court believed they had used their powers to kill someone, or to harm animals or damage property.

It was not being a witch that was considered the main crime: it was using supernatural power to harm others. Nowadays, such punishment might seem illogical, but remember that most people in the sixteenth century believed it was possible to injure or kill others by using supernatural powers.

Why ... ?

The story of witchcraft raises some interesting questions in the history of crime and punishment.

Issue	Possible explanation
Why were accusations typically made by wealthier people against poorer people?	The accusations were a sign of increased inequality in the village. There was tension between the poor and those who were a little richer than them: the poor asked for help more often; the wealthy felt threatened by the demands of the poor. Remember that at this same time the rich were also clamping down on the poor in the laws against vagabonds (see pages 74–75).
Why were most of the accused old women?	This was a sign of social upheaval in village life. The old ties that bound people together as communities or as families were being loosened. Old women would once have been cared for and even respected as wise women. Now they were seen as threatening because they were different. It is one more example of the way that vulnerable or NON-CONFORMIST members of society are sometimes scapegoated as criminals.
Why did people become worried about witches in this period?	Because of religious change. Old beliefs and practices were being transformed. Extreme new beliefs were being preached. Protestants preached that the Devil and his servants were all around trying to draw good Christians away from God. This is backed up by the fact that accusations declined and witchcraft laws were repealed once religious belief became more settled.
Why did accusations tail off in the seventeenth century?	This was a time of increasingly rational thinking. Belief in witches didn't disappear, but educated people (who usually had to judge accusations of witchcraft) were less likely to believe charges of witchcraft than in earlier periods. Another reason was that people were becoming increasingly prosperous. This reduced the tensions in villages. The rich helped the poor more and there were probably fewer requests for help.

The rise and fall of the highwayman

HIGHWAY ROBBERY WAS one of the most infamous and feared crimes of this period. It was not a new crime, but it became much more frequent during this period because there were increased opportunities for travel and many people were wealthier.

Image

The popular view of highwaymen is a glamorous one: daring, masked, well-dressed, 'gentlemen of the road'. They were polite to their victims, especially women, and did not use violence. They did not need to. Few people resisted them. Passengers were all too ready to hand over their purse and even carried two purses in case of robbery. Highwaymen could escape quickly on horseback.

Dick Turpin

Dick Turpin, born in 1705 in Essex, became involved in smuggling before joining a gang of housebreakers famous for their violence. Then he became a highwayman, joining forces with another highwayman, Tom King, apparently after trying to hold him up! The two men worked together so successfully that a reward of £100 was offered for their capture.

Turpin was ruthless, robbing women travelling alone and killing at least one man who tried to capture him. In May 1737 Turpin and King were cornered. Turpin escaped but King was killed by a shot from Turpin's gun. Was it an accident, or Turpin's way of stopping King from talking?

Turpin fled to Yorkshire where he scraped a living as a horse thief. He was arrested after an argument

Reality

In reality, many of them were treacherous, cruel and violent. One highwayman's mask slipped during a robbery and he was recognised by a woman. He cut out her tongue to stop her reporting him. Dick Turpin was typical. You can read about his crimes below.

Highwaymen were greatly feared by ordinary travellers. They were seen as a major danger by traders, largely because they disrupted trade. The worst areas for highway robbery were around London on the main routes to the capital. Highwaymen even ventured into the edge of the city. Horace Walpole, a writer, was shot at in Hyde Park and commented: 'One is forced to travel, even at noon, as if one was going to battle.'

over shooting a cockerel. The authorities did not know who he was. To win his freedom, Turpin wrote to his brother for references, but did not send enough postage so his brother rejected the letter. That was Turpin's unlucky day. At the postmaster's office Turpin's old schoolmaster saw the letter and recognised the writing. He informed the magistrates and they passed the news on to those holding Turpin that they had captured the notorious highwayman. Turpin was executed for horse-stealing in York in 1739.

A hundred years after his death, a poem about Turpin made him the most famous highwayman of all. It glamorised his life and included the story of Turpin riding his horse, Black Bess, to its death as he raced from London to York in a day. In fact, Turpin never owned a horse called Black Bess, nor rode from London to York in a day.

SOURCE 1 Two frames from a nineteenth-century version of the story of Dick Turpin

Why did highway robbery grow and then decline?

Highway robbery grew because of increased travel and increased wealth. The interesting thing for the history of crime and punishment is why highway robbery declined. How far were the ferocious punishments of the Bloody Code responsible? How far was it other factors such as better law enforcement?

■ TASK

Here you can see different factors in the rise and fall of highwaymen.

1. Seven of these factors explain the development of highway robbery in the 1700s. List these seven factors.
2. If the government wanted to put an end to highwaymen, which two factors could it do something about? Explain what it could do.
3. The other factors explain the disappearance of highwaymen. Which are they?
4. If you were a highwayman, which one of these developments would you fear most? Explain why.
5. Highway robbery was a growing danger in the early 1700s at a time when punishments for theft were savage. Do you think that the Bloody Code played an important part in stamping out highway robbery or were other factors more important?

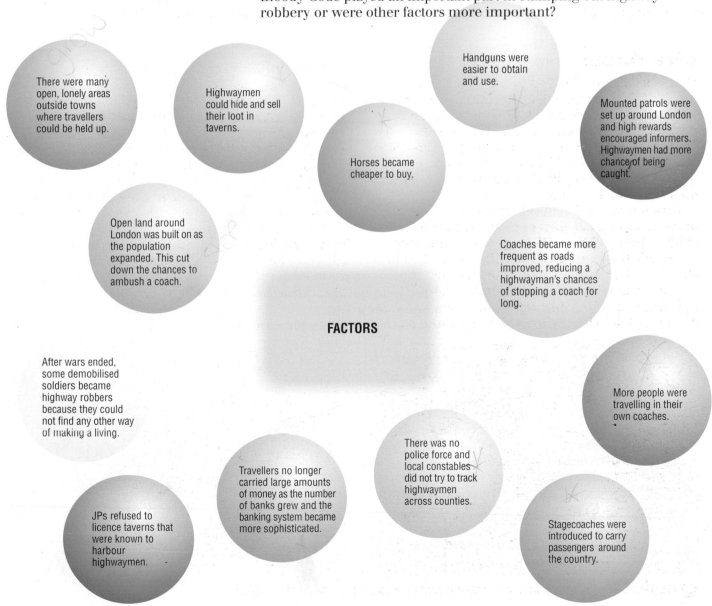

There were many open, lonely areas outside towns where travellers could be held up.

Highwaymen could hide and sell their loot in taverns.

Handguns were easier to obtain and use.

Mounted patrols were set up around London and high rewards encouraged informers. Highwaymen had more chance of being caught.

Horses became cheaper to buy.

Open land around London was built on as the population expanded. This cut down the chances to ambush a coach.

Coaches became more frequent as roads improved, reducing a highwayman's chances of stopping a coach for long.

FACTORS

After wars ended, some demobilised soldiers became highway robbers because they could not find any other way of making a living.

More people were travelling in their own coaches.

JPs refused to licence taverns that were known to harbour highwaymen.

Travellers no longer carried large amounts of money as the number of banks grew and the banking system became more sophisticated.

There was no police force and local constables did not try to track highwaymen across counties.

Stagecoaches were introduced to carry passengers around the country.

Was poaching really a crime?

IN THE 1700s some of the most unpopular laws were those which banned poaching.

- Only landowners whose land was worth £100 a year could hunt and they could hunt anywhere. £100 was a large sum of money, ten years' income for a labourer and more than many doctors, for example, earned in a year.
- Other landowners, with land worth less than £100, could not even hunt on their own land.
- In 1723 the Black Act said that hunting deer, hare or rabbits became a capital crime punishable by death. Anyone found armed, disguised or with blackened faces in any hunting area was assumed to be poaching and could also be executed.
- Possessing dogs or snares that could be used for hunting was punished by a £5 fine or three months in prison.

Critics of these laws believed they were simply there to protect the interests of rich landowners.

SOURCE 1 All these extracts are taken from D. Hay, 'Poaching and the Game Laws on Cannock Chase' in D. Hay (ed.), *Albion's Fatal Tree*, 1975. Dr Hay researched poaching on the Earl of Uxbridge's estates in Staffordshire

66 *a) There were hundreds, perhaps thousands of encounters [between poachers and keepers]. In the fifty years after 1750 the estate stewards mentioned some 200 poachers by name and dealt with at least four times that number. About a third were killing deer, another third were poaching rabbits or hares. The rest were a mixed bag of anglers, labourers keeping illegal guns or dogs and men taking birds or burning the heath – an offence against the game because it destroyed their cover.*

b) For the men of Rugeley, Longdon and Cannock, poaching was a 'custom of the manors' that they and their fathers had followed long before the Pagets [the landowners] acquired the land in the sixteenth century. It meant sport, money, a bit of meat.

c) Faced with gamekeepers who were armed with the law, attracted by rewards and backed by a great landlord, the poachers sometimes resorted to combination and violence. While some men dug in the warrens, others posted on near-by hills would watch for spies and blow horns in time to allow escape.

d) Over a third of the men caught by the keepers came from the villages of Longdon and Rugeley, over two-thirds from within three miles of [the Earl's house] and all the evidence suggests that this small community of labourers, colliers and farmers was united solidly in defence of poaching. The keepers met a wall of silence when they tried to make enquiries but found that word spread like lightning when they obtained a search warrant and that suspects had escaped with 'the apparatus' just before they arrived.

e) Occasionally the solidarity against the keepers broke down. Fear of a death sentence caused one of the burglars of the [Earl's] deer barn to reveal his accomplices. Someone else seeking a reward ratted on three poachers when the keepers agreed not to reveal any names. An alarmed father forced his sixteen-year-old son to reveal the man who had 'enticed' him to hunt deer.

f) Most poachers were poor, if only because most Englishmen were poor. Of the 121 men caught by the keepers for whom there is evidence of their work, 30 per cent were poor labourers, colliers and weavers, 12 per cent are described as servants and 14 per cent were tradesmen or artisans. Twenty per cent were 'middling men', several curates, a clerk and 21 farmers. The remaining number were qualified sportsmen hoping for sport on another gentleman's property.

g) The eighteenth-century poor have not left a literature about the joys of poaching. The excitement of snaring hares, eluding keepers and shooting deer were very real pleasures for Thomas Brown and his friends. Although it was risking a £10 fine (and therefore a year in gaol, for few could pay it) some men kept hidden in their cottages the heads and antlers of deer they had felled, trophies of the chase.

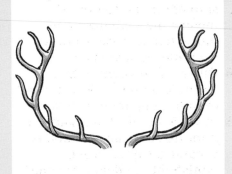

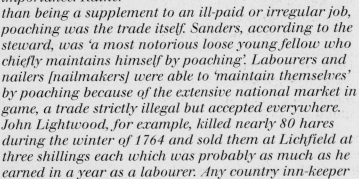

h) For a number of the villagers hunting had an even greater economic importance. Rather than being a supplement to an ill-paid or irregular job, poaching was the trade itself. Sanders, according to the steward, was 'a most notorious loose young fellow who chiefly maintains himself by poaching'. Labourers and nailers [nailmakers] were able to 'maintain themselves' by poaching because of the extensive national market in game, a trade strictly illegal but accepted everywhere. John Lightwood, for example, killed nearly 80 hares during the winter of 1764 and sold them at Lichfield at three shillings each which was probably as much as he earned in a year as a labourer. Any country inn-keeper could supply almost any quantity of game and stage-waggoners on the great roads acted as agents for London buyers.

i) The great majority of men in rural England considered the game laws a great injustice. Middling men were convinced that a law banning everyone but major landowners from hunting was an oppression and doubtless this view was held by the mass of labourers and cottagers. 'Every magistrate knows,' said a writer on hunting, 'that it is the common defence of the poacher, that it is very hard that he should be punished for taking what he had as good a right to as any man.'

j) Farmers and tradesmen made up the juries at courts. As one steward complained 'there is no answering for a common jury as they have in general a strong bias in favour of poachers, being professed enemies to all laws that relate to the Game. **"**

■ TASK

There is to be a debate in the House of Commons about poaching. You are an MP who thinks the laws against poaching are too severe and should be changed. You have to prepare a speech to convince other MPs.

You can get the information you need from extracts a)–j) opposite which describe poaching on the Earl of Uxbridge's estates in Staffordshire. You will have to choose your evidence carefully, however, since some of the evidence could be used by your opponents who think that the harsh laws against poaching should stay just as they are.

Why did the Bloody Code fail to stamp out smuggling?

DURING THE SEVENTEENTH century, governments increased taxes on imported goods to raise extra money. These import duties were unpopular because they raised the price of many desirable goods. They were also very hard to enforce. With several thousand miles of unguarded coastline around Britain it was fairly easy to smuggle in goods, and there was a ready market among people who didn't see why they should pay higher prices. Indeed, like poaching, there were many who did not see smuggling as a crime at all. Many thousands of people were involved in smuggling. Under the Bloody Code the government made smuggling a capital offence (of course!).

■ TASK

You are a revenue (customs) officer investigating smuggling in Sussex, one of the worst areas for smuggling. You have been asked by the government to report back on how best to stop or reduce smuggling. Under the Bloody Code smugglers are punished by hanging. Your job is to decide whether the threat of the death penalty is adequate or whether other policies might have more effect than the threat of hanging. Using the evidence on this spread, present your report, either orally or on paper. Make sure you back up your recommendation with evidence. Use these questions to help structure your report:

a) Which goods are smuggled?
b) Who are the smugglers?
c) How well-organised are the smugglers?
d) Do the smugglers have much local support?
e) Why do people become smugglers?
f) Do people think smuggling is a serious crime?
g) What is the best way to stop smuggling?

1. 'The smugglers pass to and from the seaside, 40 and 50 in a gang in the day time, loaded with teas, brandy and dry goods. Above 200 mounted smugglers were seen one night on the beach waiting for the loading of six boats. They march in a body from the beach about four miles, then separate into small parties.'

2. 'The smugglers came to London about two or three in the morning and could sell to dealers from 1000 to 2000 pounds weight of tea and be out of London by six in the morning.'

4. 'Not one pound in 20 of smuggled tea is seized' said a former smuggler. Three million pounds weight of tea was smuggled into Britain each year, three times as much as was legally imported.

3. Smugglers also sold their tea to 'duffers who go on foot and have coats in which they can quilt a quarter of a hundred weight of tea and bring it to London and these duffers supply the hawkers who carry it around town and sell it to the customers.'

5. 'The officers of the Customs were too few to encounter them. The smugglers were not afraid of the army. If a smuggler was taken and the proof against him clear, no magistrate dare commit him to gaol. If he did he was sure to have his house or barns set on fire if he escaped with his life.'

SOURCE 1 How smuggling was organised in Sussex. The quotations are extracts from real reports from the period

SOURCE 2 If revenue officers or the army seized a cargo, smugglers often got it back by force. This picture shows the Hawkhurst gang seizing tea from the customs house at Poole in 1747. On another occasion smugglers searching for a cargo of tea in Dover 'rode through the town about 5 o'clock in the afternoon with pistols cocked in their hands, swearing and threatening destruction to the Officers of the Customs and to blow out their brains and burn their houses [if they did not get the tea back]'

Who were the smugglers?

In 1748 103 people were listed as 'wanted' for smuggling. Over 70 per cent of them were labourers, fewer than 10 per cent were small farmers and the rest were tradesmen such as butchers and carpenters. However, wealthy people also took part. Robert Walpole, later Prime Minister, smuggled wine into the country while he was a government minister using a government ship.

Why did people become smugglers?

For farm labourers it was a quicker (and more exciting) way to make money than farm labouring. A smuggler could earn six or seven times a farm labourer's daily wage in a night. Anyone who helped smugglers to carry goods from ship to shore could expect to earn nearly twice a labourer's daily wage. The result was that farmers had difficulty recruiting workers in some places on the south coast. In Suffolk in 1749 and in the 1780s, when the army put a temporary end to smuggling, smugglers turned to highway robbery and housebreaking rather than earn a living by farming.

Not all smugglers were farm labourers. In Sussex some came from the cloth industry which was declining in the early eighteenth century. Fishing and iron-making in Sussex also employed fewer people than a century earlier.

Attitudes to smuggling

SOURCE 3 Samuel Wilson, a Sussex grocer who had received smuggled tea, speaking to a committee of Parliament in the 1740s

" … the generality of the people on the coasts are better friends to the smugglers than they are to the Custom House Officers. "

SOURCE 4 Abraham Walter, a tea dealer who had been a smuggler, speaking to a committee of Parliament in the 1740s

" It is extremely dangerous for the Custom House Officers to attempt to seize [smuggled] goods in the coast counties because smugglers are very numerous there and can assemble a great number whenever they need. Nine persons in ten in the area would give them assistance and do lend the smugglers their horses and teams to convey their goods. "

SOURCE 5 The *Gentleman's Magazine*, 1747

" About 24 smugglers well-armed and laden with smuggled goods rode through Rye, Sussex and stopping at the Red Lion to refresh, fired several times to intimidate the inhabitants and observing one, James Marshall, a young man too curious of their behaviour, carried him off. "

SOURCE 6 John Taylor, the keeper of Newgate prison, 1747

" The common people of England in general fancy there is nothing in the crime of smuggling … the poor feel they have a right to shun paying any duty [tax] on their goods. "

SOURCE 7 From a letter from the Duke of Richmond to Sir Cecil Bishop, 1749

" I have often heard you say and with great truth, that the common people of this country have no notion that smuggling is a crime. What then can the government do to show them their error but to punish the guilty? Accessories are to be punished as well as [the smugglers themselves] for you know very well that the common notion in the country is that a man may stand by and see crimes committed and even assist in them and be unpunished if he does not commit the crime with his own hands. "

SOURCE 8 A churchman reporting the words of Richard Mills who was hanged for smuggling and murder

" … as to the charge of smuggling, he owned that he had been concerned in smuggling for a great many years and did not think there was any harm in it. "

Changes in crime: Review Tasks

■ REVIEW TASK 1

New crimes, new opportunities for crime

Pages 70–89 have been investigating the reasons for and the response to developments in crime 1500–1750. This page gives you the chance to summarise your conclusions.

Your teacher will give you a chart like the one below.

A Population growth

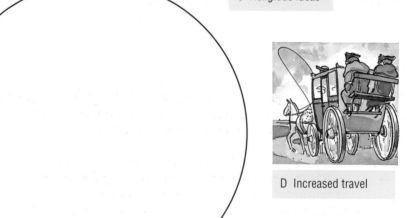

B Increased wealth and increased poverty

C Religious ideas

I Political change

D Increased travel

H Invention of printing

G Commerce – business and trade were growing rapidly

F Landowners' attitudes

E Taxation

1. Write one of these crimes in the central circle on your chart.

   ■ Vagabondage
   ■ Drinking and not attending church
   ■ Witchcraft
   ■ Highway robbery
   ■ Poaching
   ■ Smuggling.

2. You now can work out how the different factors linked together to cause this crime. If you think that, for example, increased travel helped to cause highway robbery, then draw a line from increased travel to the central box. Do this for all the factors that helped bring about your chosen crime. You will need to refer back to earlier pages in this section.

3. Were there any connections between the factors? For example, was the growth in population linked to poverty? If you can see any connections then draw lines between them.

4. On a separate piece of paper list all the factors that played a part in causing the crime. Then write a short essay to explain how the crime came about. Explain how each factor played its part and whether any of them were interlinked. Finally decide whether one factor was more important than the others.

■ REVIEW TASK 2

You will remember a set of questions from page 8. You are now going to apply these to one of the crime case studies on the last nineteen pages. For your chosen crime, answer these questions.

1. Is it a **new crime** or one that has become more common?
2. What is the **motivation** of the person committing the crime?
3. a) Would this crime be regarded as **a crime today**?
   b) If so, would it be seen as a severe crime or a lesser crime?
4. a) **How severely** were the offenders punished?
   b) How does their punishment compare with the punishment of other crimes of their contemporaries?
5. a) **Why** were they punished this way?
   b) What was the motivation of the person determining the punishment?
   c) What does that tell us about the attitudes of people in that period?

You can get a table from your teacher to record your answers, then ask the same questions about another kind of crime you have studied on pages 70–89.

Crime – the statistics

YOU MAY BE feeling dizzy after reading about all these new crimes. They will give you the impression that England was riddled with crime. That was probably what many people believed at the time. But first let us take a step back and look at the overall picture of crime.

Crime rate

Records suggest that crime rose in the 1500s then fell steadily from the early 1600s. Source 1, for example, shows crime in Cheshire.

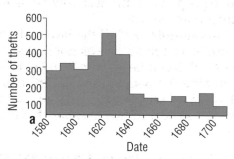

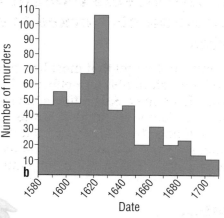

SOURCE 1 The number of cases of
a) theft and other property offences, and
b) murder, heard in the Cheshire courts between 1580 and 1709

A similar pattern can be found elsewhere. In Devon, courts heard about 250 serious cases a year in the early 1600s but only 38 in the early 1700s. The rate of murders in Devon fell from eight per every 100,000 people to just one per 100,000 in the early 1700s. One major reason for this was the long run of good harvests in the later 1600s. The population rate had stabilised. More work was available. These factors combined to reduce levels of crime.

However, whenever you think about the crime rate, remember the dark figure! We cannot know exactly how many crimes were committed because many crimes would not have been reported. Source 1 shows that 'recorded crime' decreased but many minor thefts are not recorded here.

Surges in crime

Despite this general downward trend, all through this period there were sudden surges of crime, particularly in the years following bad harvests (see Source 2). Similar rises happened when wars ended and the soldiers came home. During wars crime decreased, but when wars ended there was a surge of men looking for work and, finding none, often turning to crime.

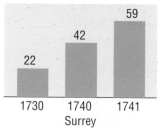

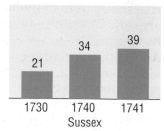

SOURCE 2 Prosecutions (in thousands) for theft and other property offences in Surrey and Sussex 1730–41. Food prices had been low during the 1730s. Then two bad harvests were followed by the very cold winter of 1739–40. The river Thames froze, stopping coal arriving from Newcastle for the south-eastern counties. Work was also hard to come by and those who struggled by in the good years found themselves in desperate conditions

Types of crime

Most crime was theft of money, food and belongings, usually of low value. Violent crimes were a small minority of cases. This pattern of crime had not changed since the Middle Ages. However, some crimes and criminals (such as you have studied on pages 72–89) became widely known, because they were new, or got a lot of publicity in pamphlets and broadsheets that had not existed in the Middle Ages.

1. Explain how
a) weather
b) war
c) changes in population
    affected the crime rate in the late 1600s.

Why did the law-makers introduce the Bloody Code?

YOU NOW KNOW a lot about the crime and punishment in the period 1500–1750. We are going to return to the question we started this chapter with. Why did punishments become bloodier in this period?

To answer this we must try to see the world through the eyes of the law-makers of the time. It was chiefly landowners who were members of the Houses of Parliament. It was they who made the laws and set the punishments. So in looking for an explanation of the Bloody Code one of the most important things is to understand the law-makers' attitude to crime and punishment.

1. Law-makers were worried about crime

Recorded crime was in fact falling through the 1600s as you can see from page 92. However, not many people at the time would have believed that. If you think your life or property is at risk, it will not reassure you much to be told that murders or thefts are down by ten per cent! Whatever the period, it is human nature to see crime as a serious problem. And in this period there was plenty of evidence to alarm the public about the levels of crime.

There were all those vagabonds and highwaymen.

The broadsheets gave lurid details of robberies and murders. Accounts of London trials were published regularly. Public hangings publicised crime as much as deterred people from crime. Crowds flocked to Tyburn in London to see the spectacle. The broadsheets published speeches made by criminals about to be hanged. We know today how sensational reports of just one dreadful crime can convince the public that the country is riddled with crime.

2. Changes in society made it harder to enforce the law

From the sixteenth century onwards the old social structure of Britain was slowly changing. The unifying power of the Church was declining. There was much more protest than in earlier centuries. Towns were growing. Trade was increasing. Travel was increasing. All these factors made it more difficult to enforce the law.

In the crowded and anonymous streets of growing towns and cities (particularly in London), it was easier for criminals to commit crime and harder to detect it than anywhere else in the country.

3. As rich landowners, law-makers were particularly worried about property crime

The MPs who passed the laws that made up the Bloody Code were all wealthy landowners. Some historians believe that landowners used the Bloody Code to protect their own lands and privileges. There is evidence to support this. Laws against poaching, for example (see page 86), seem designed simply to preserve the privileges of the rich at the expense of the poor.

In the same way, crimes that affected the developing economy, such as damaging toll-roads, breaking wool machines or stealing sheep, were singled out for particularly harsh punishment. As the wealthy grew even wealthier they had more to lose from crime. This was not a deliberate 'conspiracy' by the landowners but under the Bloody Code property crime was treated as harshly as murder or assault.

This sounds as if all the law-makers were completely selfish. It was not that simple. Many believed that if laws were broken, then everyone, including the poor, suffered. Therefore they used the Bloody Code to protect everyone, but at the same time to protect themselves most of all.

4. Law-makers thought that harsh punishments worked to control crime

We must not forget that most law-makers thought harsh punishments were effective in controlling crime. Ever since Saxon times the trend had been to make punishments harsher. It was the only method that had been tried. In this period it was just the same: the first reaction if you wanted to stop a crime – any crime – was to make the punishment harsher.

But ...

Remember that the Bloody Code was not introduced all in one go. It reflected a trend over time. Different groups of people over a long period of time all thought in a similar way.

■ Isn't it nice to find a page without a Task! But don't relax too much. You can use the information on this page to help you with the Task on page 97.

Who will hang?

■ TASK

This is a game with a purpose. By playing it you can revise what you have learned about punishments in the 1700s and how strictly those punishments were used.

Your objective is to escape the death penalty. By the end of the game you will have found out which of the real people below did escape it and why they did so.

When you have finished playing the game, write your answers to these questions:

1. For what kinds of crime were people hanged in the 1700s?
2. Why did some people escape hanging?
3. Which people were most likely to be hanged?
4. Was the Bloody Code as harsh as it sounds?

How to play

1. Get into groups of three. You will need a counter to move around the board.
2. Each of you choose one of the characters shown below and place your counter on your starting square.
3. Take turns to move one square each, according to the instructions given in the square.
4. When your fate has been finally decided, record:
   a) how you were punished
   b) why you were punished in that way.
5. Repeat the game using three other characters.

Characters

William York, aged 10. Start at square 13.

Elizabeth Hardy, aged 19. Start at square 2.

Charles Macklin, a famous actor. Start at square 7.

Roderick Audrey, aged 16. Start at square 18.

Doctor Dodd, one of the King's chaplains. Start at square 10.

Ann Collins, aged 20. Start at square 15.

Who Will Hang?

1	9	17
You are convicted of manslaughter. You are set free after being branded on the hand.	You do not know any respectable people who could speak to the court on your behalf. Go to square 3.	The King and government believe that forgery is a most serious crime. Go to square 3.
2	**10**	**18**
You are accused of stealing goods worth 13 shillings and sixpence. Go to square 19.	You are accused of forgery and of obtaining £4300 under false pretences. Go to square 4.	You are accused of stealing from houses. Go to square 5.
3	**11**	**19**
You are sentenced to hang and the execution is carried out.	You are sentenced to death. However, there has not been very much crime recently and the court is sorry for you. Go to square 24.	You tell the jury that your husband deserted you, leaving you alone and without work in London. Go to square 11.
4	**12**	**20**
Your wealthy and well-known friends tell the court that you have a good character and collect signatures on a petition to save your life. Go to square 20.	You drank too much. The judge thinks that you are rude when you try to defend yourself and that you do not respect him or his court. Go to square 3.	The jury finds you guilty, but recommends that you be reprieved from hanging. Go to square 17.
5	**13**	**21**
The jury hears that you trained birds to fly through open windows so that if you were caught inside a house, you could claim you were only trying to get your bird back. Go to square 9.	You are accused of murdering a 5-year-old girl. Go to square 23.	The judge decides that you are to be imprisoned until a final decision is made. You could still be sentenced to hang. Go to square 14.
6	**14**	**22**
You are desperate to speak up for yourself in court. To give yourself courage you have a drink of gin. Go to square 12.	After 9 years you are reprieved from hanging when you agree to join the navy and leave the country.	Your acting skills come in useful. You show great respect for the judge and say how sorry you are for the accident. Go to square 1.
7	**15**	**23**
You are accused of killing another actor in an argument. Go to square 16.	You are accused of stealing goods worth a pound, but you are innocent. Go to square 6.	The jury hear that you planned the crime carefully and carried it out in cold blood. Go to square 8.
8	**16**	**24**
The court recommends that you should hang, but the judge discusses your case with other judges because of your age. Go to square 21.	Your wealthy and well-known friends tell the court you that have a good character. Go to square 22.	You are reprieved from hanging and sentenced to transportation to America.

Did the Bloody Code increase the number of executions?

UNDER THE BLOODY Code, with so many extra capital crimes, you would expect the number of executions to go up. Strange though it seems, the number of executions actually fell considerably, as you can see in Sources 1 and 2. In the early 1700s there were about 200 executions each year in England and Wales, although at times there was a sudden flurry of executions if the government or local justices believed the numbers of crimes were increasing. The most obvious explanation for the fall in executions was the falling number of recorded crimes.

But there was a variety of explanations, some linked to the savagery of the Bloody Code itself.

■ Juries were unwilling to find people guilty of some crimes because they thought the punishment was too great. Therefore around 30 per cent of accused people were acquitted. Many more were found guilty of lesser crimes such as stealing goods of a lower value.
■ Many others were pardoned or let off because witnesses spoke about their good character and normally law-abiding behaviour. Charles Macklin, a famous actor, who murdered another actor during an argument, had plenty of wealthy witnesses to speak for him and he was set free after being found guilty of manslaughter. His punishment was branding on the hand.
■ Anyone who showed remorse and respect for the court was likely to escape hanging. One girl, desperate to plead her innocence, built up her courage with a drink at dinner. Unfortunately she drank too much and got carried away with her protests. The judge decided that she showed no respect for the court. She was hanged.
■ Another reason for the fall in executions was the development of other punishments, particularly transportation to the American colonies. Many criminals were offered the chance to join the army or navy, especially during the wars against France from the late 1680s to 1714. William York, who was ten years old when he was found guilty of murdering a five-year-old girl, escaped execution after he agreed to leave England and go to sea. However, this was only after he had spent nine years in prison, with the death penalty hanging over him. The judges recommended he should hang but his youth saved him.
■ Some criminals were much more likely to be executed than others. Regular thieves and cold-blooded murderers went to the gallows as did anyone who did not have rich or respectable friends to plead for them to the judge. So too did

horse-thieves at a time when horses were the main form of transport and counterfeiters and forgers at a time when commerce and business were growing and a wealthy merchant class was emerging.

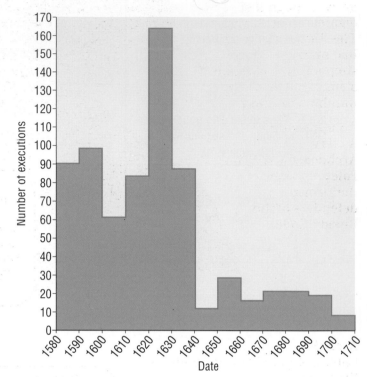

SOURCE 1 The number of executions in Cheshire 1580–1709

SOURCE 2 A comparison of executions in Devon and London. The numbers are the averages for executions in each year in the decades listed

	1600–10	1700–10
London	150	20
Devon	25	3

1. Was the number of executions rising or falling under the Bloody Code?
2. Which criminals were most likely to hang?
3. Which criminals were most likely to escape hanging?
4. Why did juries often acquit accused criminals?
5. Did punishments become bloodier under the Bloody Code?

Arguments about the Bloody Code

The number of capital crimes continued to grow through the eighteenth century. The Bloody Code had many supporters. It also had a small but growing number of critics.

A supporter

A clergyman, Archdeacon William Paley, was one of the strong defenders of the Bloody Code.

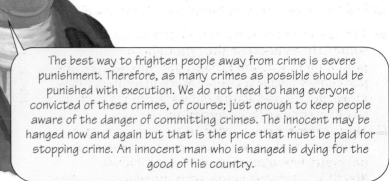

The best way to frighten people away from crime is severe punishment. Therefore, as many crimes as possible should be punished with execution. We do not need to hang everyone convicted of these crimes, of course; just enough to keep people aware of the danger of committing crimes. The innocent may be hanged now and again but that is the price that must be paid for stopping crime. An innocent man who is hanged is dying for the good of his country.

A critic

Later in the 1700s, opposition to the Bloody Code developed among a handful of MPs and writers. Sir William Meredith was one of these MPs.

The Bloody Code and all the public executions do not deter criminals. If they did, would there be such crowds and laughter at executions? To combat crime it is more important to have effective ways of catching criminals. If we increase their fear of being caught then they will think twice about committing the crime. It is also ridiculous to have so many capital crimes which do not lead to executions. It would be better to say that the penalty is transportation when that is the punishment that is usually used in the end.

6. What do Paley and Meredith agree about?
7. What do they disagree about?

■ TASK

An article has been written in the *Gentleman's Magazine* saying that the laws are too severe and most of the Bloody Code should be ended. Transportation should be used instead of execution.

Write a reply from Archdeacon Paley defending the existing laws. If you can, defend the execution of Mary Jones (page 65). You can refer to earlier material in this chapter as well as on this page.

You can get a sheet from your teacher to help you plan your reply.

*H*ow effective was law enforcement in this period?

■ TASK

In this period some measures were taken to improve law enforcement. The charts below give you information about policing and trials at this time. Your task is to decide which of these methods were new and which were continuities from the past.

1. Draw a table like the one opposite and record each of the features of law enforcement under either 'Continuities' or 'Changes'. You will need to refer back to what you have found out about the Middle Ages on pages 36–39.

	Continuities since the Middle Ages	Changes since the Middle Ages
Policing		
Trials		

2. Which changes do you think made trials fairer?
3. In which area do you think there was most change 1500–1750: policing or trials?

Policing

Hue and cry

If the hue and cry was raised, citizens still had to turn out to search for and try to catch the criminal. The constable was expected to lead the hue and cry. The local *posse comitatus* could also be called out to search for criminals.

Constables

Constables were still the main defence against crime. Two men were chosen from among the wealthier citizens of towns and villages to be constables for a year at a time. They mostly dealt with everyday matters, such as begging without a licence or breaking the Sunday laws, and they inflicted some punishments such as whipping vagabonds. They also took charge of suspects and made sure they were held in prison until their trial.

Watchmen and sergeants

Watchmen were employed in larger towns to patrol the streets both in the day and at night. They were poorly paid and often of little use. They were expected to arrest drunks and vagabonds and were allowed to peer into windows to check no one was breaking the law. In towns SERGEANTS were employed to enforce market regulations by weighing goods and collecting fines.

Citizens

Citizens were expected to deal with crimes themselves. If someone was robbed, it was his responsibility to get an arrest warrant from a magistrate, track down the criminal and deliver the criminal to the constable.

Rewards

Rewards were offered for the arrest of particular criminals. For highwaymen, £40 was offered – a sum equivalent to a year's income for middle-class families.

Thief-takers

Thief-takers made their living from tracking down criminals and collecting rewards. They were often former criminals themselves and set up innocent victims, tricking them into crime for the rewards. The most famous thief-taker was Jonathan Wild (see pages 100–101).

The army

The army was used to put down protests or other riots or to capture gangs, particularly of violent smugglers. The use of the army in dealing with protests was very unpopular because it seemed that the government was simply overpowering the people and ignoring their concerns.

Trials

Courts

There was a variety of courts.

Royal judges visited counties to hear serious cases at the assizes. Justices of the Peace (also now known as magistrates) were the mainstay of the system of courts and held quarter sessions four times a year.

Church courts dealt with crimes by churchmen and anyone who could claim benefit of clergy.

Manor courts dealt with local, minor crimes such as selling underweight bread, failing to mend roads, drunkenness or fathering illegitimate children.

Habeas Corpus

The HABEAS CORPUS (meaning 'you have the body') Act was passed by Parliament in 1679. It stopped the authorities from keeping a person in prison indefinitely without charging them with a crime. Now anyone arrested had to appear in court within a certain time or be released. The Habeas Corpus Act allowed people to criticise the king and government without fear of being seized and locked up for ever without trial. However, it did not stop governments from manufacturing evidence at trials to keep their critics quiet.

Benefit of clergy

It was still possible for people accused of crimes to claim benefit of clergy and so be tried in a church court. But as so many more people could read by the 1600s, the law was changed to prevent those accused of serious crimes from claiming benefit of clergy.

Lawyers

From the 1720s lawyers were used more often to prosecute cases, although they were still not used regularly. The development of prosecuting lawyers led, from the 1730s, to the appearance of defence lawyers. Until then, people accused of crimes had not had lawyers to defend them because it was believed that an innocent person did not need a lawyer to produce clever excuses. Lawyers were only used in the highest courts.

Juries

In the early 1600s juries dealt with a number of cases at a time rather than giving verdicts for individual cases. By the early 1700s, however, juries were deciding cases one at a time. It was thought that this would give fairer verdicts.

Speed of cases

Each case took on average ten to fifteen minutes at the most.

Jonathan Wild: Thief-taker General

1. Wild came to London as a servant but was sent to prison in 1710 for debt. There he learned from other criminals.

2. When released, Wild became a city official, pledged to track down and arrest criminals.

5. In 1716 Wild became known as the Thief-taker General after using his informers to break up gangs of footpads and burglars, and arresting a number of highwaymen.

I'm in control now, you'll rob where I say.

6. This allowed Wild to build up his power over London's criminals, taking control of the remaining gangs. Now they robbed Londoners to Wild's orders, but he still seemed a respectable official.

You'll not escape this time. It's the gallows for you.

8. Sheppard became a popular hero for his escapes, but each time Wild caught him. When Sheppard was executed, Wild's popularity fell.

9. Eventually the authorities trapped Wild with a charge of receiving stolen property. Although the usual penalty was transportation, he was hanged in 1725.

3. At the same time he paid thieves to burgle houses and bring him the details of their loot.

For a small fee I can get everything back for you.

4. Wild then visited the people who had been burgled, saying he could get their belongings back – for a fee. He was trusted because of his official position. He never handled the goods himself so could not be charged with receiving stolen property.

7. In 1724 Wild captured Jack Sheppard, a famous housebreaker. Sheppard then escaped four times, once through six bolted iron doors using just his handcuffs and an iron bar.

10. After Wild's death, there was a surge in robberies and other crime in London.

Why no police force?

The career of Jonathan Wild might seem to you to demonstrate the need for a police force. The odds in favour of getting away with crime were still heavily in favour of the criminal. Sir John Fielding, a London magistrate, wrote that 'not one in a hundred robbers are taken.'

Yet at this time there was great opposition to the idea of a professional, paid police force.

- Many people feared that a police force would mean the **end of their freedom** to express their ideas or to criticise the government. The police would be used by the government to stamp out any political opposition.
- Others **feared the expense** in setting up a police force. Instead, they preferred to rely on constables and thief-takers even though these methods were clearly not able to deal with the amount of crime, especially in towns like London.
- Others did not see the need for a police force at all. They did not think it would work. They still believed that the best way to tackle crime was to **make punishments even bloodier**. Criminals were not afraid of constables so they had to be made afraid of the punishments that awaited them if they were caught.

1. Who could arrest thieves?
2. Why was there no police force in England in the early 1700s?
3. Read the story of Jonathan Wild in the story strip.
a) What crimes did Wild commit?

b) Why was he called the Thief-taker General if he was a criminal?
c) Does the career of Wild show that a police force was needed or was not needed? Explain your answer.

Women, crime and punishment

IN THIS PERIOD most crime was committed by men. This is typical of most periods of history. Between 1500 and 1750 records suggest that women were involved in 15–20 per cent of crimes. Most of these crimes were minor ones such as petty theft, failing to attend church or having an illegitimate child. Women involved in more serious crimes such as burglary tended to have male accomplices.

A few women criminals, such as those in Sources 1 and 2, achieved notoriety. Mary Young, alias Jenny Diver, was an infamous criminal who claimed to have invented the 'pregnant pickpocket'. She had false arms and a stomach made and hid her real arms under her clothes. Sitting next to people in church she picked their pockets while all the time her 'hands' were in view! She was sentenced to transportation, but returned to England, and was caught and finally hanged in 1740.

SOURCE 1 Mary Frith, usually known as Moll Cutpurse, a London thief and gang leader in the early 1600s was not typical of women who appeared before courts

Were women punished more harshly than men?

There were often different punishments for men and women. Men expected women to behave respectably and obediently, so they punished them more harshly for crimes which challenged this image of women. For example:

- When a husband and wife were accused of drunkenness in 1633, only the woman was sent to the stocks to be humiliated.
- Women were also more likely to be punished for adultery than were men, partly because it might result in the local community having to pay for the upkeep of an illegitimate child.
- The cucking (or ducking) stool was used to punish women for brawling or arguing in public. There was no similar punishment for men.
- Women convicted of murdering their husbands were not simply hanged. They were burned to death as a sign that this was the worst kind of murder because it was seen as 'treason' against the 'ruler' of the household.

Women and the courts

Women could not be JPs, constables, lawyers, court clerks or members of the normal juries. Women could give evidence as witnesses and could bring cases to court as the victim of crime. Special juries of married women were assembled when a woman facing the death penalty claimed she was pregnant.

SOURCE 2 Mary Blandy, executed for murder in Oxford in 1752

1. 'Women were not treated equally by the law at this time.' List two examples to support this statement.
2. Why were Moll Cutpurse and Jenny Diver not typical of women criminals?

Summary: Crime and punishment 1500–1750

Headline: More capital crimes but fewer executions!

The big change in this period was the Bloody Code. The number of capital crimes increased from less than 50 to over 160. But remember that although there were more capital crimes there were actually fewer executions.

Crime

There was much continuity with the Middle Ages in the main crimes of theft and violence. Even some 'new' crimes, such as highway robbery, only seemed new because they became much more common and more publicised.

New crimes such as vagrancy did appear, but dramatic though they were, they made up only a small proportion of crimes.

In the late 1600s crime was probably falling, so the amazing thing about the Bloody Code is that it was introduced when the crime rate was lower than it had been for at least a century! However, many people believed that crime, and especially violent crime, was on the increase. Broadsheets and public executions helped to increase this anxiety, as did occasional riots and the activities of infamous highwaymen.

Causes of crime

The diagram below shows some of the reasons why crime was a problem between 1500 and 1750.

1. Which of these reasons were a particular problem between 1500 and 1750?
2. Which crimes were created by the attitudes of the law-makers?

Attitudes to crime

Attitudes in the Early Modern period can be summarised like this:

- Local communities were still expected to police themselves using constables and the hue and cry. However, some people, especially in London, were beginning to look for new methods.
- Governments could not afford the costs of police or prisons as punishments and there was a lot of hostility to the idea of a police force.
- People believed that crime of all kinds was increasing and this required more severe punishments.

- Many landowners believed that their land and rights needed to be protected strongly by the law.
- Punishments were harsh and took place in public to frighten others away from committing crimes.
- Some people were beginning to ask whether severe punishments actually did reduce the amount of crime.

■ TASK

Complete the empty columns on your own copy of the table below, summarising the changes and continuities in crime and punishment since the Middle Ages.

What methods did they use to tackle crime?

	Medieval England	Continuities 1500–1750	Changes 1500–1750
Laws	Laws dealt with all levels of crime from treason against the King to selling under-weight bread in the market. Local laws were laid down by the lords of the manor.		
Policing	There was no police force. Tithings and the hue and cry were the main methods of catching offenders. The sheriff and posse chased criminals on the run. Leading villagers were appointed as constables. These methods were effective if there were witnesses to crimes, but were much less effective at solving crimes with no witnesses.		
Trials	Trial by jury was used for most offences. Trial by ordeal was abolished in 1215. From the 1100s royal judges travelled around the country, dealing with serious cases. Trials lasted about 15 minutes. County courts were held by JPs who were leading landowners. Each manor had a weekly court run by the local lord.		
Punishments	Capital punishment was the most common punishment in royal courts and was used for many offences including theft. Hanging and other punishments were carried out in public to scare possible offenders. Fines were the most common punishments in manor courts. Prisons were only used for people awaiting trial. The stocks, pillory and whipping were also used for minor crimes.		

Obstacles to crime!

Here is another obstacle course like the one on pages 21 and 53. It focuses on: **How did people try to solve the problem of crime?**

Here you can see the methods in use by 1750. The barriers are the methods that governments tried to use to prevent crime: methods of catching criminals, trials and punishments. As you can see, these methods were not successful in stopping crime.

3. Which method was relied on most to stop crime?
4. Why were these methods chosen rather than others?
5. Compare this picture with the medieval 'obstacle course' (page 53). In what ways are they:
a) the same
b) different?
6. Chapter 5 deals with the period 1750–1900. During those years much of the Bloody Code was abolished, imprisonment became the major punishment and police forces were created. Do you expect these changes to have a major impact on crime?

■ REVIEW TASK

Why was Mary Jones hanged in 1770?

This is the question you started this chapter with. Now you can come back to it and organise your ideas to write an essay answering this question. You can get a sheet from your teacher to help you plan the essay.

1. What crime did Mary Jones commit?

2. How had the laws become more severe in the 1770s?

3. Was she hanged because crime was increasing:
a) generally at this time
b) for a brief period in that area?

4. Why did people believe that crime was increasing?

5. Which of these reasons was most important in explaining why Mary Jones was hanged?
a) her crime
b) the Bloody Code
c) the crime rate
d) people's fears of crime

A sad story

History, more than any other subject, is about real people but it can be easy to forget that. The people in the past often seem like chess pieces that we move around when we are writing books or essays, but who had no lives of their own. However, occasionally people in history leap off the page and feel as real as the families and friends that we see every day.

For me, Mary Jones was one of those people. I was stunned when I first read her story. It was both shocking and heartbreaking. For weeks I was unable to get her out of my mind. I could not understand the cruelty of attitudes that condemned her to death.

Her story made such an impact on me that I did something I had never done before – I wrote a poem. I didn't intend to, but I'd been on a course where we were practising different kinds of writing, including poetry, and I woke up one morning with the beginnings of a poem in my head. So here it is. It isn't the sort of thing you expect to find in a history book but perhaps it's a reminder that people in the past were once just as alive as we are now.

It is worth stopping for a moment whenever you start a new topic to make someone from the past come alive in your mind. That way, history will become more enjoyable and you will have a greater understanding of the people, their thoughts and decisions. One of the main reasons for studying history is, after all, that it helps us to understand other people better.

The Bloody Code and the future

A series of important developments took place between 1500 and 1750 that were to influence the system of justice in England in the future. These included:

■ the introduction of the Riot Act in 1715
■ the introduction of the Habeas Corpus Act in 1692
■ the use of lawyers in trials
■ the first realisation that severe punishments did not cut crime
■ the use of transportation and the continued absence of police and prisons.

Mary, Mary, dancing and laughing
plays with her daughter 'til bed,
Mary, Mary, yawning and sleepy
awaiting her husband's return,
Mary, Mary, anxious and fearful
searching the streets for her man,
'Mary, Mary', clamours her neighbour
he's been taken, pressed for the fleet.'
Mary, Mary, hungry and tearful
out in the street with her bairn,
Mary, Mary, no work, no husband
can't pay for their room or their food,
Mary, Mary, desperate for money
fingers some cloth in a shop,
Mary, Mary, seeing the shopkeeper
replaces the cloth on the shelf,
Mary, Mary, held by the thief-taker
'there's too much of this thieving just now'
Mary, Mary, trembling and fearful
waiting in prison for trial,
Mary, Mary, crying, collapsing
hears the judge but thinks of her child.
Mary, Mary, dancing and choking
hanged by the neck 'til she died.

CHAPTER 5

CRIME AND PUNISHMENT 1750–1900

Why was there a revolution in punishment and policing 1750–1900?

IN CHAPTERS 1–4 of this book you have studied over 2500 years of crime and punishment. Through that time rulers and governments had nearly all chosen the same solution to the problem of crime – harsh or bloody punishments, preferably in public, which were meant to frighten people away from crime.

Now get ready for some major changes.

1. **By 1850 the Bloody Code had been swept away.** The only crimes punishable by death were murder and treason and the number of executions had fallen to an average of eleven a year. Not only that, public executions ended in 1868 and transportation was abolished soon after.
2. **Prison sentences became the most common punishment** for serious crime and prisons were totally reformed from chaotic, squalid death traps to efficient and tightly controlled institutions.
3. **Professional police forces were set up,** beginning with the Metropolitan Police in 1829. Village constables had struggled for centuries to deal with crime. Now they were replaced by professional police whose sole job was to prevent crime and catch criminals.

If this book had been written 30 years ago, the answer to the key question for this chapter would have been fairly simple. It would have looked like the cartoon on the right. Most of the credit would have been given to reformers, such as Elizabeth Fry, John Howard and Sir Samuel Romilly (see pages 128–129 and 131) for persuading Sir Robert Peel, the Home Secretary in the 1820s, to make the great changes that abolished the Bloody Code, begin prison reform, and introduce professional policing. But was it really like that?

Nowadays, historians think that there were more reasons for the revolution in punishment than simply the work of reformers. This makes the investigation more difficult for you, but perhaps it will also be more interesting!

Here are the other main factors to consider:

■ **rising crime** and **rising fear** of crime
■ **changing attitudes** to the Bloody Code and punishment in general
■ **the role of government** – increasing intervention and greater wealth

Your task is to work out why each factor was important.

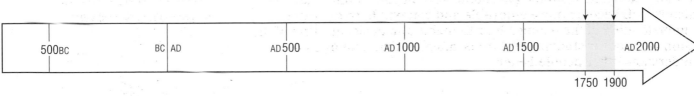

How did life change during the Industrial Revolution?

GREATER SOCIAL CHANGE took place in Britain during the period 1750–1900 than ever before. This page summarises some of the main changes.

These changes were gradual, but they completely altered the way most people lived. This revolution also had an effect on punishment and policing.

Towns

In 1750 there were 9.5 million people in England and Wales. Most people lived in villages scattered throughout the countryside. By 1900 the population had risen to 41.5 million. Many people now lived in towns, where they were crowded together in poor housing.

SOURCE 1 An engraving of a London slum in 1870 by Gustave Doré. Other cities were similar or even worse. Here is Engels' view of Manchester in the 1840s: 'Heaps of refuse, offal and sickening filth are everywhere interspersed with pools of stagnant liquid. A horde of ragged women and children swarm about the streets and they are just as dirty as the pigs which wallow happily on the heaps of garbage and the pools of filth. On average, 20 people live in each of these little houses of two rooms, an attic and a cellar. One privy is shared by about 120 people'

Wealth and taxes

Two centuries of trade and industrial growth had made Britain a wealthy country. Income tax was introduced for the first time in the 1790s to help pay for the war against France. During the 1800s governments collected higher taxes to pay for reforms that would improve people's lives.

Voting

In 1750 only one in eight men had the right to vote in a general election. By 1885 nearly all men were able to vote. As a result, governments began to make reforms, such as improving housing and health, which would win them votes from ordinary people.

Work

In 1750 farming had been the way nearly everyone earned a living. By 1900 factories or workshops were the main place of work.

■ TASK

The diagram shows some of the changes that happened at this time. Which of these changes do you think might have led to:

a) changes in the amount of crime or the types of crime
b) the development of professional police
c) more lenient punishment
d) different kinds of punishments?

As you work through this chapter you can see if you were right.

Education

In 1750 only a minority of children went to school but by 1880 the law said that all children up to the age of thirteen had to attend school. By 1900, 95 per cent of the population could read or write compared with only 70 per cent in 1850.

Harvests

Food prices had always depended on the quality of the harvest. If the harvest was bad, then the poor were in danger of starvation. By the 1800s the harvest was not so vital. Food could be imported cheaply and quickly from abroad, thanks to the changes in transport.

Protest and revolution

The French Revolution at the end of the eighteenth century had rung warning bells for British MPs. Every protest or demonstration looked to them like the first sign of 'The British Revolution' and in the years after 1815 there was much protest.

Acceptance of government intervention

For centuries British people had resisted the government meddling in local affairs or telling town or rural councils what to do. They had resisted any attempts by the government to raise money. In the early nineteenth century governments were increasingly involved in reforming and changing life in Britain. Part of the reason was the long French war which had forced the government to raise money. Governments were now raising more money in taxes and also allowing local authorities to raise local taxes such as those that paid for the police.

Ideas and attitudes

During the 1700s, there was a period known as the Enlightenment, when philosophers and thinkers argued that the human race could improve its living and working conditions, and become better educated. They believed that everyone was capable of behaving thoughtfully and logically, rather than wildly and instinctively.

In the mid-1800s Charles Darwin developed his theory of evolution. He said that humans were descended from primates such as apes. This led some people to believe that criminals came almost entirely from a criminal class that had not evolved as fully as the rest of the population.

ABOLITION OF THE BLOODY CODE

How much crime?

YOU KNOW FROM your study of earlier periods that it is difficult to be sure about how the crime rate changes. You can see a number of problems facing us on the opposite page. However, despite these problems, historians believe that the graph in Source 1 is fairly accurate.

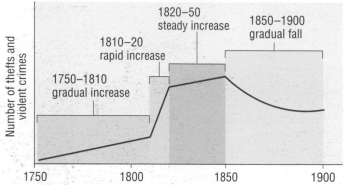

SOURCE 1 A graph showing the trends in crime, 1750–1900

What kinds of crime?

Minor theft still accounted for 75 per cent of recorded crime. Only ten per cent of crimes involved violence. Murders were rare and the murderer and victim usually knew each other.

Who were the criminals?

There were some 'professional' criminals who committed spectacular robberies and there were also gangs of smugglers, but, as in earlier periods, most crime was the work of first-time offenders or occasional criminals. Seventy-five per cent of convicted criminals were men, mostly in their teens and twenties.

Why did crime rise rapidly 1810–20?

The important detail in Source 1 is the rapid rise in crime from 1810. The end of the French wars led to increased poverty and unemployment, increased crime, and many protests against rising food prices and unemployment.

Fear of crime

Despite the rise in crime, Britain was not overrun with crime, but many people believed it was. They thought that crime was rapidly increasing and growing much more violent. From 1810 until the 1840s they were also worried about revolution. But whatever the period or the crime rate there was widespread fear of crime, particularly among the ruling classes and the middle classes as you can see from Source 2.

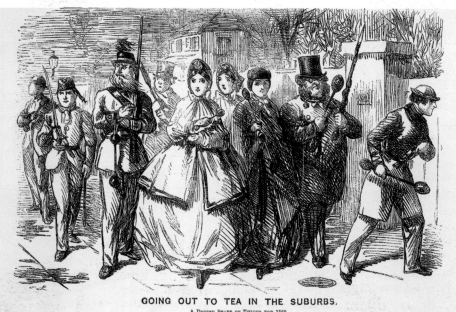

GOING OUT TO TEA IN THE SUBURBS.
A PRETTY STATE OF THINGS FOR 1862.

SOURCE 2 A *Punch* cartoon on the fear aroused by the Garotting Crisis of the 1860s. Garotting involved partly strangling the victim so that he or she could be easily robbed. There were a few cases around 1861; then in 1862 an MP was garotted near the House of Commons. Newspapers stirred up an outcry, blaming criminals who had won early release from prison for good behaviour (see page 129)

Why is it difficult to be certain about the crime rate?

This should be an easy question to answer. For this period there are lots more books on crime and the government published crime statistics every year after 1810.

Yes, we can get a broad idea, but there are still lots of problems about the evidence.

Problem 1: exaggeration in contemporary sources

Media such as newspapers do not give an accurate picture of crime. They concentrate on violent crimes, but most crimes were thefts of goods worth only a few pence.

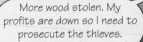

Problem 2: unreported crime

The statistics only tell us about the number of prosecutions. We don't know how many crimes were actually committed because many were not reported. Remember, the number of unknown crimes, called 'the dark figure'.

Problem 3: crackdown

Sometimes we can't tell if there were more crimes or whether people were just cracking down on crime because they had become alarmed about it or been told to do so.

More wood stolen. My profits are down so I need to prosecute the thieves.

And with all these demobbed soldiers about, they need to be taught a lesson.

We've gone easy on vagrants until now, but we've just been ordered to crack down on them.

Problem 4: new laws, new crimes

New laws created new crimes. For example: between 1870 and 1890 half a million people were prosecuted for not sending their children to school.

So ...

If there are all these problems, can we be certain of anything about crime between 1750 and 1900?

Yes, Source 1 on the opposite page is reasonably accurate. We can be sure of that, even if the 'dark figure' means we don't know everything about crime during this period.

How did people explain the increase in crime?

IN THE NINETEENTH century, people became increasingly interested in **why** people committed crime. Sources 1–10 contain some of the explanations for crime.

■ TASK

1. List all the different explanations for crime which are suggested by Sources 1–10. For example: poverty, alcohol, hunger. Some sources may suggest more than one explanation. Write each explanation on a separate slip of paper.
2. Working in groups, sort these explanations into categories. You can decide what categories to use, but if you are stuck for ideas try: blame the criminals themselves; blame the criminals, circumstances; blame evil influences on the criminal.
3. For each category, suggest what measures could be taken to remove this cause of crime.

SOURCE 1 J.W. Horsley, *Prisons and Prisoners*, 1898. Horsley was the chaplain at Clerkenwell prison in London. He was also a campaigner against all drinking of alcohol

66 *Half the causes of common assault and three-quarters of assaults on the police were committed by drunken persons. Cruelty to animals and children – of these, half might fairly be considered caused by drink. Then there are the cases which are indirectly caused by drink, for example, thefts by or from drunken persons. The conclusion that drink causes half of all crime directly and one-quarter indirectly is a moderate estimate.* 99

SOURCE 2 M.D. Hill, a Birmingham judge, gave evidence to Parliament in 1852 on juvenile crime

66 *A century and a half ago there was scarcely a town where a poor person was not known to the majority of the townspeople. In small towns there must be a sort of natural police. The individual lives under the public eye. But in a large town he lives in absolute obscurity which to a certain extent gives safety against being punished.* 99

SOURCE 3 W.D. Morrison, the author of a book on juvenile crime, believed that poverty led to crime. Conditions like those shown on page 108 were common in many towns

66 *Insufficient food, insufficient shelter, insufficient clothing, degrade men in their own eyes and in many cases their conduct falls to the same miserable level as their economic surroundings.* 99

SOURCE 4 Edwin Chadwick, Report of the Royal Commission on a Constabulary Force, 1839

66 *We have investigated the origin of the great mass of crime and we find one common cause, namely the temptations of profit from a career of theft as compared with the profits of honest and even well-paid work. The idea that any considerable number of crimes are caused by poverty we find disproved at every step.* 99

SOURCE 5 The *Morning Star*, a London newspaper, 18 January 1861

66 *Owing to the continuance of the frost and all outdoor labour being stopped, the distress and suffering among the labouring classes are truly horrible. On Tuesday night an attack was made on a large number of bakers' shops. On Wednesday night an attack was made upon many of the bakers' shops and eating houses. A great many thieves mingled with the mob and many serious acts of violence were committed.* 99

SOURCE 6 John Glyde, *The Moral Condition of Ipswich*, 1850. Glyde was a self-educated craftsman from Suffolk

66 *It is to our poor neighbourhoods and to the neglected children roaming the streets that we must look if we would check the current of crime. There must be a change of habit from some kind of idleness to some kind of industry. Vices and virtues are directly connected with idleness or industry.* 99

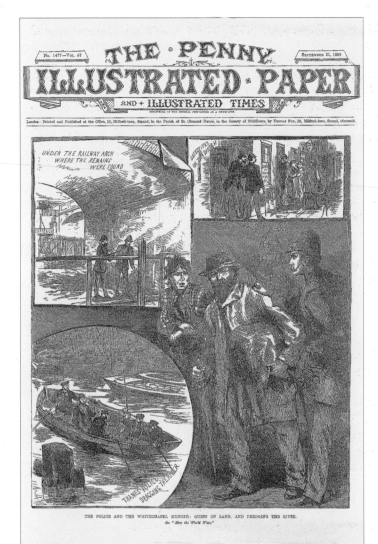

THE POLICE AND THE WHITECHAPEL MURDER: QUEST ON LAND, AND DREDGING THE RIVER.
See "How the World Wags."

SOURCE 7 A 'penny dreadful'. In 1884 *The Times* newspaper said of an eighteen-year-old who had shot a policeman that 'his mind had been corrupted by reading trashy literature'. In 1885 a magistrate said: 'There is not a boy or a young lad tried in our courts whose position is not more or less due to the effect of this unwholesome literature on his mind.' They were referring to the 'penny dreadfuls' – magazines which were devoted solely to crime; newspapers which included gruesome stories about crimes and best-selling books about criminals which glamorised the lives of the criminals

SOURCE 8 John Stone of Leicester who was accused of stealing a watch in 1822 said in his defence

" I am a poor stocking weaver in distress. I was travelling into Leicestershire after having been to London to offer myself for a soldier but was not tall enough. My parents are in distress, my father out of employment. I have eight brothers and sisters. "

SOURCE 9 Professional sports developed in the 1870s. Rivalry between fans developed and this led to violent incidents, such as the one reported by a newspaper of a match between Burnley and Blackburn in 1890.

" The referee was mobbed at the close [of the game]. The police could not clear the field. The referee had to take refuge under the stand and then in a neighbouring house. Police reinforcements arrived and eventually the referee was hurried into a cab and driven away, followed by a howling, stone-throwing mob "

SOURCE 10 These photographs are of prisoners in Bedford gaol. During the later 1800s there was a theory that the criminal class had not fully evolved – criminals inherited their criminal characteristics and could not escape from a life of crime. Members of this criminal class could be identified from the shape of their heads, their desperate, fixed expressions and their 'animal' appearance. This theory was based on Charles Darwin's theory of evolution. By 1870 all prisoners' photographs were filed with records of their background and crimes to help identify this criminal class

Why was the Bloody Code abolished in the 1820s and 1830s?

Decade	Death sentences per year	Executions per year	% of those executed who were executed for murder
(1780–1805	The number of hangings had been falling steadily.)		
1805–14	443	66	20%
1815–24	1073	89	18%
1825–34	1218	53	23%
1835–44	199	13	77%
1845–54	57	9	100%

SOURCE 1 Executions 1805–54. The figures show averages for each year in that decade. Those sentenced to death but not executed, were usually transported

You have already solved one puzzle about the Bloody Code – why it developed at a time when the crime rate was falling. Now it is time to solve a second puzzle. Why was it abolished in the 1820s and 1830s when the crime rate was rising and fear of crime was very high?

In earlier centuries the government responded to rising crime and increased fear of crime by making punishments even more savage. The pattern then had been: increased fear of crime leads to harsher punishments. But this did not happen in the nineteenth century. Instead, increased fear of crime led to the introduction of different punishments. Why?

The Bloody Code was abolished largely through the reforms of Sir Robert Peel who was Home Secretary in the 1820s. However, you will know enough about history to realise that it was not enough to say he caused this big change on his own. Now we will examine the causes that led him to make these reforms.

Key dates in the abolition of the Bloody Code

1789	Last woman burned for murdering her husband.
1806	Sir Samuel Romilly entered Parliament.
1808	Romilly gets a law passed abolishing death for pickpocketing.
1820	Last beheading – of the Cato Street conspirators who tried to assassinate the entire government.
1820–1830s	Abolition of nearly all capital crimes.
1841	Only murder and treason remained as capital crimes.
1868	Last public hanging took place.

■ TASK

It is the 1820s. You are Sir Robert Peel, the Home Secretary. You have decided that the time has come to reduce the number of crimes that are punishable by hanging. On the right you can see his rough notes outlining reasons why Parliament should abolish the Bloody Code.

Use the sources and information on page 115 to help you write the speech Peel will make in Parliament, explaining:
a) why the code needs to be reformed
b) what reforms you are going to make
c) how those reforms will help.

* We should be introducing better police. Criminals need to know they will be caught and punished.
* Let's be enlightened. It's better to reform prisoners than hang them.
* The Bloody Code isn't working. Crime is still going up. Public executions are no deterrent.
* The Bloody Code isn't being used anyway. People think the punishments are unfair.
* Alternatives are available, such as transportation.
* Unfair punishments are dangerous. They could trigger revolution.

Public executions were not working

Severe punishments were meant to frighten people into keeping the law, but they did not work. While executions were carried out, the crowds laughed and drank. London's magistrates admitted in 1783 that 'all the aims of public justice are defeated. All the effects of example, the terrors of death, the shame of punishment, are lost.'

During the 1700s the crowds at executions grew larger, partly because newspapers publicised them more widely. Some factories closed on execution day.

As crowds grew, the government felt that it was becoming difficult to keep order. There was always the danger of escape or rescue if criminals were popular, or the crowd thought them innocent. There was also an increasing rsk of protest riots if there were mass hangings when offenders were sentenced to death for minor crimes.

UNDER THE SCAFFOLD,
OR
THE HANGMAN'S PUPILS !

SOURCE 2 A cartoon of crowds at a public execution, 1867

Criminals were being taken long distances from gaol to be hanged on the edge of towns. Later, executions were moved to imediately outside the gaols to reduce the chance of problems.

Juries would not convict

Even in the early 1700s only 40 per cent of those convicted of capital crimes were hanged. By the 1800s with a much increased crime rate this had fallen to ten per cent. Juries became increasingly unwilling to convict people of minor capital crimes because they thought the punishment unfair and out of proportion to the crime.

If courts were finding offenders not guilty simply because the punishment awaiting them was unfair, then the Code was actually undermining the law. It was not protecting the property of the wealthy and middle class.

With courts unwilling to convict them, criminals would feel even more confident of escaping punishment and might be more likely to commit crimes.

Ideas about punishments were changing

The enlightened view of punishment was that it should match the crime and not be unduly brutal; criminals could be reformed by the correct punishment in to thoughtful human beings.

SOURCE 3 One reforming MP, Sir William Meredith, complained to Parliament in 1770

66 … a man who has picked a pocket of a handkerchief worth thirteen pence is punished with the same severity as if he had murdered a whole family. None should be punished with death except in cases of murder. 99

SOURCE 4 In 1767 Cesare Beccaria's book *Of Crimes and Punishments* was published in English. Beccaria said

66 Current punishments do not stop crime. Instead of making a terrifying example [by hanging] a few criminals we should punish all criminals and punish them fairly. We need punishments that fit the crimes. Instead of relying on the death penalty, criminals should be imprisoned and do hard labour that is visible to the public. 99

Politicians had already begun to look for different punishments which would be more effective because they would be used regularly and so frighten people away from crime. Transportation had emerged as the main alternative to capital punishment. The majority of those transported had originally been sentenced to death then had their sentence reduced.

Transportation: Success or failure?

IN OCTOBER 1995 Neil and Sandra Marshall, on holiday from Australia, arrived in Nottingham, curious to see the town where one of their ancestors had lived. In Nottingham they visited the Shire Hall, once the town's courthouse and prison and now the site of the Galleries of Justice museum. To their complete astonishment they found themselves witnessing a recreation of the trial of Neil's great, great-grandfather, Valentine Marshall.

For 80 years, from the 1780s to the 1860s, transportation to Australia was a vital part of the system of punishments. Valentine Marshall was one of the 160,000 people sentenced to transportation to Australia as a punishment.

On pages 117–119 you will explore the reasons why transportation became a common punishment and you will consider how successful it was. You will first look at transportation in overview and then explore the case study of one transportee, Valentine Marshall.

■ TASK

In the early 1850s the government had to decide whether to continue transporting prisoners to Australia. At the end of this investigation it will be your job to help the government decide what to do.

Step 1
Use the questions below to guide you through the text and sources on pages 117–123.

1. Why was Australia used as a convict settlement?
2. When was transportation to Australia most common?
3. Which criminals were transported?
4. What was a ticket of leave?
5. The table below shows reasons why transportation was used as a punishment. Make a copy and fill it in to assess how far the aims of transportation were achieved.
6. Do you think transportation was a success for:
a) the government
b) the prisoners?

Reasons for transportation	How far was this aim achieved? Give evidence for your judgement.
1. To provide a punishment which was less harsh than hanging so that courts were prepared to convict offenders.	
2. To provide a punishment that was still harsh enough to terrify criminals.	
3. To reduce crime in Britain – by removing the criminals.	
4. To claim Australia for Britain.	
5. To reform criminals through hard work.	

SOURCE 1 The growth of transportation. After a slow start during the French wars (1793–1815) transportation to Australia increased rapidly in the 1820s and 1830s. The peak year was 1833 with 36 ships and 6779 prisoners

Step 2
When you have finished working through the text and sources, write a paper that will be read by the members of the government:
a) listing the reasons for and against ending transportation
b) giving your own opinion about whether transportation should continue or end.

How did transportation to Australia begin?

In the 1780s the British government had faced a crisis. Transportation had already been in use as a punishment for 100 years. But the government could no longer transport convicts to America because the colonies there had won their independence. Therefore, prisons and HULKS (ships used as prisons, see page 118) were rapidly becoming overcrowded. Another colony was desperately needed to take Britain's criminals.

Several colonies, including the West Indian islands, were considered. The last was the scarcely known Australia, discovered in 1770 by James Cook. There was little possibility of sending anyone to find out whether Australia would be a good convict settlement – the round trip would take eighteen months!

The first fleet set sail for Australia in May 1787. Eleven ships left Portsmouth, carrying 1020 people of whom 736 were convicts, sentenced to transportation for seven years, fourteen years or life. The youngest was nine-year-old John Hudson, the oldest 82-year-old Dorothy Handland. Most had committed minor offences; for example, Thomas Chaddick had stolen twelve cucumber plants.

Eight months later, they landed in Australia. Forty-eight people had died on the voyage, a surprisingly low number, given that transportation to Australia was new and poorly planned.

Few of the convicts had any useful skills. There were just two brickmakers, two bricklayers, six carpenters and a stonemason – and shelter was needed for over 1000 people! It was a small miracle that they survived to welcome the next fleet two years later.

Why did the government introduce transportation to Australia?

1. An alternative was needed to hanging. This was widely felt to be too extreme a punishment for minor crimes and courts were unwilling to convict people. Imprisonment was not considered a suitable alternative at this time because of the cost. Transportation was the 'middle' punishment between the extremes of execution and the milder whipping or pillory, which were less used by this time.

You're sending me where?

2. Australia was unknown. The government hoped that the idea of being sent to an unknown place at the edge of the world would terrify people so much that they would not break the law.

3. Transportation of criminals had one advantage in common with hanging. It would reduce crime in Britain by completely removing the criminals.

4. Transportation would help Britain to claim Australia as part of her empire and to build up control over the region. This would stop France or other rivals gaining whatever resources Australia had.

5. Transportation would reform the criminals. They would be forced to work and learn skills that would be useful when they were freed.

Who was transported to Australia?

A typical convict arriving in Australia was a young man of 26 who had been convicted several times for theft, usually of food, clothing, or other goods of a small value. He had grown up in a town but had no skills or regular job.

Eighty per cent of the convicts sent to Australia were thieves, and most had committed more than one offence. Only three per cent had been convicted of violent crimes.

Far more men than women were sent to Australia: 25,000 women were transported, about one-sixth of the total.

People who had taken part in political protests were a small minority of the transported prisoners. Governments regularly used transportation as a punishment for rebels and protesters. Many of the protesters you will read about in Chapter 6 ended their days in Australia. Chartists demanding political reform were transported, as were the Tolpuddle Martyrs who had joined a workers' union. Irish rebels were also frequently transported for refusing to accept British rule.

SOURCE 2 A chain gang of convicts in Australia in the early nineteenth century

SOURCE 3 Black-eyed Sue and Sweet Poll of Plymouth, taking leave of their lovers who are being transported; an engraving made in 1792

What happened to criminals who were sentenced to transportation?

1. Waiting

Prisoners were transferred to hulks or gaols until enough prisoners were gathered together for a voyage. While they waited they worked in chains.

2. The voyage

The conditions on the voyage were cramped and unpleasant, but by the 1830s only one per cent of convicts died on the voyage. By now the journey took less than four months.

3. Arrival

On arrival, convicts were assigned to settlers. Their sentence became whatever work their master gave them. The masters provided food, clothes and shelter.

4. Early release for good behaviour

Good conduct won a 'ticket of leave' (early release) for prisoners. They regarded their ticket of leave as their right and masters who refused tickets were hated. The ticket gave prisoners a real motive for good behaviour and a sense of opportunity they never had in Britain because they could see the chances to build a new life all around them.

Reform of prisoners had been the least important reason behind the development of transportation but it worked. Convicts transported to Australia were much more likely to lead law-abiding lives after their release in Australia than convicts who were sent to prison in Britain in the same period.

5. Punishment for bad behaviour

Prisoners who committed more crimes were flogged or sent to distant settlements where treatment was harsh.

Transportation: For and against

By the 1830s, transportation was costing £0.5 million per year. Prisons were more widely used than they had been in the 1780s and were cheaper to run.

The settlers in Australia had set up societies to protest against the 'dumping' of convicts in their country. They wanted to end the idea that everyone in Australia had been transported as a criminal.

Transportation was a successful punishment. Courts were quite prepared to use this form of punishment.

SOURCE 4 A letter dictated by Richard Dillingham to his parents. He had been sentenced for taking part in protests in 1830–31. He was assigned as a gardener to the colony's architect, a kind and considerate man

> *As to my living I find it better than I ever expected thank God. I want for nothing in that respect. As for tea and sugar I could almost swim in it. I am allowed a pound of sugar and quarter of a pound of tea per week and plenty of tobacco and good white bread and sometimes beef, sometimes mutton, sometimes pork. This I have every day. Plenty of fruit puddings in the season of all sorts and I have two suits of clothes a year and three pairs of shoes a year. I want for nothing but my liberty but it is not the same with all that come as prisoners.*

Australia was by now clearly established as part of the British Empire. No other country was likely to try to claim control of Australia.

Transportation was 'no more than a summer's excursion to a happier and better climate', said Lord Ellenborough in 1810.

Transportation was now seen as more of an opportunity than a punishment by many people in Britain. Wages were higher than in Britain once prisoners had won their ticket of leave.

Crime had not fallen in Britain since transportation to Australia began. It had increased, probably quite considerably.

SOURCE 5 Edward Carr, an official in Tasmania, 1831

> *It is true the convicts are sent out here as punishment. But it is equally true that it is not in the interests of the master to make his service a punishment but rather to make the condition of the convict as comfortable as he can afford. The interests of the master contradicts the object of transportation [to punish the criminal].*

Transportation had been very successful in reforming convicts. Many took the opportunity to live peacefully and find work in Australia. Only a minority of convicts transported to Australia came back to England when their sentence was served.

In 1851 gold was discovered in Australia. A gold rush began with thousands of people in Britain trying to find the money to buy a ticket to Australia.

Valentine Marshall: A case study in transportation

Valentine Marshall was just one of the 160,000 people transported to Australia. What can we learn about transportation from his story?

■ TASK 1

You have been asked to prepare an exhibition on Valentine Marshall's life. The exhibition needs to be in two parts:

■ his trial
■ his life in Australia.

Use the material on pages 120–123 for your exhibition. You will need to think of a title and how you will present your findings in the most interesting way. You could prepare a timeline of his life, or tape an imagined interview with Marshall, looking back on his life. You also need to build in material from the rest of pages 116–119 on transportation.

SOURCE 6 Based on a drawing of Valentine Marshall in a broadsheet published in the 1830s

The 'crime'

Seventeen-year-old Valentine Marshall stood in the dock at the Shire Hall, Nottingham. He and two others were accused of setting fire to Colwick Hall three months earlier, in October 1831. Valentine, the prosecution said, had been caught up in rioting that had also led to the burning of Nottingham Castle.

The riots had begun after news arrived that the House of Lords had voted against giving more men the right to vote. At the time only one man in eight had the right to vote. Many ordinary people hoped that if they had the right to vote, then governments would have to improve their living and working conditions. The news from London destroyed those dreams.

Next day, a peaceful meeting was held in Nottingham in support of reform but when rumours spread of riots in Derby and other towns, the situation turned ugly. Colwick Hall, the home of an opponent of reform, was attacked and then the crowds surged towards Nottingham Castle, the home of the Duke of Newcastle, another enemy of reform. The castle was ransacked, furniture destroyed and the whole castle set ablaze. The army had to restore order.

The riots shocked the government and the authorities in Nottingham. They were determined to root out the leaders. Rewards were offered for information and, when names were discovered, soldiers were sent to make arrests.

The trial

The special court met in January 1832. The whole trial lasted seven days, an unusually long time. Twenty-eight men, including Valentine Marshall, were accused of crimes connected with the riots and 20-year-old George Beck was accused of leading the rioters.

■ TASK 2

Look at the evidence given by witnesses A–H. Would you find Marshall:
a) guilty of riot and arson of Colwick Hall
b) guilty of aiding and assisting in setting fire to Colwick Hall
c) not guilty of either charge?

The evidence

The evidence given by witnesses A–H is taken from the *Nottingham Review*. These are brief extracts from a much longer account of the evidence.

WITNESS A William Musters, the son of the owner of Colwick Hall

> … as near 5 o'clock as possible the mob was approaching by the front of the house …

WITNESS B John Freeman, shoemaker

> I saw Valentine Marshall there, against the oval gate opposite the house, a piece of wooden fence in his hand. I saw Marshall at the time the mob was breaking in. The butler from the Hall and his wife live next door to us. I do not know whether I mentioned Marshall was there at the Hall until I went before the magistrate two or three weeks later.

WITNESS C Richard Balderson

> I am an outdoor servant of Mr Muster's. I saw Marshall in the mob in the front of the house.

WITNESS D Valentine Marshall, the accused

> I was never near Colwick Hall that day. I went up to town to the meeting. I returned and went home to my dinner. I went out after dinner to Mrs Miller's. Then I went home and stayed 'til a little after six. I went to the top of the street and I heard that the Castle was on fire. I stopped looking at the blaze and returned home at eight or nine.

WITNESS E Mrs Marshall, the accused's mother

> He dined at home and stayed in until nearly dark.

WITNESS F Jane Miller

> I saw Marshall on the day a little after six. I live two doors from his mother. He bought a pennyworth of apples from me.

WITNESS G Mary Allen

> I live next door to Mrs Marshall. I saw him in our house between seven and eight in the evening.

WITNESS H Michael Fisher, John Lancaster, William Baldwin, John Sharp and Thomas Gadd gave Marshall an excellent character.

A report in the *Nottingham Review*, 20 January 1832

> A youth who admits he has been a thief and has been repeatedly charged with theft is the principal witness against eight different individuals charged with firing the castle or the silk mill. In the case of Colwick Hall one witness is a youth who has been in prison at least twice and whom his own brothers declare they will not believe on oath.

Did Marshall have a fair trial?

The trial of Beck, Marshall and the others was unusually long, lasting seven days in all. Separate days were spent on each incident with one day given to the trial of the three men charged with attacking Colwick Hall. However, the length of the trial does not mean that it was fair. The government and the local authorities in Nottingham were determined that someone should be punished for the riots. The judges sent from London were not going to free all the prisoners because the evidence was weak.

SOURCE 7 Extract from a letter from the Duke of Rutland to Lady Shelley, 18 January 1832

> 66 *The juries at Nottingham have been summoned, and threatened, so as to mete out but very partial justice …* 99

SOURCE 8 The words of Judge Littledale at the trial of George Beck, reported in the *Nottingham Review*, January 1832

> 66 *If such outrages are to remain unpunished there is an end to all security of property and person. It therefore becomes necessary for the sake of property and of the country to enforce the powers of the law to its fullest extent against some of those who have been found guilty. It is a painful duty for Judges to have to select persons as the objects of punishment. They do not inflict punishment for the sake of revenge but because the examples to be made will prevent other persons from violating the law by the commission of such crimes.* 99

The evidence was very weak. Twenty-eight men were accused of taking part in the riots but the majority were freed. Either the cases were dismissed by the judges because the evidence was non-existent or they were found not guilty by the jury. That still left nine men including Marshall. What kind of trial did they face?

The men were defended by a lawyer, paid for by public collection. But the defence lawyer had to overcome major problems. Until the trial began he had no idea what evidence the prosecution would bring against the accused. He had built his defence case as the trial was in progress, whereas the prosecution had had time to prepare every stage of its case.

The verdict

It took the jury just five minutes to find Marshall guilty of aiding and assisting in setting fire to Colwick Hall. He could have been hanged, but the judges recommended mercy and he was sentenced to transportation for life, along with three others. George Beck and four others were sentenced to hang.

The guilty verdict was extremely unpopular in Nottingham. Many people believed the men were innocent. The witnesses against them were either the mill owners or their employees who may have lied to save their jobs. Other witnesses were almost certainly paid to appear in court to testify against the accused. The jury was made up of landowners who had been frightened by the riots and so it is not surprising that they took just five minutes to decide their verdicts.

After the trial local people began a petition to save the five men sentenced to death. Between 15,000 and 25,000 people signed the petition that was presented to Parliament. Two men did have their death sentences repealed but nothing could save Beck, Armstrong and Hearson. They continued to declare their innocence until their execution. They were publicly executed. At the hanging the crowds chanted: 'Murder! Murder!'

SOURCE 9 This letter, together with verses on Marshall's innocence, were published in a broadsheet in Nottingham in 1834

SOURCE 10 While Marshall was in prison in Nottingham he scratched his name on the wall of the exercise yard. You can still see his name today if you visit the court and prison, now part of a museum, the Galleries of Justice

The transportation

Shortly after the execution of Beck, Armstrong and Hearson, Valentine Marshall was taken from prison to begin his sentence of transportation.

He was held on a hulk for a short period and then put on board a transport ship for the voyage that took four months. By July 1832 he was in Hobart, the convict settlement in Van Diemen's Land (Tasmania).

Valentine spent the rest of his life in Tasmania but he did not remain as a prisoner. Like other convicts, he was 'assigned' to a settler for whom he had to work. Valentine's CONDITIONAL PARDON came quickly, just over four years after he had been sentenced. This meant he was free to find work of his own, but if he committed another crime he would have to return to his sentence. He stayed away from crime and was granted a full pardon in 1842. By then he was working as a gardener, and had also married a woman named Letitia Riley with whom he had a son and daughter.

OUR CONVICTS WHAT WE DO & WHAT BECOMES OF THEM.

SOURCE 11 Convicts working in Tasmania. The text below the picture reads as follows: The above represents a hard labour gang in Tasmania, performing a species of work which used to be imposed on them some years since. It consisted of carrying bundles of shingles or wooden tiles. Each man carried two of them weighing 28 pounds [about 13 kilograms] a piece. The distance they had to walk generally averaged about 30 miles [48 kilometres] daily. This inhuman labour is now abolished

Valentine Marshall's colonial record

19 July 1832	Arrived in Hobart, aged seventeen.
10 January 1833	REPRIMANDED for disobeying orders while working as a messenger at Hobart gaol.
22 March 1833	Returned to government work at the request of his master, Mr Field.
22 February 1836	Reprimanded for disobeying orders while working as a court official at Hobart gaol.
22 June 1836	Received conditional pardon.
17 November 1837	Fined six shillings for assaulting Jane W.
22 March 1838	Reprimanded for striking his wife.
24 May 1842	Free pardon.
1887	Died aged 72.

SOURCE 12 Valentine Marshall in old age, the image of a law-abiding citizen of Hobart, Tasmania

THE REVOLUTION IN PRISONS

Why was there a revolution in prisons during the Industrial Revolution?

TRANSPORTATION WAS NOT the only alternative to hanging. Some people thought that imprisonment was a better alternative. But there were major problems with the prisons at this time.

Problems in the 1700s

■ TASK

It is 1783. Sir George Paul, the Sheriff of Gloucestershire, has asked you to help him prepare a report on prisons. He is keen to reform prisons.

You should:
a) list the problems in prisons in the 1780s. You could use the following headings: staff, prisoners, accommodation, health
b) for each problem suggest a solution.

Use Sources 1–9 for your research.

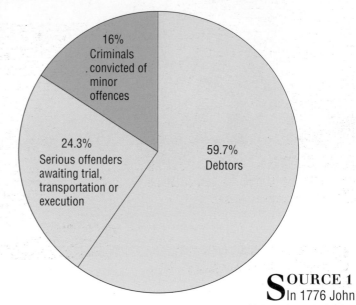

SOURCE 1 In 1776 John Howard carried out a census in the prisons of England and Wales. This pie chart shows what Howard discovered about the reasons why people were held in prisons

SOURCE 2 Some details from John Howard's book, *The State of the Prisons in England and Wales*, 1777

66 *a) Many prisoners who were found not guilty could not get out of prison because they could not afford the discharge fee set by the gaoler.*
b) Debtors' prisons had few warders and the prisoners could not be chained or forced to work. In the Marshalsea prison in London, butchers and other tradesmen came into the prison to sell food or play skittles with the prisoners in the prison drinking room. A chandler had four rooms in the prison. He used one as his workroom and shop, two for his family and sub-let the last room to other prisoners.
c) In prisons where debtors were mixed with serious criminals, the warders let the criminals have the same privileges as the debtors. There were not enough warders to keep them separate.
d) Prisoners already in a cell forced new prisoners to pay a fee to them known as 'garnish'. Warders did little to stop this. 99

TABLE OF FEES

Nottinghamshire. At the quarter sessions held at the Shire-Hall, 14th January 1760.

	S.	D.
For lodging and board of each prisoner when he lodges and diets with the gaoler, by the week	7	0
For each when he hath a room and bed of the gaoler and diets himself, by the week	2	0
For each when he hath a room of the gaoler, and finds his own bed and diet *per* week	0	6
For the discharge of each prisoner	13	4
And to the turnkey for the same	1	4

SOURCE 3 Table of fees charged at Nottingham prison in 1760. Prison warders were not paid by the government. They earned their money by charging the prisoners fees for rooms, food and anything else that was needed. Fees were also charged for seeing doctors. About 1000 prisoners a year died of diseases caught in prison

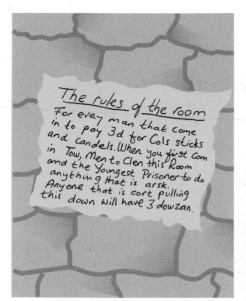

SOURCE 4 A notice pinned on the wall of Yarmouth prison

> The rules of the room
> For every man that come in to pay 3d for Cols sticks and candels. When you first Com in Tow, Men to Clen this Room and the Youngest Prisoner to do anything that is arsk. Anyone that is cort pulling this down will have 3 dowzan.

SOURCE 5 Extracts from the report on Gloucester gaol by John Howard, 1777

> " a) Gaoler – Salary: None
>   Chaplain – Salary: £40
>   Surgeon – Salary: None
> b) 1 June 1777
>   Total prisoners: 16 debtors, 24 criminals.
> c) There is only one small day room, twelve feet by eleven [3½ × 3 metres], for men and women criminals. The ward for debtors is nineteen feet by eleven [6 × 3 metres], has no window so part of the plaster wall is broken down for light and air. The night room for male criminals is close and dark and the floor so ruinous that it cannot be washed. The whole prison is much out of repair. There is no proper separation of the women. Five or six children have lately been born in the gaol.
> d) Many prisoners died here in 1773. Eight died about Christmas of smallpox. "

SOURCE 6 A former prisoner at York giving evidence to a government committee

> " All sorts of characters were together. There was much talk about crime and instructing one another in all manner of wickedness. The effect of all this was to make a man ten times worse than before and he would be sure to return to a life of crime. "

SOURCE 7 A prison cell in Nottingham gaol. This cell housed three prisoners. There was only just room for three hammocks, slung side by side

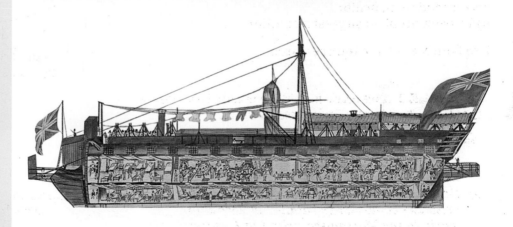

SOURCE 8 Hulks were introduced as a short-term solution to an emergency when transportation to America ended in the 1770s. However, they continued to be used as prisons until 1857 and in 1840 the hulks held over 70 per cent of prisoners in Britain. Conditions in the hulks were as bad as the worst prisons and the death rate among prisoners was one in three. This shows a prison hulk in 1810, holding Norwegian prisoners of war

SOURCE 9 Reformers like John Howard and Jonas Hanway believed that

> " Prisons should reform criminals. Prisoners should be visited daily by churchmen and be kept in SOLITARY CONFINEMENT so that they cannot learn more about crime from other prisoners. "

Changes in the 1800s

In the 1800s many changes were made in prisons to overcome the problems described on the previous two pages. Here you can see pictures of prisons in the nineteenth century. These all show the effects of reforms made in the 1800s, but the question is: 'What reforms were made?'

a

c

b

d

e

f

g

■ TASK

You have two tasks.

1. Look carefully at the photographs and note down your conclusions about:
   a) what prison life was likc in the 1800s
   b) what reforms had been introduced
   c) what the purpose of reform was.
2. There were two approaches to imprisonment in the 1800s – the *silent* system and the *separate* system which you will find out more about later. Which photographs do you think show features of which system?

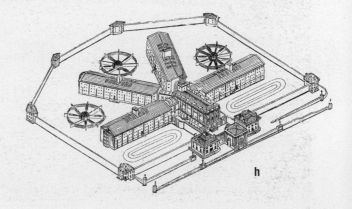

h

Why did prisons change so much in the 1800s?

IN 1750 PRISONS played only a minor part in the system of punishment. John Howard's survey in the 1770s showed that there were only 4000 people in prison in the whole country and of these, 60 per cent were in prison for debt. Over the next 100 years there were three major changes:

☐ Imprisonment became the normal method of punishing criminals.
☐ Reforming prisoners became an aim of punishment.
☐ The huge increase in prisoners led to the government taking over and reforming the whole prison system.

In the 1700s prisons were run by towns and counties with no rules about their organisation. By the 1870s government inspectors checked prisoners' work, diet, health and every other aspect of prison life.

Key dates

1777 John Howard's book, *State of the Prisons in England and Wales*, was published.
1815 Gaolers were paid out of taxes, ending the charging of fees to prisoners.
1835 The first prison inspectors were appointed.
1839 General rules for all prisons were provided by the government.
1842 Pentonville prison was built. It was intended to be a model prison for others to copy, keeping prisoners in almost permanent isolation from each other.
1857 The government ended the use of hulks as prisons in Britain.
1864 Penal Servitude Act ensured that prisoners faced the harshest possible conditions. Corporal punishment was reintroduced in prisons.
1878 The government took over control of all prisons.

Why did reformers want to change prisons?

Howard's book showed how dangerous prisons were. They were often schools for crime, turning young prisoners into hardened criminals.

Conditions were so bad that many prisoners died of disease. Reformers such as Howard wanted significant changes in prisons, including:

☐ running water
☐ clean and hygienic conditions
☐ each prison to have a doctor
☐ prisons to provide the same food for all prisoners instead of allowing prisoners to buy food

■ the end of fees paid to gaolers
■ regular visits to prisoners from churchmen
■ prisoners should work hard
■ prisoners should have to spend considerable time in silence and alone so that they would change their attitudes to crime.

All were introduced, but there were arguments about three issues, as you can see below.

The great debates

1. Separate or silent?
How should prisoners be kept in prison? In the 1700s prisoners mixed freely with each other. This was one of the major problems, as older prisoners passed on their experience of crime to youngsters. Everyone agreed that prisoners should not be able to mix freely, but how far should this go? Were they to be kept completely separate from each other or allowed to mix, in silence?

2. Work – useful or pointless?
There were two different ideas about the kinds of work prisoners should do. By the 1860s governments preferred prisoners to do pointless tasks because they believed it was more of a punishment.

3. Time off for good behaviour?
By the 1850s, prisons had developed a clear system for serious criminals serving at least four years in prison:

■ the first year spent in solitary confinement
■ the next three years spent doing hard labour in silence
■ if prisoners were well-behaved their sentences were reduced: this was like the ticket of leave system used in Australia for criminals who were transported.

1. In what ways did governments become involved in the prison system?
2. Explain the reasons behind each of these reforms:
a) stopping prisoners paying fees to gaolers
b) hard labour
c) keeping prisoners in isolation
d) regular visits by churchmen.
3. Why was the ticket of leave system ended?

■ TASK

After studying page 129, put yourself in the shoes of a prisoner in 1860.
a) Would you prefer the separate or silent system?
b) What kind of work would you prefer?

Separate

Reformers wanted to keep prisoners in individual cells where they worked, prayed and had religious teaching. They left the cells only for religious services and for exercise. Even then they were not allowed to see other prisoners (photos e and g on page 127). Pentonville prison was built as a model 'separate' prison and by the 1850s over 50 prisons were using the system. The separate system was hugely expensive because prisons had to be rebuilt to provide separate cells. Gradually, solitary confinement became an extra punishment rather than the normal way of prison life.

Silent

Some critics said that the separate system was too harsh. There was no evidence that it reformed prisoners, and there were high suicide and insanity rates because prisoners were driven to despair by loneliness. Their solution was to let prisoners work together but in silence (photo f, page 127). This was cheaper because expensive new buildings were not needed, but it required very great discipline to be effective.

Useful work

Reformers believed this was better for prisoners because it made them more likely to work after they had been released.

Useful work was making boots, mats, prison clothes, and sewing mailbags and coal sacks.

Pointless work

Critics thought this was better because prisoners hated it and so were less likely to commit crimes that would put them back in prison.

Pointless, boring work included:

Oakum picking – pulling apart and cleaning a metre length of tarred ship's rope each day. The prison sold the strands to make string or fill mattresses which led to the saying 'money for old rope'.

The treadwheel – walking nowhere to make the wheel turn. The wheel was abolished in 1902.

The crank – prisoners in their cells turned the crank handle 20 times a minute, 10,000 times a day and kept going for over eight hours. If a warder tightened a screw it made the crank harder to turn, leading to warders being nicknamed 'screws'. This was also abolished in 1902.

Why was there a reaction?

From the 1850s, the crime rate was falling. The new, more lenient, prison system was well suited to a less crime-ridden society.

Ironically, however, just as the crime rate was falling the prison system became much tougher, thanks to some highly publicised crimes, such as the Garotting Crisis of the early 1860s (see page 110) which the press blamed on the failure of the new reformed prison regimes. The critics said that prisons were not reforming criminals but simply sending them back to the streets to commit more crimes.

As a reaction against reform, measures were introduced to make prison life as terrifying as possible. Prisoners now faced more hard labour and minimum five-year sentences for a second offence. Punishments became harsher, including whipping, electric shocks for those not working hard enough, bread and water diets and more time in solitary confinement. This harsher system continued from the 1860s for the next 30 years.

How were women and children treated in prison?

Women in prison

In 1813 Elizabeth Fry began working among women in Newgate prison in London (Source 2). Shocked by what she saw, she began a campaign to improve prison conditions for women so that there was more chance that they would be reformed.

SOURCE 1 From a report on conditions in Newgate prison in London by Elizabeth Fry. Fry visited the prison in 1813. Before she went into the cells she was advised by the prison governor to leave her watch in his office or it would be torn off her by the prisoners

Nearly 300 women, sent there for every grade of crime, some untried and some under sentence of death, were crowded together in two wards and two cells. Here they saw their friends and kept a multitude of children, and they had no other place for cooking, washing, eating and sleeping.

They all slept on the floor. At times 120 in one ward without so much as a mat for bedding and many of them were very nearly naked. They openly drink spirits and swearing is common. Everything is filthy and the smell quite disgusting.

In 1800 all criminals — men, women and children — were mixed together in large prison cells. Youngsters under seventeen committed a large number of crimes.

SOURCE 2 Elizabeth Fry visiting women prisoners in Newgate prison

SOURCE 3 A man of 43, interviewed by the journalist Henry Mayhew in the mid-nineteenth century

I ran away from home when I was twelve or thirteen. There was nine of us boys among the lot that I joined. I worked in Fleet Street and I could make £3 a week at handkerchiefs alone, sometimes falling across a wallet. I carried on in this way for about fifteen months when I was grabbed for an attempt on a gentleman's wallet. I had two months in the Bridewell prison.

Children in prison

In 1838 Parkhurst prison was opened, the first prison solely for the young. Prisoners spent four months in solitary confinement except for silent exercise, services and schooling. Then two years were spent in leg irons.

In 1850 reformatory schools were set up in the hope that they would do more to persuade children to give up crime. The persuasion included hard labour and harsh punishments.

In 1817 Fry formed the Association for the Improvement of Female Prisoners in Newgate. She visited other prisons and set up ladies' prison associations at each one.

These changes were made at Newgate and were later introduced in other prisons:

- rules for women to obey in prison
- female warders
- clothing and furniture provided
- schools for women and children in prison, focusing on religious education
- regular work for women in prison.

Further changes included:

1823   It was compulsory to have women warders for women prisoners.
1835   Inspectors were appointed to supervise conditions in gaols. Conditions on convict ships were also improved, ending the shackling of women during voyages.
1853   Brixton prison was opened solely for women.

1. What were the main changes in prison life for women and children?
2. Were these changes made to make life easier for the prisoners?

By 1900 there were separate prisons for men and women, and children were sent to Borstals where they could be reformed. The amount of juvenile crime had become much smaller with the introduction of compulsory schooling.

SOURCE 4 A teenage boy photographed while serving a sentence in Bedford prison, c.1870

The 1870 Education Act made education compulsory for children aged ten and under for the first time. Later Acts extended compulsory education to older children. This had the greatest impact on reducing juvenile crime because children were no longer on the streets in daytime.

In 1899 children were no longer to be sent to prison with adults. Instead, special reformatory prisons were set up called Borstals, after the Kent village where the first one was founded.

The punishment revolution: Summary

The big idea

The main purpose of punishment was to reform the criminal, rather than to warn others away from crime. Punishments took place in private, not public. The aim was to change the prisoner rather than just getting rid of him.

Humiliation

The pillory was little used by the 1800s. It was abolished in 1837.

TWO PRETENDED FORTUNE-TELLERS IN THE PILLORY

The stocks were little used in the 1800s. They were abolished in 1872.

Fines

Fines became much more common in the 1800s, becoming the most common punishment.

The prison revolution

- Imprisonment was used for a small minority of criminals in 1750 but by the 1860s over 90 per cent of serious offenders were sent to prison. Prisons were taken over by the government which laid down regulations and inspected the prisons.

- Prisons were reformed to improve conditions and to make punishment more effective. Men, women and children were separated, doctors were provided and fees to gaolers abolished.
- The government took over the organisation and running of prisons.
- The first inspectors of prisons were appointed in 1835.
- Prisoners had to work and also spent long periods in silence. Both methods were meant to help reform the prisoners.
- Well-behaved prisoners had their sentences reduced until the 1860s. After that, sentences became harsher with harder work, punishments and more solitary confinement.

Physical punishments

Whipping was abolished for women in 1820.

Whipping for men was less common but continued into the 1830s. It continued as a punishment for offences in prison into the twentieth century.

Capital punishment

The Bloody Code was abolished. From the 1830s the only crimes punishable by execution were murder and treason. Hanging became much less common. Public executions ended in 1868.

Transportation

Transportation was seen as a middle course in punishment between execution and fining. Between 1787 and 1868, 162,000 people were transported to Australia. Transportation ended in 1868.

■ REVIEW TASK

Why did these changes take place?

The work of reformers was only one reason why punishment changed so much in the nineteenth century. This diagram summarises the main factors for change.

On your own copy of this chart, add and label arrows to show the connections between different points.

You are going to use the ideas on these pages to help you plan and write an essay: Why was there a revolution in punishment in the 1800s? You can get a sheet from your teacher to help you.

Rising crime
Fear of rising crime led to a demand for more effective punishments.

The work of reformers
Individuals, such as John Howard and Elizabeth Fry, influenced government thinking about how prisons should be run. Reformers believed that prisoners could be reformed through hard work and religious instruction.

Main factors for change

People doubted the effectiveness of existing punishments
- The Bloody Code had not reduced crime. Many sentenced to death were given other punishments and so the law appeared ridiculous.
- Public executions did not terrify people into keeping the law.
- Prisons needed reforming to stop them becoming 'schools for crime'.

The role of government
Governments were becoming more involved in every aspect of society in order to improve conditions. Higher taxes were being raised to pay for improvements.

The role of the reformers

At the beginning of this chapter, we raised the question of how individual reformers affected the punishment revolutions. Through the chapter, you will have seen references to these three individuals. Now it is time to consider their significance.

1. Did Howard's and Fry's campaigns lead to immediate improvements?
2. Did Romilly have to fight hard to abolish hanging for many crimes?
3. Write a paragraph explaining how important these three reformers seem to have been in the changes to punishments.

John Howard (1726–90), prison reformer
Work: Howard became interested in prisons when he was Sheriff of Bedfordshire and so responsible for prisons in the county. He then made tours of prisons in Britain and abroad.

Importance: His book, *The State of Prisons in England and Wales*, was published in 1777. This provided specific evidence for the growing campaign to reform prisons. However, national reform of prisons did not begin until well after his death and took some time to spread.

Sir Samuel Romilly (1757–1818), campaigner against the Bloody Code
Work: Romilly was a lawyer and a member of the government in 1806–07. He campaigned to reduce the number of crimes that could be punished by death.

Importance: His work did lead to some capital crimes being abolished, but the number of executions was already falling and attitudes had been changing for some time. People realised that many criminals were escaping punishment because victims refused to prosecute knowing the sentence was so severe. As a result in 1808, for example, there were no votes against the ending of hanging for pickpockets.

Elizabeth Fry (1780–1845), prison reformer
Work: Fry was brought up a Quaker and worked to help the homeless before beginning her work in prisons. In 1817 Fry formed the Association for the Improvement of Female Prisoners in Newgate prison.

Importance: Fry helped to bring about the changes in Newgate which were later introduced in other prisons, including providing clothing and furniture, female warders and schools for women and children in prison which focused on religious education.

THE REVOLUTION IN POLICING

Why was the first police force set up in London in 1829?

Policing before 1829

During the 1700s old methods of policing continued, much as they had done for centuries. Constables and watchmen were still appointed in villages and towns. Some of them were efficient, but many did not have enough time or support to be effective. After all, they had full-time jobs too.

SOURCE 1 Night watchmen preparing to leave the watch house for work, c.1812

Constables did not have much chance of success in cities, especially London, where the crowded streets and houses provided ideal shelter for criminals. Therefore, new ideas about policing began to be tried out in London.

At the centre of the struggle against crime were John Fielding and his brother Henry. They were London magistrates based at Bow Street. They realised that more men were needed on London's streets to stop crime. Their measures included:

■ a civilian horse patrol to stop highwaymen. In 1805 a new patrol of 54 men was set up
■ introducing the Bow Street Runners, a team of thief-takers who patrolled the streets of London in the evenings
■ publishing the *Hue and Cry* newspaper which contained details of crimes and criminals, and of stolen property. The newspaper was circulated to magistrates and the public. This helped pass on information about criminal activities.

The failings of the system of constables

Most people now accepted that the centuries-old system of constables could not cope with increasing crime. The job of constable was still part-time and the post held for one year only. A patchwork of other types of police had appeared in London, but there was no overall organised system.

Thanks to John Fielding and other pioneers, a more organised system of preventing crime was developing in London by 1800. However, there was still no overall co-ordination of the different forces of constables, watchmen and runners. An even greater problem was that there was great opposition to the idea of a police force because:

■ people feared the cost
■ they feared the invasion of privacy
■ they thought it might be used by the government to limit freedom
■ they thought it wouldn't work.

However, the idea of a police force was slowly getting stronger, as the setting up of the Thames River Police in 1798 showed.

The breakthrough came after Sir Robert Peel was appointed Home Secretary in 1822. Peel believed that police were needed and he immediately set up a day patrol of Bow Street Runners in London. By 1829 he had won support for the setting up of the Metropolitan Police. Initially, 3200 men were recruited to police a seven-mile circle starting at the centre of London.

SOURCE 2 Sir Robert Peel, the Home Secretary who set up the Metropolitan Police, was one of the greatest administrators of the nineteenth century. He had the skills to find a solution to the problems and to win support for setting up the police force

Why was Peel able to set up the first police force in London in 1829?

Government and taxation

Governments were increasingly involved in reforming and changing life in Britain. Part of the reason was the long French war which had forced the government to raise money. Governments were also raising more money in taxes and allowed local authorities to raise local taxes such as those that paid for the police.

Increased crime and increased fear of crime

There was a widespread belief that crime and especially violent crime was increasing and was out of control. The crime rate had actually risen quite sharply in the years following the French wars.

Fear of protest

After the French Revolution governments and landowners in Britain feared that a similar revolution might take place in Britain (see pages 144–145). In the years after 1815 there were many protests about unemployment and high food prices and a revolution seemed possible. (You can see examples of these on pages 146–147.)

London

The rapid growth of towns had made the old system of constables and watchmen seem even more old-fashioned and inadequate. There were simply too many people, crammed into closely-packed houses and streets, to police in the old ways.

These problems were particularly tricky in London. Fear of crime, disorder and even revolution was strongest there.

SOURCE 3 The Duke of Wellington, speaking as Prime Minister in 1829 when the Metropolitan Police was established

66 *In one parish, St Pancras, there are now no fewer than 18 different establishments [groups trying to prevent crime], not one of which has any communication with another. The consequence is that the watchmen of one district are content with driving thieves from their own particular neighbourhood into the adjoining district.* 99

SOURCE 4 John Hopkins Warden, a constable in Bedford, 1821, writing about the existing system of constables that had lasted for centuries

66 *[A part-time parish constable] who is perhaps new to his office every year and cannot be aware of criminals' habits and plans also has his own business to take care of. He knows that his term of office as constable will soon expire so he does not give it the attention it requires.* 99

How did policing develop after 1829?

1829 The Metropolitan Police force was set up in London. It had 3200 men.

1835 A new law said that towns were allowed to set up their own police forces.

1839 A new law said that counties were allowed to set up their own police forces. Bow Street Runners and other forces in London were amalgamated with the Metropolitan Police.

1842 The Metropolitan Police set up the first detective force.

1856 It became compulsory for all towns and counties to set up police forces.

1870 Police helmets were introduced.

1884 There were 39,000 police in Britain.

1. Was the idea of a police force for London completely new in 1829?

2. Why had a police force not been set up before 1829? You could also refer to page 134 for help with your answer.

3. Write a one-sentence explanation of the significance of each of these factors in the setting up of the first police force:

   ■ fear of crime and protest
   ■ inadequacies of existing system
   ■ growth of towns
   ■ increasing government involvement.

4. Which of the factors are most helpful in explaining

a) why **pressure for a police force built up** in the period after 1815?

b) why the first police force was set up **in London**?

Changing attitudes to the police

THE IDEA OF setting up a police force had been resisted for a long time. How did people react to the police forces once they began work? Were they instantly popular or were people still hostile to them? And how did attitudes to the police change over the century?

■ SOURCE INVESTIGATION

Look at Sources 1–11 below.

1. These sources give you ideas about what the police actually did. List the tasks being undertaken by the police in these pictures.
2. What can you work out from them about attitudes to the police in the nineteenth century? Think about the following questions:
a) Which sources are hostile to the police?
b) What do they criticise?
c) Which sources show the most support or respect for the police?
d) What do they like about the police?
3. 'The reputation of the police steadily improved over the nineteenth century.' How far do you agree or disagree with this statement? Refer to the sources in your answer.

This is the Policeman mark'd 10—letter Z;
Who, anxious to prove that the peace he maintains,
Sets to work with his staff on an old woman's head,
And silenced her by the loss of her brains.

SOURCE 4 A cartoon from *Punch* magazine, 1842

SOURCE 5 Charles Dickens, *Martin Chuzzlewit*, 1844. Mrs Gamp asked

66 *Where's the pelisse? If they greased their whiskers less and minded their duties which they're paid so heavily for a little more ...* 99

SOURCE 1 A cartoon called 'Calthorpe Street Blues' from a song sheet, c.1830

SOURCE 2 A cartoon called 'Blind Man's Buff' from *Punch* magazine, 1888

PERPLEXED FARMER. *"You haven't seen such a thing as my Old Woman about, have you, Mr. Policeman?"*

SOURCE 6 A cartoon from *Punch* magazine about the work of the police at the Great Exhibition of 1851. Six million tickets were sold for the Exhibition at the Crystal Palace. Whole villages left home to explore the wonders of the 10,000 exhibits

SOURCE 3 A verse from *Punch* magazine in 1850, which accompanied a cartoon called 'Burglars Carousing'. 'Crusher' was one of the nicknames for a policeman

66 *Policeman Y to booze is gone, no watch patrols the lea,
The house that yonder stands alone invites to burglary.
The footpad prowls on heath and fen, no crusher stops his way.
Uprouse you, then, my merry men, for now's your time of day.* 99

SOURCE 7 From *Punch* magazine, 1851

" *The police are beginning to take that place in the affections of the people – we don't mean the cooks and housemaids alone but the people at large – that the soldiers and sailors used to occupy. The blue coats – the defenders of order – are becoming the national favourites. The taking of a foreign fort seems to sink into insignificance before the taking of an unruly cabman's number. Everyone has been charmed during the Great Exhibition by the way in which this truly civil power has been effective.* "

SOURCE 8 From the weekly magazine *Fun* in 1868 following the Reform Riots in Hyde Park. Richard Mayne was the chief of the Metropolitan Police

" *Richard Mayne is the leader of an organised gang of ruffians who for some time have annoyed all respectable people by 'playing at soldiers' on various occasions in public places. The miscreants wear helmets and commit other absurdities.* "

RUFFIANLY POLICEMAN

SOURCE 10 A cartoon from *Punch* magazine in 1866. There had been riots in London over political reform. Over 1200 metres of railings in London's Hyde Park were torn down and the army had to be called out to help the police. A number of policemen and demonstrators were hurt

AN UNEQUAL MATCH.

SOURCE 9 A cartoon from *Punch* magazine in 1881

WHITECHAPEL, 1888.

First Member of "Criminal Class." "Fine Body o' Men, the Per-leece!"
Second Ditto. "Uncommon Fine!—It's Lucky for Hus as There's Sech a Bloomin' Few on 'Em!!!"

SOURCE 11 A cartoon from *Punch* magazine in 1888

Nineteenth-century policing: *Success or failure?*

SIR ROBERT PEEL set up the first police force. Imagine we could miraculously bring Sir Robert back to life and interview him about nineteenth-century policing. What would he say?

> Weren't they supposed to be stopping crime? You said that was their main job.

> They did that too. Look at Source 1 – twenty-four petty thieves arrested. The police became quite effective at catching thieves. They probably prevented a lot of crime simply because they were seen on the streets. But there's only so much the police could do. They were not able to solve the problem of crime overnight.

> How did you overcome opposition to a police force?

> We had to make sure the new policemen didn't look like soldiers because of fears they would be used to interfere in the liberties of citizens. The new policemen wore top hats, blue coats (to contrast with most soldiers' red coats), no decoration (to contrast with the soldiers' badges) and carried truncheons rather than swords.
> And by the way, those hats served a double purpose – they were reinforced so constables could stand on them to look over a high wall!

> Wasn't that because they didn't stay in the police for very long?

> Staff turnover was a problem. Of the 2800 constables in 1830, only 562 remained four years later. Drunkenness was a major problem early on. It led to 80 per cent of dismissals. Then we lost 1300 who left to 'better' themselves or return to their old jobs.

> Do you think this problem would have been avoided if you'd paid them more? I have here a quotation from one of your 'ex-constables': 'What man of sober, industrious habits would consent to live in a Barrack for the pay of a bricklayer's labourer and work or watch seven days and nights in a week? It is absurd to expect it.'

> What did your police forces actually do?

> Most time was spent on routine tasks, clearing drunks and vagrants out of the streets, sorting out traffic problems and dealing with dangerous driving such as cabmen and delivery drivers who whipped their horses through the overcrowded streets.

> That's very biased, if I may say so. I had good reason for thinking that one of my police constables, if he was single, could find out of his pay of 21 shillings a week: lodgings, medical care, food at the mess, clothing and ... still save ten shillings a week. That's not bad.

SOURCE 1 Alexander Hennessey was a member of the Metropolitan Police. This is his log of arrests in sixteen years between 1857 and 1873

Reasons for arrests	*Number of arrests*
Petty theft	24
Burglary	4
Drunkenness	27
Drunk in charge of a vehicle	20
Cab driver holding up traffic	18
Assault	5
Begging	3

> But still less than a skilled worker earned. In one force, in 1836, 36 per cent had previously been general labourers and another 16 per cent had been soldiers or sailors.

> Yes, but you must realise the cost of the police was the biggest cause of opposition. Even paying them 21 shillings a week was thought to be overpaying them. In 1842 two-thirds of Bedfordshire parishes petitioned for the disbanding of the police because it was 'expensive if not inefficient'. If you want a police force you have to be prepared to pay for it.

Which many places weren't.

Exactly. In the end, they had to be forced. In 1856 it was made compulsory for every district to have a police force.

Did the police learn from their early mistakes?

Of course. There was a limit to what a uniformed policeman could do. In 1833, one of my policemen said, 'All thieves know a policeman in uniform and avoid him.' Ordinary police in uniform were watched on their rounds until they were away from the spot. So we started a plainclothes force. The commanders found that policemen in plain clothes arrested three criminals for every one taken by uniformed men.
Then we set up a detective branch in 1842, to detect criminals after a crime had been committed.

Who were willing, but not very successful, if you believe those Sherlock Holmes stories?

Sherlock who?
The point is that the police took over from the public the gathering of evidence and making prosecutions. Since Roman times these tasks had been left to the victims of a crime and had often led to crimes going unreported because to do so was simply too much bother. Now, for the first time, that burden had been lifted from the victim and taken on by the police.

SOURCE 3 A poem from the *Sunderland Echo*, February 1891, following a strike at Silksworth colliery. Police were used to protect bailiffs who were evicting miners, and 50 policemen took part in a truncheon charge. The poet has followed the style of Tennyson's famous poem 'The Charge of the Light Brigade', about a suicidal yet brave cavalry charge

" *Flash'd all their batons bare,*
Flash'd as they turned in air,
Thumping at back-skulls there,
Mauling away because
Someone had blunder'd
Pounding at ev'ry head,
Quiet folks' blood was shed;
Women and children
Reeled from the blows that sped,
Moaning and sunder'd
Then they marched back again
Gallant half hundred! "

I'd like you to read this poem from the *Sunderland Echo* (Source 3). What do you think of it?

In my time we did use London police to quell riots and protests in other parts of the country. And sometimes these policemen did cause injuries or even death. But remember, we sent the police because we believed this would be **less likely** to lead to violence than sending the army.

What was your greatest success?

The fact that the police became accepted and respected. At first, they were called 'Crushers' and 'Raw Lobsters'. By the 1850s that suspicion of the police was replaced by respect and they were more likely to be called 'Peelers' or 'Bobbies' – a generous reference to me!

But they still didn't solve the problem of crime, did they? Here is a quotation from 1897 complaining about 'the lack of police protection, the recent desperate assaults in Blackfriars Road, the frequent watch-snatching and highway robberies, the pilfering from shops and the numerous burglaries.'

With respect, that is one instance – if you want the bigger picture, just look at the statistics. Crime fell steadily for 50 years from 1850 to 1900. Give the police some credit, young man. Thieves don't rush forward to admit that they have been planning a robbery, but were prevented from carrying it out because of the presence of police. It's common sense to me that good policing stops crime.

SOURCE 2 This artist's reconstruction of a famous cartoon by Cruikshank shows one of the most common duties of early policemen

Why did the crime rate drop in the second half of the century?

WITH THE INTRODUCTION of a professional police force and a reformed punishment system, the crime rate began to fall from the 1850s, after a century or more of rising crime. The link may look obvious to you. It looked obvious to the people of the nineteenth century: the revolution in prisons, punishment and policing had reversed the trend of rising crime.

- Prisons were no longer schools for crime. Improved conditions in prisons did give more chance of reforming prisoners.
- A fairer system of punishment restored respect for the courts. Punishment was no longer a matter of chance. Criminals who were caught and convicted faced prison or a fine. There was popular approval of these sentences.

- The presence of the police deterred crime, particularly minor theft which was, and had always been, the most common form of crime.

However, you know enough about the history of crime and punishment to realise that the link is not that simple.

These reforms probably did have an impact on the crime rate, but it is likely that these measures might have been useless without underlying changes in employment, prices and wages. The period 1850–1900 was one of prosperity for many and, as you know from earlier periods, in times of poverty crime rises and in times of prosperity crime falls.

How important each of these factors was, is impossible to judge. What is clear is that they worked together to reduce the crime rate.

■ TASK

Work in groups. Six would be a good number.

You are the staff of the popular and famous *Crime Gazette*. It is nearing the end of the century and you are preparing the first edition for the New Year 1900. It will be a review of the past century: examining major events, what changed and why it changed over the last 100 years.

Here are some features you might include:

a) stories of some famous crimes of the century, with explanations of why they are significant and how they affected attitudes to crime and punishment
b) profile of and mock-interview with an individual who has influenced crime and punishment (see pages 138–139 for ideas)
c) a timeline showing the main events of the century
d) a look forward into the new century – what remains to be done?
e) some pictures that sum up important ideas about crime and punishment in the nineteenth century. For example, you could use Source 1 and add your own explanation of how policing developed through the century.

Most importantly you will need to write an editorial summing up the different factors that you think have contributed to the falling crime rate of the past 50 years. Here are some possible headlines you could use for your editorial.

- Return to harsher punishments pays dividends.
- Crime problem solved.
- Some progress but still some way to go.

SOURCE 1 A policeman (or 'peeler') dealing with troublemakers, c.1830

You might have other and better ideas. But try to make sure you are answering from a 1900 perspective.

Your teacher can give you a banner heading which you can incorporate into your work. This Task would be best tackled using a DTP computer program.

Summary: Crime and punishment 1750–1900

Headline: a revolution in punishment and policing

There were three big changes in this period.

- The Bloody Code was swept away.
- Prison became the most common form of punishment for serious crime.
- Professional police forces were set up for the first time.

Crime

Thefts were still far more common than violent crime. Most crimes were minor thefts although violent crimes received a great deal of publicity. New kinds of crimes were created by changes in the law; for example, not sending your children to school became a crime.

The crime rate increased steadily at the end of the 1700s and then increased rapidly in the period 1800–20. The rate of increase then slowed down but did keep rising until the middle of the century. After that, crime may well have gradually fallen as prosperity increased and the great majority of people had work, even if many jobs were still temporary.

The causes of crime

The diagram below shows some of the reasons why crime was a problem between 1750 and 1900.

1. Which of these reasons were a particular problem between 1750 and 1900?
2. Which crimes were created by the attitudes of the law-makers?

141

■ REVIEW TASK

1. On your own copy of the table below, fill in continuities and changes in crime and punishment 1750–1900.
2. In previous chapters there has been an illustration of an obstacle course which summarises: **How did people try to solve the problem of crime?**

   This time, you make your own. Look back to pages 21, 53 and 105. How will the 1900 obstacle course look different? Either draw or describe an obstacle course for the end of this period. Explain what is different from the course for 1750.

Nineteenth-century reforms and the future

A series of important developments took place between 1750 and 1900 that were to influence the system of justice in England in the future. These included:

■ the introduction of police in 1829
■ the use of prisons as the major punishment for serious crime
■ the idea that criminals could be reformed
■ the abolition of capital punishment except for treason and murder.

	What happened 1750–1900?	Continuities	Changes
Laws	There was an increasingly wide range of laws. As governments became more involved in every aspect of society, they made new criminal offences which had not existed before, e.g. in 1870 it became compulsory to send children to school. Parents were fined for not doing so.		
Policing	The old system of unpaid constables was replaced by professional police forces. By 1860 forces had been set up throughout the country. Detective forces followed.		
Trials	The system of trials was little changed.		
Punishments	The Bloody Code was abolished. Capital punishment was little used by 1900. The only crimes punished by execution were murder and treason. The main purpose of punishment was to punish and reform the criminal, not to warn others away from crime. Therefore, punishments no longer took place in public. Physical punishments such as whipping were abolished except in prisons. Fines were a common punishment. Prison became the main form of punishment with 90 per cent of serious offenders sent to prison. Transportation was seen as a middle punishment between execution and fines until prisons took over. Transportation ended in 1868.		

PROTEST FROM 1700 TO THE 1920s

Protesters or criminals? Why has the treatment of protesters changed since 1700?

IN CHAPTER 3 you examined the treatment of protesters from 1300 to 1700. Now you are going to follow the story into the twentieth century.

Riots and protests were common in the 1700s and early 1800s.

Not only were they common, but force was often used to end the protests. In this chapter you will investigate the changes in causes and methods of protests from 1800, and you will try to understand the changing methods that governments used to deal with protests.

- **Part 6.1: Why were protesters treated so harshly before 1850?**
- **Part 6.2: Why were protesters treated more leniently after 1850?**

■ TASK

While you are working on this chapter, keep a diary recording protests today. Use the following headings or use a chart like the one on page 146:

- The causes of protest
- The actions of the protesters
- The authorities' reactions to the protest
- Success or failure of protest.

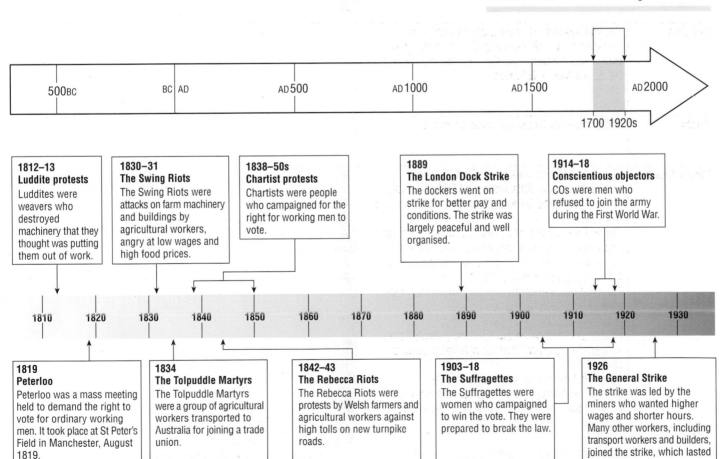

1812–13
Luddite protests
Luddites were weavers who destroyed machinery that they thought was putting them out of work.

1830–31
The Swing Riots
The Swing Riots were attacks on farm machinery and buildings by agricultural workers, angry at low wages and high food prices.

1838–50s
Chartist protests
Chartists were people who campaigned for the right for working men to vote.

1889
The London Dock Strike
The dockers went on strike for better pay and conditions. The strike was largely peaceful and well organised.

1914–18
Conscientious objectors
COs were men who refused to join the army during the First World War.

1819
Peterloo
Peterloo was a mass meeting held to demand the right to vote for ordinary working men. It took place at St Peter's Field in Manchester, August 1819.

1834
The Tolpuddle Martyrs
The Tolpuddle Martyrs were a group of agricultural workers transported to Australia for joining a trade union.

1842–43
The Rebecca Riots
The Rebecca Riots were protests by Welsh farmers and agricultural workers against high tolls on new turnpike roads.

1903–18
The Suffragettes
The Suffragettes were women who campaigned to win the vote. They were prepared to break the law.

1926
The General Strike
The strike was led by the miners who wanted higher wages and shorter hours. Many other workers, including transport workers and builders, joined the strike, which lasted for nine days.

The story so far

Why were there so many riots in the eighteenth century?

BREAD RIOT AT THE ENTRANCE TO THE HOUSE OF COMMONS. 1815.

SOURCE 1 A riot caused by high bread prices in the early nineteenth century

In 1715 the Riot Act made it a capital offence for twelve people or more to meet together and then not disperse if a magistrate read out the Riot Act. If a crowd did not disperse, then the magistrate could call in soldiers to break up the crowd. The rioters could be hanged or transported. Many were.

This Riot Act was introduced because the new king, George I, was threatened by rebellion. It was soon used against all kinds of protesters, whether they were protesting against shortages of food, sudden cuts in wages, or toll gates. Indeed, any meeting of more than twelve people, however peaceful, could be broken up under the Riot Act. The village constables were unable to keep the peace so soldiers were used for that purpose.

As almost any meeting that the authorities wanted to prevent could be called a riot, there were hundreds of such events.

In 1769 an American, Benjamin Franklin, noted: 'I have seen within a year, riots in the country about corn; riots about elections; riots about WORKHOUSES; riots of colliers; riots of weavers; riots of coalheavers; riots of sawyers; riots of political reformers; riots of smugglers in which custom-house officers and excise men have been murdered and the King's armed vessels and troops fired at.'

Franklin sounds amazed by the number of riots he had heard of during his visit to Britain from America. He was not exaggerating. A full list would have been even longer, including riots against turnpike roads, food prices, theatre prices, Roman Catholics, cider and shop taxes and even against the rumoured destruction of cathedral spires.

For ordinary people, protesting was often the only way they could make their views known. They had little influence over what the government decided. Only a very small percentage of people could vote.

Riot is a misleading description of many of these incidents. They were not wild outbursts of violence which is what we now think of as a riot. Historians who have studied a wide range of so called 'riots' in the 1700s have shown that:

■ many peaceful and legal protests such as petitions to Parliament were called 'riots'
■ many riots were organised with clear aims, rather than being violent outbursts
■ deaths and injuries were extremely rare and avoided at all costs
■ people saw riots as a normal way of working together to defend their rights.

Why was the government so worried about protests in the early 1800s?

The French Revolution of 1789 raised the stakes. Now the terrified landowners and politicians in Britain saw every protest as the beginning of the British Revolution. This fear continued throughout the first half of the 1800s. The French wars of 1793–1815 added to government fears because of the possibility of an invasion by Napoleon's army. Later revolutions in France, in 1830 and in 1848, kept alive British fear of revolution when it might have died away.

Why were the landowners who made up the government afraid of revolution? Some were certainly acting selfishly to protect their power, land and wealth. But not everyone had this one, simple motive. Lord Liverpool (Prime Minister 1812–27) and other politicians had been in France during the early days of the revolution and had seen the chaos of revolution. They genuinely believed that revolution would harm everyone by disrupting work and trade.

In the first part of this chapter you will study six different protests before 1850. Hundreds of these protesters were severely punished. Some were hanged. Many of the other leaders were transported to Australia. The main aim of the investigation is to explore why governments treated these protesters so harshly. Which of the reasons shown below do you think are correct?

Things are getting out of hand. Any moment now the violence will start. We must restore law and order for everyone's sake. Use soldiers if necessary.

If we do not stop these protests they will turn into a revolution and we know from the French Revolution what a disaster that would be.

Look at all these protests. If we give in to one protest, we will soon lose all our power and land.

The Luddites

TASK

Make your own copy of this table and complete it after you have studied each protest.

	Description	Date	Reasons for protest	Methods of protest	Authorities' reactions	Punishments of protesters	Reasons for authorities' reactions
Luddites							
Peterloo							
Swing Riots							
Tolpuddle Martyrs							
Chartists							
Rebecca Riots							

> **Luddites** were weavers and other textile workers who destroyed machinery that they thought was putting them out of work.

IN 1811 BRITAIN was at war with France, a war that had been going on for eighteen years. One result of the war was that the quantity of Britain's overseas trade had fallen. Consequently, some employers had cut their workers' wages or sacked them. Poor harvests made a difficult situation worse and food riots took place in various parts of the country. In Carlisle soldiers fired on men, women and children who had broken into a warehouse to get food. One woman was killed.

This was the background to attacks on machinery that began in Nottingham in 1812. Employers had introduced new machines called stocking-frames, which could produce goods more cheaply than people could. As a result, workers lost their jobs or had their wages cut. The workers who had lost their jobs ganged together at night to smash the hated frames. They left behind threatening messages signed by General Ludd, who was rumoured to live in Sherwood Forest, although there was no such man.

The attacks spread to Lancashire and Yorkshire. In April 1812, 150 armed Luddites attacked Rawfolds Mill, owned by Edmund Cartwright. Cartwright had been expecting the attack. As the Luddites tried to batter down the mill doors, his men opened fire.

Two attackers were killed and the rest retreated, leaving a trail of weapons behind them.

The local authorities and the government, horrified by the French Revolution of the 1790s, feared that a revolution was about to take place in Britain. A revolution would make it impossible to win the war against France and could lead to a French invasion. When the Prime Minister, Spencer Perceval, was assassinated in Parliament these fears were further increased, even though the murderer was a bankrupt merchant, not a Luddite. When the news reached Nottingham, crowds paraded round the town, beating drums and flying flags. In Leeds a leaflet was published saying:

'You are requested to come forward with arms and help redressers to redress their wrongs and shake off the hateful yoke of a silly old man and his son more silly and their roguish ministers, all nobles and tyrants, must be brought down. Above 40,000 heroes are ready to break out, to crush the old government and establish a new one. Apply to General Ludd.'

Over 10,000 soldiers were sent to stop the Luddite attacks. A law was passed making frame-breaking punishable by death. Seventeen Luddites were executed. They became heroes and martyrs to the local people. Despite the government's fears, there were probably few revolutionaries among the Luddites. Most were ordinary working people, frightened by poverty into taking the only action that might help them.

By 1813 the economic situation was improving. Food became cheaper and trade improved, increasing the number of jobs and level of wages. Luddism faded away, although this was not the end of protests about unemployment.

1. Which political events worried the government at the same time as the Luddite attacks?
2. Why would the leaflet published in Leeds have frightened the government?
3. What, according to Source 1, put an end to the Luddite attacks?
4. Complete row 1 of your table from page 146.

SOURCE 1 A contemporary illustration of Luddites attacking a stocking-frame

Luddism – the main events

1811	Stocking-frames smashed in Nottinghamshire.
1812	March – breaking of frames in Yorkshire.
	April – attacks on mills, including Cartwright's Rawfolds mill. William Horsfall, mill owner, murdered.
	May – Spencer Perceval, Prime Minister, was assassinated. Rumours of armed men gathering on northern moors. Thousands of soldiers sent to calm areas of Luddism.
1813	Seventeen Luddites executed: three for murder of Horsfall, five for the attack on Rawfolds Mill and nine for seizing weapons in raids on villages.

SOURCE 2 From the newspaper, the *Leeds Mercury*, 1812

" A correspondent from Barnsley observes that the army of General Ludd was the other day completely put to rout by the discharge of a substance called potato into the stomachs of the troublemakers. A boatload of this kind of ammunition arrived very opportunely and was distributed to the labouring class. "

■ TASK

Your teacher will give you a sheet of questions from the Editor of the *Leeds Mercury*. He wants to put them to a Luddite. You have taken part in a number of Luddite attacks and want more people to hear about the reasons for the attacks. Give your answers to the *Mercury*'s questions.

Peterloo

What happened at Peterloo?

On 16 August 1819, 60,000 people packed into St Peter's Field, Manchester. That meeting became one of the most famous events of the nineteenth century – Peterloo!

> **Peterloo** was a mass meeting held to demand the right to vote for ordinary working men. It took place at St Peter's Field in Manchester, August 1819.

SOURCE 1 A cartoon by Cruikshank, entitled 'Manchester Heroes'

■ TASK

1. Make a list of the questions you want to ask about this event.
2. What are the artists' attitudes? Are they likely to provide accurate illustrations?
3. How many of your questions can you answer from the two illustrations? Write your own account of what you think happened that day.

SOURCE 2 An engraving of the events at Peterloo made very soon afterwards and widely circulated across the country

The events at Peterloo

The day dawned hot and sunny and people streamed into Manchester from the Lancashire mill towns. Men, women and children marched hand in hand in their Sunday best, accompanied by music. Their banners demanded 'Liberty' and 'Votes for All' because they were there to demand reforms from the government.

Since 1815 bread prices had been high. Unemployment had risen, as many soldiers, returned from the French wars, had been unable to find work. Protests and riots followed, all of which had been broken up by soldiers. The people wanted lower food prices and the chance to vote in elections. They believed that if they could vote, then governments would have to listen to their demands.

In 1819 the reformers decided to hold a series of mass meetings in Leeds, Birmingham, London and Manchester. Henry Hunt, one of the most rousing speakers of the time, would address the crowd. The local magistrates were anxious. Their job was to keep order but they feared that the meeting would be the signal for the beginning of a rebellion. There were rumours that armed men had been training on the moors. They feared that Hunt would stir the crowd to violence. The magistrates had special constables to help them and a group of local soldiers, the yeomanry.

When Hunt appeared there was enthusiastic applause, flags waved, trumpets blew, and the magistrates panicked. A horn sounded and the Manchester Yeomanry rode forward. The story is taken up by Samuel Bamford, a supporter of reform who was in the crowds (Source 3).
Eleven people were killed at Peterloo. About 400 were wounded.

The events in Manchester caused great anger. Newspaper reporters in the crowd strongly criticised the magistrates for over-reacting. Cartoonists like Cruikshank showed the people as the innocent victims of the bloodthirsty soldiers and the panicky magistrates. Many people demanded that the government should punish the magistrates.

The Prime Minister, Lord Liverpool, and his government faced a difficult decision. There were still great fears of a rebellion. Perhaps the anger at the deaths in Manchester would make a rebellion even more likely? If ministers showed strong support for the magistrates, it might discourage rebels. On the other hand, people were so angry that supporting the magistrates might be the very thing that would tip the balance towards rebellion.

SOURCE 3 Samuel Bamford's account of Peterloo

66 *Their sabres glistened in the air and on they went, direct for the hustings. As the cavalry approached the dense mass of people, the people used their utmost efforts to escape but so closely were they pressed by the soldiers, the special constables, the hustings and their own numbers that immediate escape was impossible. Sabres were plied to hew a way through naked held-up hands and defenceless heads; and then chopped limbs and wound-gaping skulls were seen and groans and cries were mingled with the din of that horrid confusion.*

In ten minutes the field was an open and almost deserted space. The hustings remained with a few broken or hewed flag-staves erect and a torn or gashed banner or two drooping; whilst over the whole field were strewed caps, bonnets, hats, shawls and shoes, trampled, torn and bloody. Several mounds of human beings still remained where they had fallen, crushed down and smothered. Some of these were still groaning – others with staring eyes were gasping for breath and others would never breathe more. 99

■ TASK

Imagine that you are a member of Lord Liverpool's Cabinet. What policy are you going to recommend at tomorrow's emergency meeting? Here are your choices. Remember that the peace of the country depends on making the right choice.
a) Criticise the magistrates and force them to resign. This may show that the government is concerned about the people. However, what will your political supporters think of this policy?
b) Give the magistrates your support. Their job was to stop any possibility of rebellion and they did just that.
c) You might want to go further and make sure that other large meetings cannot take place. You could ban all meetings of, say, more than ten people. You could give magistrates powers to search houses where weapons could be hidden. What else could you do?

How did the government react to Peterloo?

The government chose options b and c. This probably seems very harsh, especially as the crowd in Manchester had done nothing to provoke the soldiers. However, the government's great fear was revolution, particularly as it had seen the chaos that had taken place in France after the French Revolution in the 1790s. Another reason why the government backed the magistrates was that, if they did not, they were afraid that it would be difficult in future to get people to act as magistrates.

The government did not consider introducing reforms to help reduce poverty and unemployment. They blamed the effects of the long war and the return of demobilised soldiers. They did not think that governments should take any action to change these conditions, but took the view that things would improve in time.

Newspapers and reformers called for an enquiry into the events of Peterloo, but the government refused. Twelve thousand additional troops were sent to the area although, such was the fear of rebellion, they were kept together in case small groups of soldiers were attacked. Hunt and others were put on trial and charged with conspiring to disturb the peace and to arouse hatred of the government. Hunt was sentenced to two and a half years in prison, three others to a year. The Manchester magistrates clearly felt the leaders had got off lightly. One magistrate told a reformer: 'I believe you are a downright blackguard reformer. Some of you reformers ought to be hanged – the rope is already round your neck.'

The government's main response came with the Six Acts (see below). They were intended to stop any chance of meetings turning into rebellion and to stop the spread of reforming ideas amongst the people. You can see the details of these Acts in the chart below. The Six Acts were severe but they were only in place for a year. By then the demand for reform among the majority of the people had begun to fade in cities like Manchester. Lower food prices and more work reduced the discontent.

1. Why did Lord Liverpool and his government support the magistrates?
2. Who was officially blamed for Peterloo?
3. Why were the Six Acts passed by Parliament?
4. Why was a tax put on newspapers?
5. Do you think that the government's reaction was harsh?
6. Complete row 2 of your table from page 146.

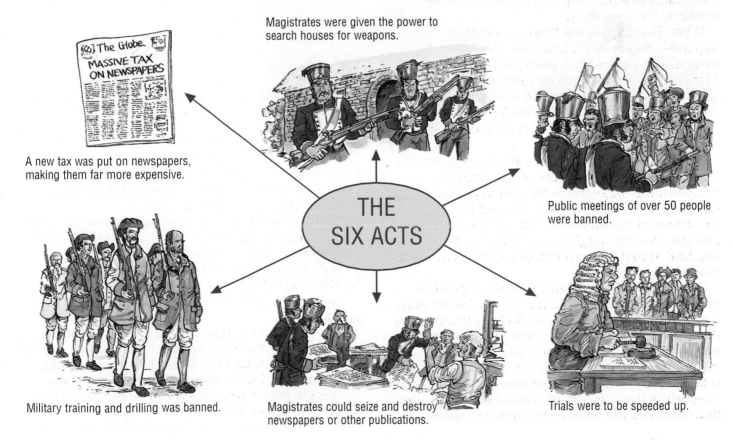

A new tax was put on newspapers, making them far more expensive.

Magistrates were given the power to search houses for weapons.

THE SIX ACTS

Public meetings of over 50 people were banned.

Military training and drilling was banned.

Magistrates could seize and destroy newspapers or other publications.

Trials were to be speeded up.

The Swing Riots

ONE MORNING IN November 1830 John Benett, the MP for Wiltshire, was woken with the news that his house was about to be attacked. Four hundred farm labourers were approaching, armed with hammers and crowbars. They smashed their way into the barns and broke up the threshing machines used on his farm.

This was just one incident in the Swing Riots that raged across the south of England late in 1830. There were 1500 such incidents of machine-breaking, arson and riot in just four months. The leader of the movement was a fictional figure, Captain Swing, but the real members were young men, mostly skilled farm workers and craftsmen, who had never been involved in any crime. They were angry about poverty and because the landowners, who had helped the poor in times of hardship, no longer thought that helping their workers was their responsibility.

The Swing Riots: attacks on farm machinery and buildings by agricultural workers angry at low wages and high food prices.

SOURCE 1 An account by the Duke of Wellington, Prime Minister during the Swing Riots

" I persuaded the magistrates to put themselves on horseback, each at the head of his own servants and gamekeepers armed with horsewhips and pistols and to attack these mobs, disperse them, destroy them and take prisoner those who could not escape. "

SOURCE 2 The sentences handed out to Swing rioters

Total accused	1976
Acquitted	800
Executed	19
Transported	505
Prison	644
Fined	7
Whipped	1

SOURCE 3 A contemporary painting of a mob burning hayricks in Kent, 1830

The problems were low wages and high bread prices. Bad harvests had forced up food prices. Wages had fallen because farmers had introduced new machinery. Anyone who tried to make up for low wages with a little poaching was given a long prison sentence or transportation to Australia, if caught. Unable to vote, the workers had no other way to influence the government than their campaign of machine-breaking and rick-burning at farms belonging to prosperous landowners.

The government was determined to end the riots. In Europe there had been a series of revolutions and in Britain protests were beginning again over political reform. Hundreds of labourers were arrested. Petitions were collected, pleading for mercy and pointing out that the men had not used violence against anyone. Despite this, the Swing rioters were punished more severely than any other group of protesters. The government wanted to stamp out any possibility of revolution. Local magistrates were outraged that their farmworkers had dared to riot and passed heavy sentences.

1. What did the methods of the Swing rioters have in common with the Luddites?
2. Which other events affected the government's attitude to these riots?
3. How severely were the Swing rioters punished?
4. Complete row 3 of your table from page 146.

■ TASK

Your teacher will give you a sheet of questions from the Editor of the *Wiltshire Gazette*. He wants to put them to someone who attacked Benett's farm. You want more people to hear about the reasons for the attacks. Give your answers to the *Gazette's* questions.

The Tolpuddle Martyrs

The Tolpuddle Martyrs were a group of agricultural workers transported to Australia for joining a trade union.

IN 1833 A group of farm labourers in the village of Tolpuddle, in Dorset, met in secret. When they were sure they were not being watched the ceremony began. Each man was blindfolded in turn. Then they swore an oath, led by George Loveless, the local Methodist preacher. They swore to keep their union a secret and to work for the aims of the union, the Friendly Society of Agricultural Labourers.

It was not illegal to belong to a union or a 'combination' as unions were called. In 1824 the laws banning unions had been repealed. However, many employers were increasingly worried about the growth of unions. They believed that unions would interfere with their freedom to run their businesses however they liked. They were particularly anxious about the Grand National Consolidated Trades Union (GNCTU) set up in 1833 which aimed to bring all workers together to fight for better conditions.

Despite the men's oath of secrecy, the local farmers heard about the new union and set about breaking it up. They had strong memories of the Swing Riots and believed unions of farmworkers would lead to more attacks. They used a law that was really meant to apply only to the navy, saying that taking secret oaths was illegal. Even though joining a union was not against the law and they had not planned a strike or threatened anyone, Loveless and five others were arrested and charged with taking illegal oaths. Their sentence was seven years' transportation to Australia. As a result, unions were badly hit. The GNCTU broke up and it was another 20 years before unions revived.

SOURCE 1 From a book written in 1838 by George Loveless about the Tolpuddle case

❝ *The whole trial disregarded justice and decency. The greater part of the evidence against us was put into the mouths of witnesses by the judge. He told the jury that if such Societies [unions] were allowed to exist it would ruin masters, cause a stagnation in trade, destroy property. The jury was selected from amongst those who are most unfriendly towards us.* ❞

SOURCE 2 The words of Robert Scott, the master in Australia of James Brine, one of the martyrs

❝ *I understand it was your intention to have murdered, burnt and destroyed everything before you and you are sent over here to be severely punished and no mercy shall be shown to you.* ❞

SOURCE 3 In Australia the Tolpuddle men were forced to walk to the farms where they would work. Thomas Standfield, aged over 50, had to walk 150 miles (241 kilometres). Three weeks later his son, John, who was also transported, gave this description of his father

❝ *... a dreadful spectacle, covered in sores from head to foot, and as weak and helpless as a child. He slept in a 'watch-box' 6 feet by 18 inches [2 metres × 45 centimetres] with a small bed and one blanket with nothing to ward off the wind and had to walk four miles [6½ kilometres] for his rations.* ❞

The Tolpuddle men did not serve their full sentences. There was a widespread campaign saying that they had been unfairly convicted and they were released and returned to Britain in 1836.

SOURCE 4 The transportation of the men led to protest meetings including this one attended by 25,000 people in London. A petition demanding their release was signed by 250,000 people. What can you tell from this engraving about the protest meeting?

1. What does Source 1 tell you about landowners' attitudes to the Tolpuddle men?
2. How were the Tolpuddle men treated in Australia?
3. Did the harsh treatment of the Tolpuddle men achieve the government's aims?
4. Complete row 4 of your table from page 146.

The Chartists

How did governments react to the Chartists?

In 1832 the Reform Act gave men owning property worth £10 the right to vote, but that still excluded the majority of men and all women. As a result, a new campaign for the right to vote began in the 1830s. The campaigners called themselves Chartists because they wanted the government to agree to their People's Charter. Another reason for protest was the Poor Law of 1834 which ended payments to help the poor unless they moved into workhouses where families were split up and had to wear workhouse clothes which made poverty look like a crime.

1. According to Source 1 what problems existed in the political system?
2. From your knowledge of the political system today, which of these reforms were eventually introduced?

Support for Chartism spread rapidly in the late 1830s. There were over 80 Chartist Associations for women alone. What made Chartism a mass movement was hunger and unemployment. However, Chartism was mainly 'a knife and fork, a bread and cheese' movement. In years when food prices fell, support for Chartism also fell. In the more prosperous years after 1848, support for the Charter almost disappeared, although nearly all its objectives were eventually achieved.

Chartist methods

The Chartist leaders could not agree on the best way to influence the government. The majority favoured peaceful methods: distributing pamphlets, mass meetings and persuasion. Another group believed that peaceful methods would not work and that more violent methods should be used. Overall, Chartism was a peaceful movement, although the government remained anxious in case it led to rebellion. Now we will look at the two key events in the history of Chartism and how the government responded to these crises.

The Newport rising 1839

In November 1839 about 3000 armed coalminers and ironworkers marched on the town of Newport, probably intending to hold a meeting in support of the Charter and to protest about the arrest of Chartist leaders. The authorities were alarmed by information about men purchasing weapons and practising military drills. The threat of violence led to soldiers opening fire on the protesters who seemed to be trying to take control of the town. Over 20 Chartists were killed.

In the following months, around 500 Chartist leaders were arrested and many were imprisoned for over a year. The leaders of the Newport rising were sentenced to death but the sentence was reduced to transportation. Between 1839 and 1848 over 100 Chartists were transported to Australia.

The new police forces were used to combat possible violence in other places at this time. London police were sent to several northern towns and to Wales, but in some areas this only made the situation worse because people resented the arrival of outsiders. In the town of Llanidloes the arrival of the 'Peelers' sparked off three days of rioting in protest.

> **Chartists** were people who campaigned for the right to vote for working men.

> **SOURCE 1** The People's Charter demanded six political reforms
>
> 66
> 1. *A vote for every man aged 21 and over*
> 2. *Secret ballots*
> 3. *The abolition of the property qualification for MPs*
> 4. *MPs to receive salaries*
> 5. *Constituencies to be of equal size*
> 6. *Elections to be held every year* 99

The pattern of Chartism

1837–39	In 1839 the first Chartist petition was presented to Parliament. Three bad harvests in a row had pushed wheat prices to over 60 per cent higher than in 1835.
1841–42	High unemployment led to the second petition in support of the Charter in 1842.
1847–48	High food prices led to the third petition to Parliament in 1848.

SOURCE 2 The procession through London in 1842 when the Chartist petition for reform was taken to Parliament. The House of Commons voted heavily against receiving the petition. Widespread strikes followed in the north, but there was no nationally organised outbreak of violence. What can you tell from this illustration about Chartism?

The last petition, 1848

1848 saw revolutions in several European countries. In Britain, inspired once more by hunger, the Chartists claimed that five million people had signed their petition. A mass meeting was called in London, which the leaders hoped would be followed by a march on Parliament with the petition. They hoped that such a show of power would force the politicians to accept their demands for reform.

The government's reaction was decisive. The planned procession was banned. The Duke of Wellington (Commander in Chief of the army) organised London's defence against the threat of revolution. He placed cannon on London's bridges. Ten thousand soldiers stood by in readiness, although they were kept out of sight so as not to provoke violence. Thousands of special constables were also recruited to police the expected crowds.

This show of strength and determination ended any threat of violence. The Chartists' leaders agreed not to lead a mass march to Parliament. Instead, they took the petition there themselves, in a cab.

In fact, it had been signed by only around two million people and there were many forged signatures, including those of Queen Victoria and Wellington.

The crowds watched in 1848 but they did not rebel. There were a few conspirators intent on revolution but they were arrested and imprisoned. The government's policy of arresting, imprisoning and transporting anyone connected with violence had been effective, even if it was probably an over-reaction. Governments had also shown that they would make reforms to improve people's standards of living. In 1846 Sir Robert Peel's government had ended the Corn Laws and so had helped to bring down the price of bread. As a result, support for the Charter had been widespread but largely peaceful. There was never enough united support for a rebellion to be successful.

3. When did the Chartists get the most support?
4. Why did support for Chartism fall away?
5. Was there a real chance of rebellion in 1848?
6. Complete row 5 of your table from page 146.

The Rebecca Riots

The Rebecca Riots were protests by farmers and agricultural workers in Wales against high tolls on the new turnpike roads.

1. In May 1839 the tollgate on the road to Efailwen was destroyed.

2. The gate was rebuilt but destroyed again in June and July by the same people – Rebecca and her daughters.

3. The 'women' were really local farmers, angry at their growing poverty. They felt there was no other way to hit back. There was no single leader. Several leaders appeared as Rebecca at different times. They probably took the name from a Bible story.

5. The farmers were also paying rents, taxes and tithes to the Church of Wales even if they belonged to other churches. They also feared the new workhouses.

There's nothing I can do to prevent the tollgates.

6. The farmers felt that nobody was on their side, least of all the local magistrates and major landowners.

7. Violence spread in the 1840s. Barns and hayricks were burned and the workhouse at Carmarthen destroyed.

You'll never catch Becca.

9. The government sent 1800 soldiers to calm the area.

Reward £500
For any information leading to the capture of rioters

10. Seventy London policemen were also sent and rewards of £500 were offered for information.

11. A handful of leaders were arrested. Five were sentenced to transportation to Australia.

4. They attacked the tollgates because they were suddenly having to pay several tolls on one journey. The new turnpike roads were run by different companies and each levied its own tolls.

8. The violence attracted criminals eager to take advantage of confusion. In 1843 a woman tollgate keeper was killed.

12. The original farmers began to leave the movement, angered at the way criminals had used the Rebecca Riots. The Prime Minister, Sir Robert Peel, set up an enquiry. A Roads Board was set up to take over the turnpikes and tolls. By the mid-1840s west Wales was peaceful again.

Summary chart: Protest 1800–50

Reasons for protest	Protest was the only way of influencing the politicians who ran the country. No women and only a minority of men could vote in general elections. Hunger and poverty led to protests at different times, but as soon as a good harvest lowered food prices, the protests faded away. Some people protested for the vote or other reforms.
Methods of protest	Very varied: on the one hand, protesters destroyed or burned property; on the other hand, they held mass meetings, organised petitions and held peaceful marches and processions.
Authorities' reactions	The authorities main concerns were to keep law and order, and not to give in to the protesters. The old methods of law enforcement, such as the system of constables, relied on local support. The constable was helpless if the local population refused to co-operate with him. From 1700 to the 1830s the government relied increasingly on the Riot Act and the army to deal with protest. From 1829 the Metropolitan Police were sometimes used. The use of local police forces in the 1840s was sometimes more successful.
Punishment of protesters	The leaders of protests were punished severely through imprisonment and particularly transportation. Governments believed that the best way to stop people causing trouble was to send them as far away as possible for as long as possible.
Reasons for authorities' reactions	Governments could have responded to protests by making the reforms the people wanted but, as you have seen, they did not do this until the 1840s. They feared that reforms would be seen as a sign of weakness and therefore would only encourage revolution. Governments feared losing control. Governments did not believe that they should interfere with the economic situation to improve people's lives. All the illustrations on page 145 were correct. Ironically, for all the government's fears, a revolution was never likely. The failure of the Chartist march in 1848 suggests that the chances of rebellion were low.

1. What did these protesters have in common with the Luddites and the Swing rioters?
2. How did the government's reaction differ from its reaction to the Luddites and the Swing rioters?
3. Complete row 6 of your table from page 146.
4. Look back to the cartoons on page 145. Which of them do you think best explains the authorities' reactions to each protest you have studied?

WHY WERE PROTESTERS TREATED MORE LENIENTLY AFTER 1850?

THERE WERE FEWER protests in the 1850s and 1860s, a time of greater prosperity and employment. Governments had also begun to introduce reforms that were starting to improve working conditions and tackle poverty. Nevertheless, many of the causes of protest remained. Only a minority of men and no women could vote. Many people were poorly paid and likely to suffer unemployment if trade declined. Workers had little power to defend themselves.

■ TASK

The rest of this chapter looks at four case studies of protests in the period 1850–1930. All were treated more leniently than the earlier ones. Here are some of the reasons why. Your task is to find evidence to support these explanations.

Different methods of protesting were used. Protests were better organised and tried to win public sympathy.

Parliament did not feel threatened just because workers were protesting against bad pay and conditions.

There were a lot of different groups protesting about different issues. The government couldn't force all these protests to stop.

The London Dock Strike of 1889

' ... men ravening for food fought like madmen for [work]. Coats, flesh, even ears were torn off, men were crushed to death in the struggle.'

That was how the dockers' leader, Ben Tillett, described the scene when employers needed dockers to work for just a few hours. The London dockers were amongst the poorest paid workers in the country in the 1880s and even when they had work it might only be for a day or a few hours. Employers hired and fired them depending upon whether a ship needed loading or unloading.

The result was that many dockers earned less than £1 a week at a time when surveys showed that a family needed a minimum of £1.50 a week for just enough food, clothing and shelter. There was no trade union to help the dockers because the only unions were for skilled craftsmen. Nobody thought that unskilled workers could afford to pay union subscriptions or afford to go on strike.

In the 1880s three strikes showed that unskilled workers could stand up for themselves and improve their conditions. The Matchgirls' Strike showed the way and just the threat of a strike by gasworkers at the London Gas Company led to their working hours being cut from 70 to 50 a week. The most important action was the Dockers' Strike of 1889.

The dockers went on strike to win:

- an increase in pay from 5d to 6d an hour – 'the docker's tanner'
- 8d an hour overtime
- a guaranteed minimum of four hours work a day.

The strike lasted five weeks. Hardly anyone expected it to succeed. The dockers only had 7s 6d in their strike fund at the beginning. However, the strike was superbly organised by Ben Tillett, John Burns and Tom Mann. They collected funds, distributed food to families and persuaded other workers not to break the strike. Daily meetings were held to keep up the men's morale. Dock gates were picketed to stop the employers smuggling in other workers. After five weeks the employers gave in and agreed to the dockers' terms.

One vital part of planning the strike was staying on good terms with the police. Two thousand extra policemen were moved into the area to keep the peace. The dockers' leaders, particularly John Burns, made every effort to welcome the police, talk to them and win their trust.

Strikers were careful not to threaten or intimate other workers as this was against the law. The result was that fewer than 20 dockers were arrested in a strike lasting five weeks. The strikers' peaceful methods won them wide support and ended the employers' hopes that the police would stop the picketing.

SOURCE 1 Ben Tillett, *Memories and Reflections*, 1931

" *To obtain employment we are driven into a shed, iron-barred from end to end, outside of which a foreman or contractor walks up and down with the air of a dealer in a cattle market, picking and choosing from a crowd of men, who, in their eagerness to obtain employment, trample each other underfoot, and where like beasts they fight for a day's work.* "

SOURCE 2 James Gray, a dock labourer, giving evidence to a parliamentary committee in 1888

" *As a rule I have to struggle for employment. Yesterday I earned 2s 3d; this is the first work I have done since last Friday. I have been down at the London docks every morning at the usual hour of calling on, half past eight, and I have been unsuccessful in obtaining employment until yesterday. Yesterday I was there from 8.30 until 11.30. At 11.30 there were something like 350 men waiting for employment. A contractor came to the gate for I think it was fourteen men and of course there was a struggle between us men at the gate who should be lucky enough ...* "

SOURCE 3 There was a daily procession of dockers through London during the strike. Tillett wrote later

" *Our daily processions were not only demonstrations and advertisements for our cause but we collected contributions in pennies, sixpences and shillings from the clerks and City workers who were touched by the emblem of poverty and starvation carried in our procession – the 'dockers' dinner', a herring and dry bread ...* "

1. Why were the dockers on strike?
2. What methods did they use to win support?
3. How did the strikers put pressure on the employers to agree to their demands?
4. Why did the police remain on good terms with the strikers?
5. Do events during the Dock Strike show that attitudes to protest had changed since the 1840s?
6. Look at Source 3 on page 139. Were all protests treated leniently?

The Suffragettes

THE CAMPAIGN FOR women's suffrage began in earnest in the 1860s. (Suffrage means the right to vote.) Committees all over the country organised petitions and meetings; 1300 were held in 1877–78 alone. In 1897 these local groups formed a national organisation, the National Union of Women's Suffrage Societies (NUWSS – also called the Suffragists), led by Millicent Fawcett. More meetings and petitions followed, but most male politicians simply ignored these polite demands.

In 1903 some Suffragists lost patience. Emmeline Pankhurst formed the Women's Social and Political Union (WSPU) in Manchester. The WSPU, whose motto was 'Deeds not Words', rebelled against the male government of Britain. Mrs Pankhurst and her followers quickly became known as the SUFFRAGETTES.

SOURCE 1 Emmeline Pankhurst's description of Suffragette activities one afternoon in March 1909

" It was exactly half-past five when we alighted from the cab and threw our stones, four of them, through the window panes [of 10 Downing Street]. At intervals of fifteen minutes, relays of women who had volunteered for the demonstration did their work. The first smashing of glass occurred in the Haymarket and Piccadilly and alarmed both pedestrians and police. A large number of women were arrested, and everybody thought that this ended the affair. But before the police had reached the station with their prisoners, the ominous crashing and splintering of plate glass began again. [Fifteen minutes later] the third relay of women began breaking the windows in Oxford Circus and Bond Street. "

■ TASK

You are a member of a government committee trying to decide how to deal with the Suffragettes.

1. As part of your research, list:
a) the peaceful tactics
b) the violent tactics
   used by the Suffragettes.
2. Decide which of these ways of dealing with the suffragettes you will recommend:

■ imprisonment
■ fines
■ transportation
■ ignore them
■ increased policing in London
■ arrest of all leaders without charges.

Suffragette methods of protest

The Suffragettes ran a much more high-profile campaign than the NUWSS. Their methods included heckling at public meetings, organising processions, and publishing posters and leaflets that were dropped from airships. When this failed to win women the vote, the Suffragettes, led by Emmeline Pankhurst and her daughters, began to use more extreme methods.

For a time, according to the *Daily Mail*, 'any unaccompanied lady in sight, especially if she carried a hand bag, became an object of menacing suspicion'. In London they chained themselves to the railings of 10 Downing Street.

By 1913 their tactics had moved beyond breaking windows and setting off fire alarms, and their campaign had spread from the centre of London. This is a sample of activities in May and June 1913:

31 May	Railway telegraph wires cut in Cardiff and Monmouth.
2 June	Post boxes in Lewisham set on fire.
3 June	Acid poured onto the greens of a golf course near Doncaster.
4 June	Emily Davison tried to stop the King's horse at the Derby (and was killed in the attempt).
5 June	Purple dye poured into reservoirs near Bradford.
9 June	The grandstand at Hurst Park racecourse in Surrey set on fire.
9 June	A cricket pavilion in Middlesex set on fire.

When Asquith, the Prime Minister, visited Dublin an axe was thrown, narrowly missing him. Bombs were planted in railway stations and in Westminster Abbey and an explosion led to a fire at the home of David Lloyd George, the Chancellor of the Exchequer.

The government's response

Many MPs were shocked by the growing violence. They were also very worried about giving in. Asquith believed that if he gave in to threats, it would encourage other groups to use violence to threaten the government. The government faced serious threats, particulary from rebellion in Ireland and lengthy strikes in coal and other vital industries.

Therefore, the government tried to curb the Suffragettes' campaign. Window-breakers and other protesters who refused to pay fines were sent to prison.

In prison some Suffragettes went on hunger strike and the government decided to force-feed them, rather than take the risk of them dying.

SOURCE 2 Sylvia Pankhurst's description of being force-fed in Holloway prison

" *Six wardresses flung me on my back on the bed, and held me down firmly by shoulders and wrists, hips, knees and ankles. Then the doctors came stealing in … A man's hands were trying to force open my mouth; my breath was coming so fast that I felt as though I would suffocate. His fingers were striving to pull my lips apart – getting inside. I felt them and a steel instrument pressing round my gums, feeling for gaps in my teeth. I was trying to jerk my head away, trying to wrench it free … I braced myself to resist that terrible pain. 'No, that won't do' – that voice again. 'Give me the pointed one!' A stab of sharp, intolerable agony. I wrenched my head free. Again they grasped me. Again the struggle. Again the steel cutting its way in, though I strained by force against it. Then something gradually forced my jaws apart as a screw was turned; the pain was like having the teeth drawn. They were trying to get the tube down my throat, I was struggling to stiffen my muscles and close my throat. They got it down, I suppose, though I was unconscious of anything then save a mad revolt of struggling, for they said at last: 'That's all!' And I vomited as the tube came up … Day after day, morning and evening, the same struggle.* "

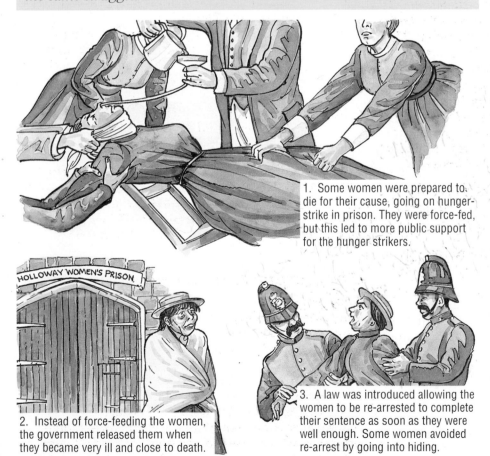

1. Some women were prepared to die for their cause, going on hunger-strike in prison. They were force-fed, but this led to more public support for the hunger strikers.

HOLLOWAY WOMEN'S PRISON

2. Instead of force-feeding the women, the government released them when they became very ill and close to death.

3. A law was introduced allowing the women to be re-arrested to complete their sentence as soon as they were well enough. Some women avoided re-arrest by going into hiding.

SOURCE 3 The 'Cat and Mouse Act'. The government seemed to be playing with the hunger-strikers like a cat plays with a mouse

SOURCE 4 In November 1910 the most dramatic confrontation between police and Suffragettes took place outside Parliament after the government delayed a compromise that would have given some women the vote. Police tactics were aggressive and many women were injured. Twenty-nine women complained of indecent assault by policemen. This is how one woman described her experience

" *For hours I was beaten about the body, thrown backwards and forwards from one policeman to another. Often seized by the coat collar, dragged out of the crowd, only to be pushed helplessly into a side street while he beat one up and down one's spine until cramp seized one's legs, when he would then release one with a violent shove. Once I was thrown with my jaw against a lamp-post with such force that two of my front teeth were loosened.* "

1. List the methods used to oppose the Suffragettes' campaign.
2. Why did the government introduce the 'Cat and Mouse Act'?
3. The police remained on good terms with the dockers during the 1889 strike. Why do you think there was more police violence towards the Suffragettes?

Votes for women
1918 Women over the age of 30 were given the right to vote.
1928 Women over the age of 21 were given the right to vote.

The conscientious objectors in the First World War

IN THE FIRST WORLD WAR 16,000 men refused to join the army because they were conscientious objectors (COs). Nearly all refused to fight on religious grounds. Some conscientious objectors believed that war itself was wrong and refused to support it in any way; others simply did not want to kill other human beings. Many COs who refused to join the army agreed to do other war work, such as driving ambulances at the front line, which was extremely dangerous.

About 1500 refused to take any part in the war. All of them were interviewed by special courts called tribunals. If they still refused to take any part in the war, they were imprisoned. Sources 1 and 2 describe the way COs were treated. Their right to vote was also taken away and not returned until 1923, five years after the war ended.

SOURCE 1 The recollections of Len Payne. He and his family were Quakers, members of the Society of Friends which was firmly opposed to war

66 *I was reading a Quaker journal and saw that a No-Conscription Fellowship was being formed and we joined this. We held secret meetings in cafés and other places in Leicester and sometimes our meetings were broken up by the police. The first tribunal was dominated by a military officer who barked out all the time so that the rest of the members had little chance of saying anything.*

On my way from a No-Conscription Fellowship meeting I was pushed off my bike and arrested by two policemen. Taken to the local police station, my clothes were taken from me and I slept the night on a hard board in a cell. In the morning I was taken before a magistrate and a military escort took me to a barracks. Here khaki clothes were forced on me. There were about twelve of us including my brother and we refused to drill properly. For this we were sentenced to 28 days tied spreadeagled to the wheel of a gun. As they had no guns we were given solitary confinement in completely darkened rooms.

I was court martialled and sent to Newcastle prison. This old prison was a great shock, rows and rows of cells and when the door of my cell slammed on me the bottom seemed to fall out of my little world and I wondered if I would survive. I was in this cell 23 hours out of every 24. There was a tiny window high up, a hard wooden plank bed, a bucket for a toilet and dreadful food. We met other COs only in the exercise yard where we were forbidden to talk. 99

In the Second World War government attitudes were less harsh. COs religious consciences were respected and they were not persecuted as they had been in the First World War. This time COs were sent to prison only as a last resort. A greater effort was made to give them other kinds of work such as in farming or industries vital to the war effort. However, the public again treated COs with hostility. Some COs were sacked from their jobs and others were attacked in the street.

1. Why did COs refuse to fight?
2. Why did refusing to fight in wartime become a crime in 1916?
3. How were COs treated when they refused to take any part in supporting the war?
4. Why do you think they were treated so harshly in the First World War?
5. How were COs treated in the Second World War?

SOURCE 2 In 1916 a group of COs were taken to France where they were ordered to take part in training. When they refused they were court martialled and faced the threat of the death sentence for disobeying orders now that they were in the war zone. One of them, Howard Marten, described what happened

66 *The court martial seemed to have an atmosphere of hostility, but I heard in a side-room as we were waiting one officer say to another 'you know it would be monstrous to shoot these men.' My statement was based on the wrongfulness of war from a Christian standpoint. We were then dismissed and a few days later we were paraded at the Henriville camp at the side of a huge parade. There must have been well over a thousand men there. We were called out singly and our crimes read out. I was the first and I was 'sentenced to suffer death by being shot' – a long pause – 'confirmed by the Commander in Chief' – again a long pause and I really thought that was that – after another long pause – 'but the sentence has been commuted by the Commander in Chief to one of penal servitude for ten years.'* 99

SOURCE 3 From A. Calder, *The People's War, Britain 1939–1945*. The Peace Pledge Union was opposed to war and tried to persuade people not to fight

66 *Six Peace Pledge Union organisers were on trial for putting up a poster which said 'War will cease when men refuse to fight. What are YOU doing about it?'. The magistrate dismissed the case saying, 'This is a free country. We are fighting to keep it a free country.'* 99

The General Strike of 1926

THE MOST DRAMATIC political event of the 1920s was the General Strike of May 1926. For nine days, miners, transport workers, builders, printers and many others, totalling two and a half million workers, stayed out on strike. The strike began with the miners. Since the First World War had ended in 1918 demand for coal had fallen. As a result, mine-owners' profits had also fallen. In 1926 the owners demanded that miners work eight hours a day instead of seven, and accept a ten per cent wage cut, with more wage cuts to follow.

When the miners refused to agree, the owners went ahead with a lock-out, closing the pits in the hope that hunger would drive the miners into accepting the deal. Instead, the Trades Union Council called the General Strike, keeping an agreement already made with the miners' union. A power struggle began between the unions on one side and the mine-owners and the government on the other.

You will recall how the memory of the French Revolution and fear of revolution influenced the way governments dealt with protest in the nineteenth century. In the 1920s a similar fear prevailed following the Bolshevik (Communist) Revolution in Russia. All over Europe, Communist parties had gained support following the success of the Russian Revolution and many leaders in Britain feared that workers would rise up and create a revolution in Britain.

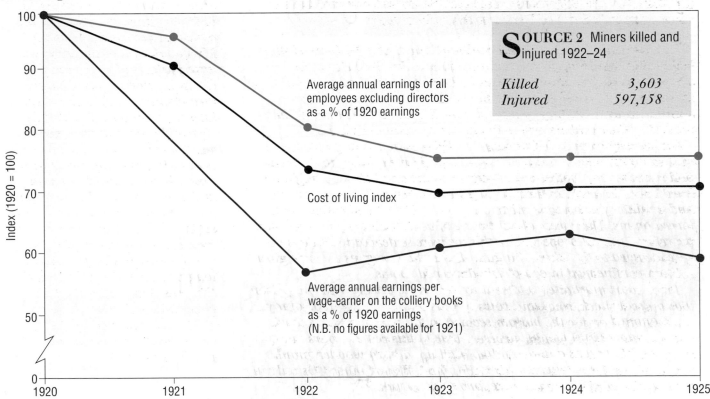

Average annual earnings of all employees excluding directors as a % of 1920 earnings

SOURCE 2 Miners killed and injured 1922–24

| Killed | 3,603 |
| Injured | 597,158 |

Cost of living index

Average annual earnings per wage-earner on the colliery books as a % of 1920 earnings (N.B. no figures available for 1921)

Index (1920 = 100)

SOURCE 1 This graph shows the changes in the living standards of miners in comparison to other groups

■ TASK

1. Complete a table like this to record the tactics used by the two sides in the General Strike.

Tactics used by the strikers	Tactics used by the government

2. Which tactics were the same as those used in or against protests in the nineteenth century?
3. Which tactics were new?
4. How important do you think the new tactics were in winning support?
5. Explain how far the police response to the strikers was similar to the police response to the 1889 Dock Strike or to the Suffragettes.

What tactics did the strikers use?

SOURCE 3 Strikers on their way to a special church service at St Andrew's Church, Plymouth. Strike leaders were determined to avoid violence. They sent out a strong warning against riots or damaging property. They were concerned that the government would use spies posing as strikers to start violence

Daily meetings were held to keep strikers and their families in touch with news and to keep up their morale. In many places the meetings turned into social events with sports, concerts, meals, picnics and hymns being sung. This all fostered a strong spirit and commitment among the families.

Every effort was made by the strikers to stop traffic moving around the country on the roads.

Every effort was made to stop traffic driven by volunteers. Some trams were overturned. One group of strikers greased a railway line on an uphill section and the volunteer drivers did not have the experience to get their trains up the slope. A train was derailed in Northumberland, but only because the volunteer driver ignored strikers' warnings that rails had been removed. No one was seriously hurt.

A union messenger in Scotland wrote: 'We had, in Scotland, brought both road and rail transport to a stop. At least in the areas that mattered. This was an effort by all the unions when it came to Glasgow – they had a wonderful organisation in relation to road traffic. They had to come to us to get anything through. We wouldn't let them through with goods. In the end they didn't even try. We wouldn't starve anyone out though.'

THE
BRITISH WORKER
OFFICIAL STRIKE NEWS BULLETIN
Published by The General Council of the Trades Union Congress

| No. 1. | WEDNESDAY EVENING, MAY 5, 1926. | PRICE ONE PENNY |

IN LONDON AND THE SOUTH

Splendid Loyalty of Transport Workers

WONDERFUL RESPONSE TO THE CALL

General Council's Message : Stand

SOUTH WALES IS SOLID!

Not a Wheel Turning in Allied Industries

SOURCE 4 The *British Worker* was published by the unions, although they had not planned a newspaper until the government published the *British Gazette*. It was widely distributed, selling a million copies on 11 May. It was only four pages long because the government had taken over supplies of newsprint

BLACKLEGS and volunteers were jeered or stared at in silence. There was little violence, although in Edinburgh women emptied slop buckets out of windows over the heads of special constables.

How did the government try to stop the strike being a success?

Volunteers worked as traindrivers and signalmen on the railways. Volunteers were largely from the middle and upper classes. Many had enough money not to need to work for a living and some thought that beating the strike was a game. They were often incompetent. There were a number of collisions on the railway, leading to four deaths, 35 people being injured and serious damage to engines.

Soldiers were moved into camps outside cities but were rarely used. The navy was used to break the strike by bringing in food. In Hull a naval captain marched his men into the town with rifles and fixed bayonets to stop trams being overturned.

Special constables were recruited from the middle classes. Some were members of the British Fascist movement who wanted to destroy the strike. In London, food lorries were escorted by convoys of soldiers and armoured cars. They were not needed because there were no serious food shortages, but it made good propaganda for the government.

The British Gazette

Published by His Majesty's Stationery Office.

No. I.   LONDON, WEDNESDAY, MAY 5, 1926.   ONE PENNY.

FIRST DAY OF GREAT STRIKE

Not So Complete as Hoped by its Promoters

PREMIER'S AUDIENCE OF THE KING

Miners and the General Council Meet at House of Commons

FOOD SUPPLIES

No Hoarding: A Fair Share for Everybody

HOLD-UP OF THE NATION

Government and the Challenge

NO FLINCHING

The Constitution or a Soviet

COMMUNIST LEADER ARRESTED

Mr. Saklatvala, M.P., Charged at Bow Street

SEQUEL TO MAY DAY SPEECH

THE "BRITISH GAZETTE" AND ITS OBJECTS

Reply to Strike Makers' Plan to Paralyse Public Opinion

REAL MEANING OF THE STRIKE

Conflict Between Trade Union Leaders and Parliament

SOURCE 5 The *British Gazette* was the government newspaper during the strike. It was edited by Winston Churchill who was extremely hostile to the strike. About two-and-a-half million copies a day were produced by the end of the strike. It provided news about what transport was running. Its information about the number of trains running was far from accurate, but this and other anti-strike propaganda helped the government to build support

At the beginning of 1926 there were over one-and-a-half million radio sets in Britain. The government decided not to take control of the BBC, but because the law courts had said the strike was illegal, the BBC refused to let the union leaders speak on the radio. It also refused to allow the leader of the Labour Party to speak, or to let the Archbishop of Canterbury appeal for a compromise until the strike was nearly over. However, the radio did help calm fears about food shortages and violence. By the end of 1926 there were over two million radios.

SOURCE 6 Vic Feather, a union organiser who later became leader of the TUC, said about the special constables

66 *They weren't dedicated to serve the community like the regular police, but because they hoped 'to keep the bastards down'. We didn't really come up against them much. There was a bit of pushing and shoving but the police kept the special constables out of it really, they didn't respect them.* 99

How did the police respond to the strike?

SOURCE 7 An eye-witness account by striker Harry Watson, from Margaret Morris, *The General Strike*, 1976

‘One morning we heard that troops were unloading ships and that lorries were coming up the Victoria Dock road, manned by troops. Sure enough, up came lorries with barbed wire all around their canopies and troops with guns sitting behind the barbed wire. The people were jeering and booing but that was the extent of their reactions. It was quite good-humoured.

Then the police started pushing from behind and they kept pushing and pushing us into the road. This led to arguments and before we knew it the police were laying about us with their truncheons. That caused more anger. There was a real explosion for about half an hour. We had to hit back to defend ourselves from what the police were trying to do to us – there were quite a few broken arms as a result of the blows we were subjected to.’

The next day the strikers went prepared for trouble and armed themselves on the way with iron railings ripped out of garden walls. Again the lorries with troops to guard them came up and again the police lined up, some in front but most at the back of the onlookers. Again the pushing began but this time before the police could start anything the crowd turned on them and started laying about them with the iron railings. That day it was the police who were injured.

SOURCE 8 From Margaret Morris, *The General Strike*, 1976

Bill Ballantyne recalls that the Carstairs strike committee took the line that there was no point in making enemies of the police: ‘If they left us alone, we would leave them alone.’ The police there were just as anxious to avoid trouble: the Chief Constable approached Bill and explained that they ‘didn’t want to use batons or anything like that’; he thought it essential to keep the temperature down and so he suggested a football match. As Bill Ballantyne says, ‘that develops in the country, you get to know the policemen and they know you’. he played centre forward and the strike committee scored three goals against the police.

These two extracts paint very different pictures of the way the police responded to the strikers. Source 8 is more typical of what happened. The police tried to avoid confrontations. In many areas strike leaders and local police chiefs successfully worked together to avoid violence. This was easier when the police were local men who knew the strikers.

Trouble between police and strikers was more likely in London where the government wanted to show that it was still in control, as you read in Source 7. There were also baton charges by police on strikers in Newcastle when both sides alleged that the other side had attacked first. There were other small-scale incidents in the north-east of England and in Glasgow, but generally the strike saw good relations between police and strikers. However, 5000 arrests were made during the General Strike for disorder, picketing or inciting others to break the law by joining the strike. Over 1000 people were imprisoned. The Northumberland strikers who removed rails that led to a train derailment (see page 164) were each sentenced to between four and eight years in prison despite their warning to the volunteer driver not to take the train on the line.

SOURCE 9 A policeman protects the volunteer driver of a London bus during the General Strike

How did the General Strike end?

The strike was effective. Public transport was stopped in many areas and food prices rose by over 50 per cent. Growing shortages of food meant that a crisis was approaching and at that stage the TUC accepted a compromise and called off the strike.

The government had made the strike appear to be a challenge to the way the country was governed, rather than simply a dispute between miners and mine-owners. The *British Gazette* and the BBC had both helped to portray strikers as traitors. Even one of the union leaders, J.H. Thomas, said: 'God help us unless the government won.'

The TUC thought the compromise to be reasonable. It gave them the chance to back away from appearing to challenge the elected government. However, the miners rejected it because it did not promise any improvements at all in their wages or conditions. They carried on their strike for another seven months, but were eventually forced to accept worse terms than they had been offered before the strike began.

Two new developments played a large part in winning the battle for the government. One was the radio which the government used to spread selected news and opinions – hostile to the strike. The other was the motor car – thousands of people could travel to work in their own cars and were not dependent on public transport.

UNDER WHICH FLAG?

JOHN BULL : ONE OF THESE TWO FLAGS HAS GOT TO COME DOWN—AND IT WON'T BE MINE.

SOURCE 10 An extract from the *British Gazette* published by the government on 6 May 1926

" *The General Strike is in operation, expressing in no uncertain terms a direct challenge to ordered government ... The strike is intended as a direct hold-up of the nation to ransom.* "

SOURCE 11 An editorial in the *York Herald*, 3 May 1926

" *The General Strike is tantamount to an attempt to seize the reins of government and is very near the border line of treason to the state ...* "

1. Read Source 10. What was the government's attitude to the strike?
2. Was it successful in persuading others to see the strike in the same way?
3. What do the arrests and imprisonments tell you about the government's attitude to the strike?
4. a) Were the strikers in 1926 treated more or less harshly than protesters in the early 1800s?
   b) Why do you think the treatment had changed?

SOURCE 12 A cartoon published in the magazine *Punch* on 12 May 1926. For nearly 100 years the figure of John Bull (on the left) had been a symbol of Britain's strength and superiority

Summary: Protests from 1700

THE OPENING TASK on page 143 suggested that you should keep a diary of protests while you were working on this chapter. This page gives you the chance to compare the way protests today are handled with the protests you have studied in this chapter.

■ REVIEW TASK

The causes of protest

SUFFRAGE FOR WOMEN 1912

The right to vote

Poverty and hunger

Workers' rights and conditions

Protecting jobs

1. List the causes of the protests you have studied on pages 146–167.
2. List the causes of protests today.
3. Explain the diferences and similarities between the two lists.

Methods of dealing with protests

The army

National police

Local police

4. When did governments use
a) the army
b) the police
   to deal with protests you have studied on pages 146–167?
5. Who deals with protests today? Why?
6. Explain the differences and similarities between modern methods of dealing with protests and those used in the nineteenth century.

Punishments for protesters

Execution

Transportation

Prison

You shall pay a fine of £200.

Fines

7. Why were protesters punished harshly in the early 1800s?
8. In what ways are protesters punished today?
9. Why have punishments become more lenient since 1850?

CHAPTER 7

CRIME AND PUNISHMENT IN THE TWENTIETH CENTURY

Why have there been so many arguments about punishment and policing since 1900?

IN THE SECOND half of the twentieth century reported crime rose steeply. Crime and punishment always were controversial topics, but this apparent crime wave made them even more so. Crime and punishment became hot political issues. Some called for harsher punishment; others for better policing. Some blamed government policies for rising crime; others blamed decaying moral values.

The debate continues today. We can't (and won't try to) judge the rights and wrongs of different viewpoints today. If you have been keeping a crime and punishment datafile (see page 3) then you will have plenty of up-to-date information to feed in to your debates about crime, punishment and policing.

This chapter tries to take a cool historian's look at the changes that have taken place in this period and some of the arguments they have raised:

- Is there a crime wave?
- Why is juvenile crime rising?
- What kind of police do we want?
- What kind of prisons do we want?
- Does Britain still need capital punishment?

You will find that many of these issues and arguments today are similar to the issues from past periods. So as you study this chapter you can revise your knowledge of earlier periods as you draw comparisons or make links with the twentieth century.

Read all about it – Thefts up! Murders up! More crimes now than ever before! Don't walk the streets alone!

| 500BC | | BC | AD | AD 500 | AD 1000 | AD 1500 | AD 2000 |

1900 2000

rgument 1: Is there a crime wave?

FOR 100 YEARS, from 1850 to the 1940s, the recorded crime rate in Britain fell gradually. In the 1950s that trend reversed and crime began to rise. This increase has been much faster than the increase in population. Sources 1–3 summarise these trends.

1. Describe the pattern shown by Source 1.
2. How far does Source 2 agree with Source 1?
3. Which category of crime has shown the greatest increase?

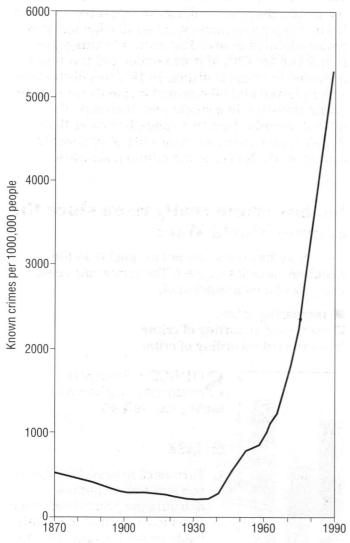

SOURCE 1 Graph showing all crimes known to the police 1870–1990. This graph has been adjusted to allow for rising population, i.e. the graph shows crime per 100,000 population

Has violent crime increased?

The answer is yes and no! Throughout the twentieth century about five per cent of recorded crimes have involved violence or sexual assault, so as crime in general has risen, violent crime has risen with it. In recent years the proportion of violent crime has increased slightly to six per cent of all crimes.

On the other hand, the ratio of murders to population has actually fallen in the last 100 years. In the 1880s there were fifteen murders per million people. In 1984 the figure stood at eleven murders per million – 25 per cent lower than in the 1880s.

Date	Murder/ Manslaughter	Burglary	Theft
1900	312	3812	63,604
1910	291	6499	76,044
1920	313	6863	77,417
1930	300	11,169	110,159
1950	315	29,834	334,222
1960	282	46,591	537,003
1970	393	190,597	952,666
1980	620	294,375	1,463,469
1996	681	1,101,000	2,280,000

SOURCE 2 Exact numbers of murders, burglaries and thefts known to the police 1900–96

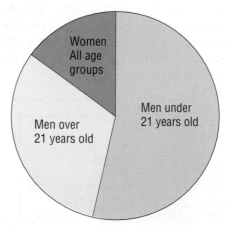

85 per cent of recorded crimes are committed by men. Over half of these are committed by young men aged 21 and under. The crime rate among teenage boys has increased faster through this century than for any other group.

SOURCE 3 Age and sex of offenders in the 1990s

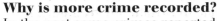

Can we trust these statistics?

Sources 1–3 are based on **recorded crime**. You know by now that such statistics are problematic.

The dark figure

The 'dark figure' of unreported and unrecorded crime has always been substantial.

In the twentieth century, unlike earlier periods, we have some idea of the scale of the dark figure because of crime victimisation surveys. One reliable survey in 1981 suggested that there were three times more thefts than were actually reported to the police and twelve times as much vandalism. So crime is certainly higher than statistics suggest.

However, and this may seem like a contradiction but it's not, the dark figure is getting less, i.e. the gap between actual crime and reported crime is narrowing. Source 4 shows this trend for burglaries. While the number of reported burglaries *went up 100 per cent*, the number of people experiencing burglary (information that comes from crime victimisation surveys) went up *only 18 per cent*. Therefore, many more people were reporting burglaries. So burglaries rose but not as spectacularly as the reported crime statistics suggest.

Why is more crime reported?

More people report house burglaries because they have to for insurance purposes. It is easier to do so since most homes have a telephone. The easier it is to report the crime, the more will be reported.

More people report violent crimes, such as rape or domestic violence, since they think the police will be more sympathetic and take them more seriously than they did in the past.

Why is more crime recorded?

In the past some crimes reported to the police would not have been recorded. The problem would have been dealt with informally and 'off the record'. The police now record more crime, more consistently. This is partly because of changes in policy, and also because computer technology has given them new, more efficient ways of doing so. The easier it is to record crime, the more will be recorded.

A startling example of how changes in recording policy can affect crime statistics is vandalism. Until 1977, when an incident of vandalism was reported to the police, the officer taking the report had to make his or her own decision whether the damage was major (defined as over £20 worth of damage) or minor (under £20). If it was under £20 it was not recorded in crime statistics. In 1977 this distinction was removed and all reported incidents got into the crime statistics. In a single year, therefore, the official records show that vandalism more than doubled, and added an extra 150,000 previously unrecorded offences to the criminal statistics.

So, has crime really risen since the Second World War?

Yes, crime has risen, but not as quickly as the headline statistics suggest. The crime rate rises because of a combination of:

- increasing crime
- increased reporting of crime
- increased recording of crime.

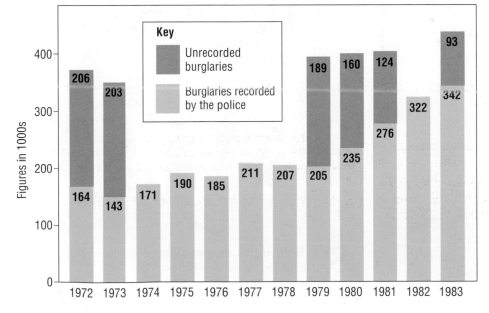

SOURCE 4 Recorded and unrecorded burglaries in Britain involving loss, 1972–83

■ TASK

1. Turn back to page 111. There you saw two historians debating the problem of crime statistics. Which of the points made by the historians about the nineteenth-century statistics also apply to twentieth-century statistics?

2. Using the information on this page, write a similar conversation about twentieth-century crime statistics.

Fear of crime

In some ways the exact statistics do not matter to the historian. What matters is fear of crime. This is what most affects punishment and policing.

In the past, there was only a limited amount of evidence to measure the fear of crime. In the twentieth century we have some firmer evidence. For example, in a 1984 survey, people were asked if they felt unsafe walking out at night. Twelve per cent of all Britons answered yes. When the same question was asked in 1997, the figure had risen to 32 per cent. So by this measure, fear of violent crime had almost trebled in thirteen years. Fear of crime was greatest in urban areas.

	% of people feeling unsafe when out alone at night	% of people who think they are very likely to be burgled in the next year
England and Wales	32	9.8
Scotland	26	5
N. Ireland	22	4.6
USA	25	4.4
France	20	5.9
Sweden	11	1.2
Average	21	4.2

SOURCE 5 From the international crime victimisation survey carried out in eleven countries in 1997

Some fear of crime is rational. It is understandable that fear of crime is greater in urban areas since crime is greater in urban areas. However, some fear of crime is ill-informed. For example, the British Crime Survey of 1997 showed that pensioners believed they were particularly at risk from violent crime. In fact, people under 29 are thirteen times more likely to be the victim of violent crime than an old person.

The media and crime

In the 1600s broadsheets first entertained readers with stories of murder. In the 1800s 'penny dreadfuls' competed for readers with lurid tales of violent crime. Today, in the same way, crime sells newspapers and wins television viewers. The more sensational, the more interest there seems to be. Violent, dramatic crimes receive wide coverage and so do crimes where the victims are particularly vulnerable, such as the elderly or the very young. These crimes make the headlines almost every day so it is easy to think that we are living in the middle of a crime wave.

New crimes? New opportunities for old crimes?

■ TASK

In your study of crime and punishment you will have discovered some change and some continuity in types of crimes across the centuries. Here are some twentieth-century crimes.

1. Which of these crimes do you regard as:
   a) new crimes
   b) new opportunities for old crimes?
      Give your reasons. Refer back to what you have studied earlier in the course.
2. Which of these crimes do you think are most feared by people today? Again give your reasons.
3. As a class, draw up your own list of crimes reported in your national or local newspapers this week. For each one decide whether it is a new crime or an old crime.

Motor car crime

One hundred years ago the car had only just been invented. Nowadays car theft is one of the biggest categories of crime, particularly among teenage boys. Motor crime includes anything from drunk driving to traffic offences. It absorbs a massive amount of police and court time. In 1996 there were nearly 1.3 million motor crimes, including theft of over half a million cars.

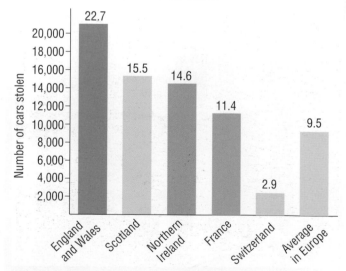

SOURCE 6 The number of cars stolen per 100,000 of the population in different countries

Hooliganism

SOURCE 7 England supporters clash with police at the Olympic stadium in Rome during a qualifying match for the 1998 World Cup

Terrorism

From the 1960s Britain has lived with the constant threat of terrorist violence. Most commonly this has been the threat of bombings by the IRA who were trying to end British rule in Northern Ireland. Other terrorist groups have also operated in mainland Britain. The actual number of attacks and the casualties they caused remain small, but the threat to public order and the nuisance caused by added security has made terrorism an ever-present worry and constant drain on police resources.

SOURCE 8 The wreckage of a London bus after a terrorist bomb exploded in 1996

Computer crime

Since so much business is now dependent on technology, computer crimes have become common. Computers have been used to steal money from bank accounts or to hack into the private records of individuals or governments to steal information. People have also deliberately introduced computer viruses to destroy vitally important information held on other computers: this can result in the ruin of a business.

Drug crime

Throughout history there has always been money to be made from smuggling or supplying banned goods. Drug smuggling and dealing is the most recent version.

Poaching

SOURCE 9 In August 1997 a Yorkshire newspaper reported an increase in deer poaching

" Deer in nature reserves have been poached and so have deer on deer farms. Venison [deer meat] has become a fashionable food in restaurants and even supermarkets. Farms and reserves near motorways are particularly vulnerable because the poachers can make a speedy getaway. "

■ TASK

Work in pairs.

You have to write a crime feature for a national newspaper. You are only allowed a headline, plus 400 words, plus a diagram or a graph. You can use the information on the last three pages, or your material from your crime datafile.

One of you has been asked to produce a sensationalist, alarming report which will sell as many copies as possible.

The other has been asked to produce a balanced analysis.

Keep your reports. You will need them for a later exercise.

Argument 2: Juvenile crime – why it happens, what to do about it!

LOOK BACK AT Source 3, page 170. Young offenders commit most crime. If society were able to tackle this group of offenders successfully, then surely it would go a long way to reducing crime. One of the big debates about crime and punishment in the second half of the twentieth century has therefore been about why juvenile crime is rising.

TASK

The statements on this page show some of the most common explanations for rising juvenile crime.

1. Study the explanations.
a) Which of these explanations are similar to earlier periods?
b) Which of them are new to the twentieth century?
2. Which of these explanations is supported by Source 1?
3. Which of these explanations make sense to you?
4. Why is it impossible to say for sure whether any of these explanations are accurate?
5. Why are explanations of crime important?
6. Which of these explanations do you think would lead the speaker to support these policies:

   harsher punishment
   more lenient punishment
   spend more money on policing
   spend more on security
   improve education
   improve the trial and court system
   tackle social deprivation in inner cities?

7. Look back at your article from the Task on page 173. Which of these explanations would best fit in your feature?

Explanations of rising juvenile crime in the twentieth century

Parents have failed their children. Children are not brought up to know right from wrong any longer. Their parents don't give them the right lead. Some parents cause the problems by sexually or physically abusing their own children.

Cars. Most theft by juveniles is theft from cars. Cars are easy targets. Stealing cars provides instant kicks. It all comes down to the way the car dominates our society.

Drugs. In 1997, in Wakefield, police estimated that 70 per cent of all theft, burglary and violent crime was drug-related. Drug addicts or drug dealers assault others to steal to obtain drugs.

Loss of community. Some people hardly know their neighbours. Young people are more ready to steal from those they don't know. Neighbours are less ready to protect and help someone they don't know.

Materialism. Adverts show young people the good life as being all about what you own. Getting money and possessions has become their sole aim in life. Crime is the quick way to get money.

Punishment is too slow. In the time young people have to wait for a trial, they can commit many other offences.

Poverty and inequality. Where is juvenile crime greatest? In urban areas. Where is deprivation and poverty greatest? In urban inner-city areas.

Unemployment. Unemployed teenagers get bored, they have time on their hands, and little prospect of a job. It's not surprising they turn to crime.

Loss of discipline. For example, until 1960 young men went straight into the armed forces for national service. That sorted them out just when they needed it. Now they have no one to discipline them.

The media. Television makes robbery and violence seem like a natural part of everyday life.

Punishment has become too soft. Young people feel they are above the law and can reoffend without fear of punishment. The courts and police do not have enough power to deal with offenders.

The education system has failed young people. Crime is most common among those who do badly at school and who believe they will never be able to get a job. A high proportion of young offenders have problems reading and many are undiagnosed dyslexics who were never given the support they needed to learn to read properly.

SOURCE 1 An extract from a report by the Chief Inspector of Prisons on young offenders

" ■ *Over 50% had been excluded from school or truanted regularly*
■ *25% were homeless*
■ *66% had no educational qualifications*
■ *66% regularly took drugs*
■ *Most female prisoners and a fair number of males had suffered sexual or physical abuse.* "

How should juvenile offenders be punished?

In the early nineteenth century, juveniles were punished as if they were adults – they could be hanged, transported, or fined. Since then, there have been two important developments.

Age of criminal responsibility

In 1908 an age of criminal responsibility (when a child could be held responsible for his/her crime) was introduced for the first time. It was set at seven. In 1933 it was raised to eight. In 1963 to ten, in 1969 to fourteen.

1. At what age do you think juveniles should be held responsible for their actions?

Separate custody for young offenders

Young offenders were separated from adults in prison. In 1901 the first Borstals were built as juvenile alternatives to prison. Today juveniles have separate courts and different kinds of punishments.

These two developments are widely accepted. What causes more argument is the question of how best to reform juvenile offenders. Is it:

- to impose a severe sentence – a so-called 'short sharp shock' – which will scare them off further offending
- to educate them in the consequences of their crime
- to use parental influence
- to distract them away from the forces that led them to crime?

2. Look at Sources 2 and 3. Which measures are favoured by each source?

SOURCE 2 The father of a young boy repeatedly cautioned for a sequence of car crimes

" For me, he could be stuck up in chains in a dungeon for a couple of days. That's all these kids need. Nathan is part of this trend of young people feeling that the law can't touch them. "

SOURCE 3 Adapted from the *Guardian*, 18 October 1997

" A scheme which brings young offenders face to face with their victims was yesterday hailed as a possible solution to the problem of youth crime, after evidence suggested it lowered the numbers of young people reoffending from 30 per cent to 4 per cent.

Charles Pollard, Thames Valley Chief Constable, said, 'We feel we need a system which isn't just about blaming people but actually holds them to account. I think the court system does not achieve this. How do you expect people to change their behaviour if the system doesn't make them realise what damage they're doing?'

Bob Gregory, an officer who specially trained for the scheme, said, 'It works because it criticises the behaviour of the offender. Going to court is obviously a difficult thing but everything tends to wash over the offender and they don't have to face the reality of what they have done.' "

■ TASK

In 1998 the government introduced the latest idea – **youth offending teams**. These teams aim to prevent young people reoffending by:

a) speeding up the justice system for young offenders
b) confronting the offenders with the consequences of their crime
c) encouraging the offender to compensate their victim in some way
d) reinforcing the responsibilities of parents
e) helping young offenders to tackle the root problems leading to their offending
f) helping the offender develop a sense of personal responsibility.

Suggest one measure which you think would help achieve each aim. You could use ideas you have gathered in your crime data-file or you could use ideas from earlier periods of history. For each measure explain how and why it would help.

Argument 3: What kind of police do we want?

How has policing changed since 1900?

By 1900 each area of Britain had its own local police force, but there were still problems.

- Police officers were badly paid and poorly trained. The only training was some military drill.
- Most of the police officer's time was spent on the beat – walking around his local area – up to 20 miles per day.
- A policeman (they were all men – there were no women police officers) operated on his own, on foot, with just a whistle to call for help.
- There were more than 200 local police forces. Each had its own rules and ways of working.
- Local record keeping was poor and there were no centralised records of criminals. It was unusual and difficult for neighbouring forces to work together.

How did this change in the twentieth century?

■ TASK

As you study these two pages complete your own copy of the table below. You might not have much to put in the third column yet. The next spread will help you with that.

Development in policing	Causes of this change	Consequences

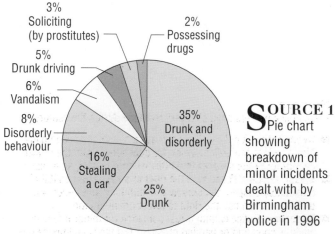

SOURCE 1 Pie chart showing breakdown of minor incidents dealt with by Birmingham police in 1996

- 3% Soliciting (by prostitutes)
- 2% Possessing drugs
- 5% Drunk driving
- 6% Vandalism
- 8% Disorderly behaviour
- 16% Stealing a car
- 35% Drunk and disorderly
- 25% Drunk

1. Compare Source 1 with Source 1 on page 138 (nineteenth-century policing). What are the similarities and differences?
2. What problems might the great variety of police work pose for training police officers?

Weapons

To distinguish them from soldiers, the first police were not armed. Nowadays, police can be issued with guns when necessary – and the number of times this happens is increasing. Police in riot gear now resemble the soldiers that they were intended to replace in the 1830s.

Ordinary officers are still unarmed. The police don't want to be armed and the public doesn't want them to be either.

In response to fears about the police being vulnerable to attack, a different style of truncheon was introduced in the 1990s and police have a range of other weapons to protect themselves or assist the arrest of a suspect such as portable canisters of CS gas which can cause temporary blindness or special riot control equipment when necessary.

Transport

From the 1930s the car and the motorbike improved police speed and effectiveness.

In the 1970s the car had greater impact. The police changed their methods of working by replacing the 'bobby on the beat' with rapid response teams of police who could be quickly called to the scene of a crime.

However, there was later a reaction to this and many forces reintroduced foot or even horse patrols as the public wanted the reassurance of seeing a police officer on the streets.

Crime detection

In 1901 the existence of blood groups was discovered so chemical analysis of blood samples could help in detection. Also in 1901 the first national register of fingerprints was set up to help identify suspects. More recently, DNA samples have been used as evidence. Security video recordings and national TV programmes have helped in identifying criminals.

Training and recruitment

The police try to attract high-quality candidates. Pay is good. A National Police Training College started in 1947. All officers now have at least fourteen weeks' training before they start work, and local forces have their own specialists for continued police training.

Women police officers were first appointed in 1920, to deal with women and young people. Increasingly, they have taken on similar roles to male police officers, although there are still fewer female police officers.

Communication

Communications technology has revolutionised police methods.

The first murderer to be caught using the new technology of radio communication was Dr Crippen in 1910. British police were looking for him after they found the body of his wife beneath the floor of their house. Crippen fled to Canada on a liner with his mistress, who was disguised and pretended to be his son. The liner's captain became suspicious of this disguise and sent a radio message to Britain. The police were alerted and arrived in time to arrest Crippen as he disembarked.

In the 1920s Morse Code transmitters were first installed in police cars and police telephone boxes (for police on patrol to call for help) were set up. In the 1930s the first two-way radios were introduced in police cars and the 999 emergency system was started. Nowadays, all officers carry a two-way radio for instant communication with their police station or headquarters.

Work

The public still see the police as 'thief catchers'. But dealing with crime is only one part of police work. A 1993 survey revealed that only eighteen per cent of calls made to the police were crime related. The rest concerned items such as lost property or noisy neighbours. A police officer is as likely to be called out to keep order at a football match, defuse an argument between a tenant and a landlord, or pick up a drunk as to try to catch a thief.

Computer records

Computers have improved local police record-keeping. There is also a centralised National Computer Record including a database of fingerprints, motor vehicle details, and information about missing persons. This is a service that can be used by all local police forces.

Specialisation

The work of the police is so varied that it is impossible for the police to be skilled in all the kinds of work they have to handle. Since 1945 the major crime prevention work has been dealt with by specialist national squads such as the Fraud Squad (1946), the Anti-Terrorist Squad (1971) and the Special Patrol Group (1965; since 1987 renamed the Metropolitan Patrol Group) which deals with inner-city riots and disturbances and threats to public order.

Powers

Basic police powers have changed very little during the century.

- **Questioning:** A police officer can ask a suspect to accompany him or her to the police station for questioning. But the officer cannot force the suspect to do this without making an arrest.
- **Arrest:** Police officers have the right to arrest a person if they reasonably suspect the person is committing an offence. An ordinary citizen has the right to arrest offenders too!
- **Reporting:** Police cannot arrest someone for minor offences such as speeding or parking offences. But they can impose on-the-spot-fines, or can report the suspect who will later be called to court.
- **Search:** Police normally need a warrant from a magistrate before they can search private property. The police have to convince the magistrate that the request is reasonable.

Organisation

The total number of police officers in Britain has increased to 126,856 (as at March 1998) over the century, but the number of separate forces has been cut from about 200 to 41. All the forces work in a similar way. And they work together on many aspects of law and order and crime prevention.

Some people want a single, national police force, but this has been consistently opposed. The reasons for opposition recall the arguments of the early 1800s. Opponents fear that a single national force would be too great a power in the hands of a government that wanted to use the police to enforce unpopular measures.

How has the image of the police changed since the 1950s?

1950s

Historians argue that the highpoint for the public image of the police was the 1950s. Of course, the police had critics, but the level of **consent** was very high. The police were symbolic of the law-abiding British nation. The popular image of the police officer, which could be seen in films and TV, and which was also widely held by ordinary people, was of a trusted authority figure who prevented crime by quick thinking and wise words. Policemen were seen as fair-minded uncles to young troublemakers but tough with real villains. In the case of young male offenders, a police officer was as likely to use a cuff round the ear and to send him back to his parents for punishment as to drag him off to the police station. The favourite nickname for the police was 'the bobby'.

SOURCE 2 Still from the TV series *Dixon of Dock Green*, which began in the 1950s

1980s

By the 1980s images of the police had changed in fiction and reality. Rising crime put police work under the spotlight and police methods were called into question. A series of scandals, involving faked evidence, forced confessions and alleged racism, eroded the reputation of the police. Rising crime also caused the police to change their tactics and they moved away from being community based to being more impersonal and technological. The rapid-response teams in their panda cars, screaming in to clear up a crime, was the symbol of the 1980s policing. The affectionate nicknames had been sometimes replaced by the angrier and critical 'pigs'.

The 1980s television police officer was presented as tough and sometimes violent, and likely to cut corners to meet his targets or to get ahead.

The image is a long way from the 1950s image of the fatherly but friendly copper, operating in a largely safe and secure world.

SOURCE 3 A still from the 1980s TV police drama *Juliet Bravo*, which was about a woman police officer

Community policing

Police officers are just ordinary men and women, but given extraordinary powers. The police must keep the consent and support of the community they serve. This was an issue in the first police forces of the nineteenth century. It remained an issue in the late twentieth century.

In his report on the Brixton riots of 1981, Lord Scarman said that one important cause of the riots was that the police had become out of touch with the community and had lost consent. It led them to introduce controversial and insensitive methods of policing.

In the 1990s many measures had been taken to help the police rebuild links with communities; for example, by visiting schools and setting up 'neighbourhood watches'. Research has shown that crime can be reduced simply by introducing neighbours to one another! Community policing aims to make the police more responsive to the local community.

One example of the tension within modern policing is the debate over foot patrols. A police officer on the beat rarely sees a crime actually being committed or arrests anyone so it might seem that they are a waste of time. However, the 'bobby on the beat' is reassuring to the public and it increases police links with the community. Many forces have reinstated the 'bobby on the beat' by popular demand.

SOURCE 4 Police holding back crowds at a demonstration in London, 1958

SOURCE 5 Police dressed in riot gear confront protesters near Downing Street, 1997

1. What image of the police do you get from current TV programmes, films and books?
2. Do newspapers cover the full range of police activities or do they present a distorted picture of the work of the police?
3. What is the attitude to the police of people in your class?
4. Why do you think the image of the police has changed?

Argument 4: What kind of prisons do we want?

SINCE THE NINETEENTH century, imprisonment has been the most common form of punishment for serious crime. The debate over how these prisoners should be treated has been the cause of much argument this century.

How did the prison regime change up to 1947?

Nineteenth-century view

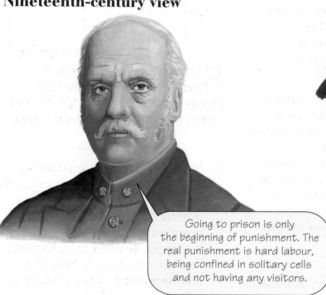

Going to prison is only the beginning of punishment. The real punishment is hard labour, being confined in solitary cells and not having any visitors.

In the late nineteenth century, prisons were run much as the first speaker describes. In the twentieth century a process of change began.

- In 1896 Broadmoor Hospital was opened to house mentally-ill prisoners.
- In 1902 hard labour on the crank and treadwheel was abandoned.
- In 1922 solitary confinement was ended. Prisoners were allowed to talk ('associate') with each other. The convicts' arrow uniforms were replaced by ordinary clothes. Prisoners were allowed more visitors.
- From 1922 onwards, diet, heating and conditions in cells improved gradually. Teachers were employed in prisons in order to give prisoners a better chance of finding work after being released.
- In 1934 the first open prison was started. In an open prison the rules were more relaxed. Prisoners were allowed to leave the prison to work. The regime was supposed to prepare inmates for ordinary life back in the community. Also in the 1930s the idea of abolishing women's prisons altogether was realistically considered.

Twentieth-century view

A person is sent to prison as punishment, not for punishment. Losing freedom is a punishment in itself. There is no need for extra punishment on top of that.

Why did it change?

The man behind many of the reforms was Alexander Patterson who played a key role in the prison service from 1922 to 1947. A range of factors made it possible for him to make these changes:

- Crime and fear of crime reduced, so there was less pressure on prisons to be seen to be harsh.
- Between 1910 and the 1930s the prison population halved because more people were put on probation instead (see page 183), and because from 1914 people were given more time to pay fines.
- Eighty per cent of prisoners were on short sentences or were one-off offenders.
- The old belief that criminals inherited their criminal tendencies was declining. Instead criminals were regarded as ordinary people who had the misfortune to be brought up in poverty, or who had criminal families and friends who had led them astray. This raised hopes that they could be reformed by better treatment and education in prison. In 1898 the aim of prisons was summed up as 'the humanisation of the individual and training for freedom'.
- Many people, including Patterson, did not believe that imprisonment deterred people from crime. In his view, the most important factor in deterring people from crime was the certainty of arrest, trial and punishment. If people did not expect to get caught, then they would commit crime. If prison did not work as a deterrent, this added further weight to his belief that the emphasis of the regime should therefore be on reforming the prisoner not punishing him or her.

How did the prison service come under strain after 1947?

More prisoners

As you can see from Source 1, the prison population rose steeply from the 1940s. This was not only the result of rising crime.

- **The average length of sentences was rising.** Ten years used to be unusual. It is now quite common for violent offenders.
- **The proportion of offenders sent to prison for certain crimes increased significantly.** For example: the proportion of drunk drivers sent to prison trebled in the 1980s; the proportion of thieves sent to prison went up by a quarter between 1977 and 1984.
- **The numbers in prison awaiting trial increased.** Some prisoners are on remand awaiting trial for as much as a year.

Less reform

Overcrowding became a serious problem in the 1980s. Leeds prison was designed to hold 624 prisoners. In 1981 it housed 1200. It had sixteen baths and three showers and the water supply was so variable that only four baths could be used at once. In some prisons overcrowding combined with a shortage of staff meant that prisoners had to spend 23 hours a day in their cells, and reform and education programmes were cut. What's more, 40 per cent of all prisoners in Britain were serving long sentences for violent crime. In such overcrowded conditions tensions mounted and led to serious prison riots (see Source 3, for example).

More prisons

Possible reactions to these problems would have been to reduce sentences and to send fewer people to prison, but in the 'fear of crime' climate of the 1980s this was not considered politically acceptable. Alternatives were considered for juveniles and minor offenders (see pages 183), but the political mood was that criminals should be sent to prison.

The government decided to build more prisons, including (for the first time since the early nineteenth century) prison ships (see Source 2) and private prisons. These private prisons were run by security companies who were paid by the government per prisoner. They housed mainly low-risk offenders and, unlike the nineteenth century, they operated under a strict set of rules.

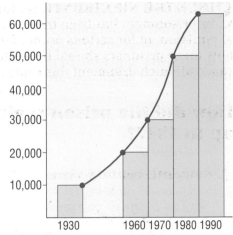

SOURCE 1 The rising prison population through the twentieth century. In the 1980s Britain had the fourth highest proportion of prisoners in Europe

1. In the history of punishment there is sometimes a pendulum effect. There is change in one direction. Then there is a reaction and change moves in the opposite direction. Explain in your own words how that has happened in the history of prisons since 1870.

SOURCE 3 Protests against prison conditions in 1990 at Strangeways prison, Manchester, caused millions of pounds worth of damage

SOURCE 2 This prison ship was moored off the Dorset coast in March 1997 and housed 500 prisoners. At the time the national prison population was growing by 350 prisoners a week. The use of the prison ship was intended to last for around three years until more prisons were built

One man's experience of prison

In 1994 professional golfer John Hoskisson killed a cyclist in a drink-driving accident. He was sentenced to three years in prison. In his book *Inside* he describes his experiences in two prisons.

SOURCE 4 Extracts from John Hoskisson's *Inside*, 1998

Wandsworth

66 *The cell door flew open and three of Wandsworth's most feared warders charged in.*

'Against the wall,' they screamed, truncheons drawn. For a split second there was pandemonium but in that time I saw Jimmy Baker, one of my cellmates, whip a small parcel of heroin out of his pocket and swallow it.

Minutes later we were all back in the cell – the beds had been overturned, mattresses split open, pictures ripped off the wall and the sheets left in a pile on the dirty stone floor.

Later Jimmy picked up his slop bucket and with practised ease retched up the contents of his stomach including the parcel of heroin he had swallowed. I told him I'd have to ask to have him move out if he smoked heroin. 'Do that and I'll knife you,' he said.

I've never been so fearful of my safety. As the night progressed he became more volatile, screaming obscenities. Sleep was impossible and I could not disengage my mind from the terror of my incarceration with this loathsome, drug-crazed creature.

Cordingley

The bonus of a C-category prison is being allowed to wear one's own clothes; the downside, was that because inmates were supposedly more trustworthy, officers left each prison landing unsupervised. Consequently the place was filthy. Stale mouldy food littered the floor, dustbins overflowed, and the windows were so dirty hardly any light filtered through.

In Wandsworth only small radios had been allowed, but here everyone seemed to have huge ghetto blasters. The noise was excruciating. The thin walls of my cell shut out none of the noise and it drowned my radio set at full volume. That first night I managed to sleep only after the walls stopped shaking at 2 am. One night at 2 o'clock I lost my rag. 'Turn down that racket,' I screamed. The reply was immediate and ominous: 'You're going to get it whitey.' For the next few days I lived in fear and spent my free time holed up in my cell. Complaining wasn't an option. Over the next year I saw many horrific incidents that arose solely because of the intolerable

noise level and the unwillingness of those who ran the prison to do anything about it.

The next day at last was my first induction – setting objectives for each prisoner. I'd been in Wandsworth for weeks but had never been introduced to this process every prisoner is supposed to undergo. I asked for education opportunities and to keep fit in the gym. I was to be disappointed. The gym was minute and decrepit with gaping holes in the floorboards. As for education, because of savage budget cuts, only 20 out of 280 inmates were on courses. No trades were taught. GCSE English was the most advanced course you could take.

Everyone at Cordingley was expected to work. I was assigned to the metal shop. The whole thing was farcical. After a cursory explanation, the supervisor left me at my huge pressing machine with just the comment: 'Do the best you can.' It took me five minutes to learn the job. Ten minutes to invent a quicker way of doing it. Fifteen before I received a warning: 'Hey you – you're working too hard.' At the end of the first week we had produced 2000 pieces; 1800 had to be scrapped because they'd been badly made.

Every week I saw prisoners released back into the outside world with nothing to show for their time inside except a £46 discharge grant. Regularly they were rearrested within days.

It's been a real eye-opener, prison. Perhaps it's now time I made some sort of comment. One thing's for certain – prison is essential. There are some dangerous people in here; the public has a right to be protected. But it's no good putting everyone in the same boat. There are good prisoners ... and someone has got to do something about the problem of drugs. An ever increasing proportion of the 60,000 angry men in prison will be getting out hooked on heroin and looking for revenge. 99

■ TASK

1. Make a list of all the things wrong with prisons, according to Source 4.
2. Source 4 is one-sided. How might the prison authorities excuse or justify each of the features the writer criticises?
3. In what ways are conditions described in Source 4 better or worse than the conditions in nineteenth-century prisons (see pages 128–129)?
4. Imagine that John Hoskisson is going to visit your class to talk about his experiences in prison. What questions would you like to ask him?

Alternatives to prison

Does prison work? A prison sentence keeps criminals 'off the street' and it shows the criminals that you are 'tough on crime'. However, prisons are a far from perfect form of punishment.

- Most prisoners reoffend – particularly young prisoners. Seven out of ten young prisoners commit more crimes.
- Prisons are still too often 'cradles for crime' where young offenders learn from older criminals, or develop drug-taking habits which lead them to further crime when they are released.
- A prison sentence does not deal with the personal or social problems that led to prisoners committing crimes in the first place. When prisoners come out they often walk back into the very situation that led them to crime in the first place.
- It is hugely expensive to house and feed the prisoner and staff the prison and prisoners' families need financial support from the government if they lose the family's main breadwinner.

It is easy to criticise prisons, but it is much harder to think of alternatives. The table below summarises some of the alternatives that different governments have tried over the twentieth century.

■ TASK

1. For each of the alternative punishments listed in the table, explain how it might help deal with the criticisms of prisons listed in the text.
2. Here a number of factors which affected the development of prisons in the nineteenth century:
   a) wealth
   b) reforming ideas
   c) religion
   d) rising crime and rising fear of crime.

For each one explain whether it also affected prisons in the twentieth century and if so how.

Alternative punishments	Special measures affecting juveniles (aged under 17)
	1900 – Borstals Introduced as alternatives to prison.
1907 – Probation introduced The person on probation had to report once a week to the police and to meet regularly with a probation officer. As long as they did not reoffend there would be no further punishment.	
1914 – Longer to pay fines Anyone needing to pay fines was given time to pay rather than being sent to prison.	
	1933 Age of criminal responsibility raised to eight.
	1948 Detention centres set up to give 'short, sharp shock' sentences.
1962 – Birching abolished Those who would previously have been birched were now likely to be fined or sent to prison.	
	1963 Age of criminal responsibility raised to ten.
1965 – Capital punishment abolished (see page 184).	
1967 – Parole introduced Prisoners no longer had to serve all their sentence if they behaved well. **Suspended sentences introduced** If offenders did not reoffend their sentence was waived.	
	1969 – Juvenile courts, supervision and care orders introduced Age of criminal responsibility raised to fourteen.
1972 – Community Service Orders introduced Criminals were required to do a number of hours work for the community.	
	1983 – Detention centres and youth custody These replaced Borstals and prison for those under 21.
1990s – Electronic tagging experiments introduced This was really a form of probation. Offenders wore an electronic tag which let police observers know where they were at any time.	

Argument 5: Does Britain need capital punishment?

The countdown

Throughout the 2500 years of this development study, execution was the ultimate punishment. But from the late 1700s its use in Britain was declining. The abolition of the Bloody Code in the 1830s meant that only murder and treason were punishable by death. In 1868 public hanging ended. After 1840 there were around fifteen executions a year – all for murder.

Attempts to abolish capital punishment altogether failed. Parliament voted against abolition in 1848, 1849, 1850 and 1928.

In 1947 the House of Commons voted for abolition, but the House of Lords threw it out. Exactly the same happened in 1956.

In 1957 hanging was abolished for all murders except:

- murder of a police or prison officer
- murder by shooting or explosion
- murder while resisting arrest.

As a result, executions in Britain fell to an average of only four a year – all for premeditated murders.

1965: the year of decision

In 1965 many people wanted to abolish execution altogether. Could Britain really have a punishment system without execution? Opinion was divided.

The debate was passionate. The topic was regularly discussed in newspapers and on television; books were published, and leading figures were asked whether they were for or against! Opinion polls were run to find out the attitudes of the people.

Can you rediscover the intensity of that debate?

■ TASK

For keeping capital punishment

We cannot do without this ultimate deterrent. Murder and violent crime will rise.

We do not execute many people. On average, only four people a year! And they have all committed cold-blooded and premeditated murders.

Unless you literally keep a murderer in prison for life that murderer can kill again when he is released. What would abolitionists say to the family of a victim who was murdered by someone who escaped execution only to kill again?

Capital punishment has police support. They believe that abolition will make criminals more likely to carry and use guns. It also has popular support. We cannot abolish capital punishment when the majority of the people in the country support it. We must reflect public opinion, not try to move ahead of it.

The only alternative abolitionists suggest is to keep murderers in prison for life. This is expensive but it is also an inhuman punishment, more cruel than death. Some people serving life imprisonment and the guards who guard them say it would have been better for them to be executed. Their life is worth nothing. The head of the prison service said this in 1930 – that a lifetime in prison made someone's life not worth living.

The British legal system seldom makes mistakes. There may be a chance in a thousand of the innocent being convicted, but there are so many safeguards that that person would not be executed – look at the numbers who have been reprieved by the Home Secretary.

Public revulsion against some crimes is so great that if we get rid of capital punishment there would be attempts to lynch murderers.

Some murders are so terrible that execution is the only way to show society's contempt and to avenge the families of the victims. Could you really live with the idea of a multiple murderer getting away with a cosy life in prison, while the lives of the victims' families are ruined for ever?

This trial abolition won't work either. Five years would not be long enough to really know the impact of the measure. They only want this trial period to bring in the faint hearted. We cannot really trial anything in that period.

SOURCE 1 The execution of Dr Crippen at Pentonville prison in 1910. Dr Crippen had brutally murdered his wife and then tried to escape the country

For abolition of capital punishment

Human beings are fallible. Our legal system makes mistakes. The wrong person could be hanged. We have no right to inflict an irreversible penalty. Think about Timothy Evans. He was hanged for a murder he didn't commit. Or Derek Bentley – does anyone now think he should have been hanged?

Execution is barbaric, uncivilised and un-Christian. We fought a war to prevent these kinds of atrocities. Execution is the kind of thing you associate with Hitler's Germany, not with Britain.

The abolition of the death penalty would actually increase the number of convictions for murder. Juries are reluctant to find people guilty because of the severity of the punishment. They would rather give people the benefit of the doubt than risk convicting an innocent person, who could be sentenced to death.

There is no evidence that the number of murders would rise following abolition. Look at the experience of other countries. For example, after Sweden got rid of the death penalty in 1920 the murder rate stayed the same. In the Netherlands it was abolished in 1870, but the murder rate was lower in the 1950s than before abolition. Some people predicted crime would rise after the abolition of the Bloody Code but that did not happen.

The death penalty places a permanent and undeserved stigma on the criminal's family.

The Home Secretary is reprieving more than half of all those sentenced to death. Execution is not being used. Between 1900 and 1954 there were 7454 murders. There were 1210 death sentences, but only 632 were carried out.

Execution is not really a deterrent to murderers because most murders happen on the spur of the moment.

The morbid fascination with execution has all the wrong effects. It degrades the population.

Prisons have improved since the 1930s. Life imprisonment might be a reasonable punishment.

People who are executed become nationally famous for their crimes and for their punishment. If they were sent to prison they would become just another statistic.

Imagine it is 1965. Parliament is about to debate the abolition of capital punishment.

The BBC is running a television debate on the subject. You have been invited to attend the debate as an expert on crime and punishment through history. These are the options being considered:

- abolish capital punishment altogether
- abolish it for a trial period
- keep it as it is.

You can choose to support any of these options. But whatever view you take, you have to present a convincing case. You must write a speech to give in the debate. You need some big points and some supporting evidence. You can get ideas from the panels below.

Remember to look at what your opponents are saying. You need to be able to refute their arguments as well as put forward your own.

Finally, you are a history expert so you will want to draw some lessons from history.

Once you have prepared your speech, run this as a class debate.

SOURCE 2 Supporters of Derek Bentley asking people to sign a petition against his execution. Derek Bentley was nineteen when he was executed in 1953 for the murder of a policeman. The person who actually shot and killed the policeman was aged sixteen, but under the law no one under eighteen could be hanged. One of the prosecution's main claims was that Bentley had shouted to the killer: 'Let him have it.' There was no definite proof that Bentley had said this. Even if he had, it could equally have been a plea for his friend to hand the gun over to the police. Despite the jury's recommendation for mercy and the fact that Derek Bentley had a mental age of ten, he was hanged. In November 1997, after a long campaign, Bentley's case was referred to the Court of Appeal to re-examine the evidence. In 1998 the verdict of guilty was quashed by the Court of Appeal

Obstacles to crime!

This is your last obstacle course. It focuses on: **How did people try to solve the problem of crime?**

Here you can see the methods in use in the 1900s. The barriers are the methods governments tried to use to prevent crime – methods of catching criminals, trials and punishments.

If you are looking for the Chapter 7 summary, there isn't one! The next chapter summarises the whole book, including this chapter.

1. What are the differences between the methods here and those in earlier periods?
2. Why did these changes take place?
3. Compare the obstacle pictures.
a) In what ways are they the same?
b) When did the greatest changes take place?
c) Why have changes kept taking place?

CHAPTER 8

CONCLUSION – EXPLAINING CHANGE AND CONTINUITY IN CRIME AND PUNISHMENT

CONGRATULATIONS! YOU KNOW and understand far more about the history of crime and punishment than you did a few months ago. This final chapter will help you to revise the information you have already covered so that you can remember it for your examinations.

This chapter also gives you the chance to look at a number of themes that are vital for understanding the history of crime and punishment.

- **Part 8.1:** Pages 185–195 give you an **overview of changes and continuities** through history in:
  - crime
  - punishment
  - law enforcement
  - explanations of crime.

- **Part 8.2:** In history you are not just interested in what happened, you are also interested in explaining why it happened. Pages 196–203 look at the **factors** that have affected crime, punishment and policing across the centuries:
  - wealth and poverty
  - urbanisation
  - mass media
  - religion
  - government
  - war
  - technology
  - trade
  - chance.

- **Part 8.3:** Some things change faster than others. Some things hardly change at all. Finally, pages 204–211 investigate the different **patterns of change** that you can see in the history of crime and punishment.

How has crime changed through history?

THIS PAGE SHOWS the main kinds of crime that have been committed across the centuries. Above the timeline are the crimes that have always been committed.

Below the timeline you can see the crimes that were particularly common at some times, but not at others. Many of these only became crimes because the government of the time decided to make them crimes.

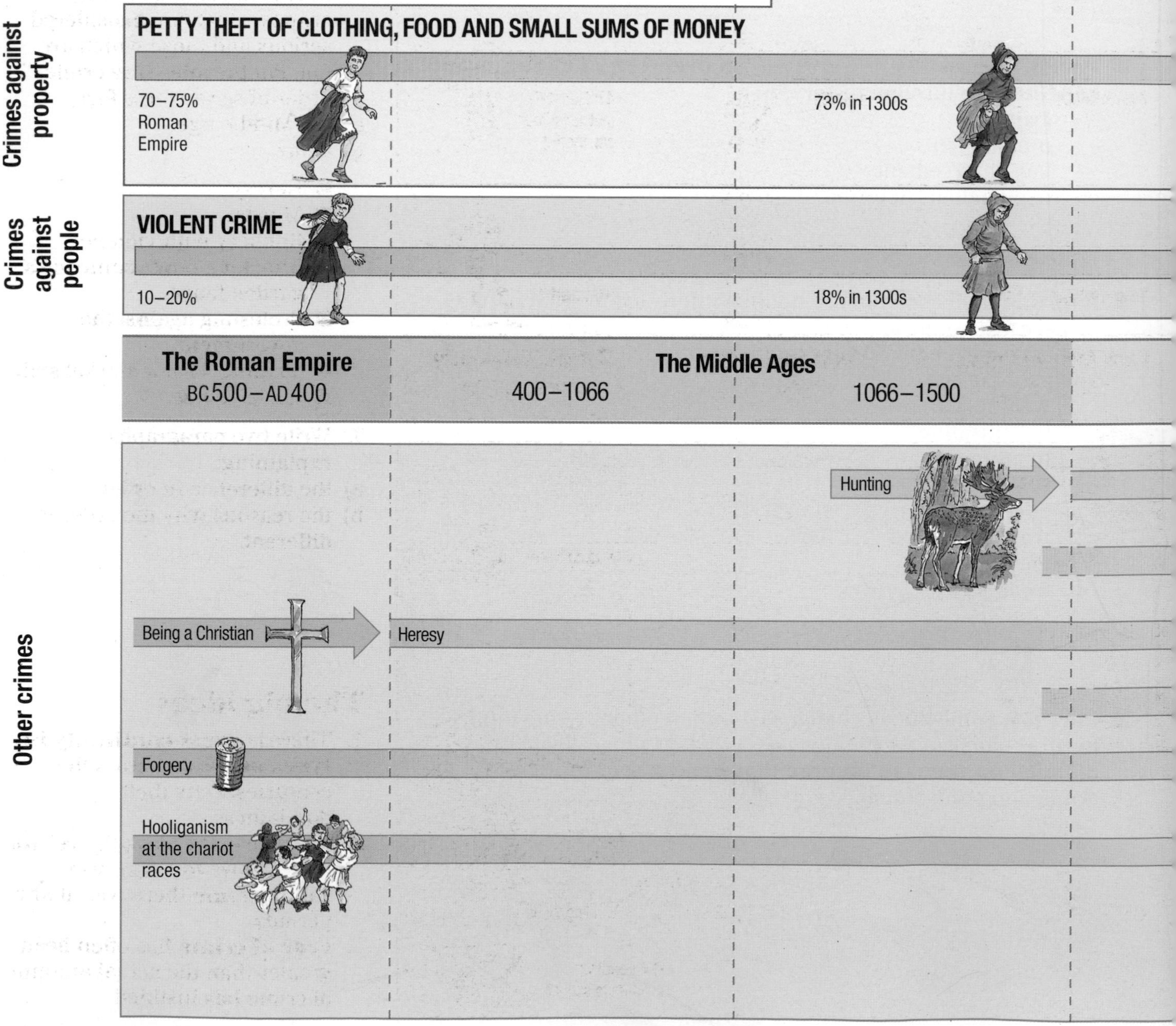

Crimes against property

PETTY THEFT OF CLOTHING, FOOD AND SMALL SUMS OF MONEY

70–75% Roman Empire

73% in 1300s

Crimes against people

VIOLENT CRIME

10–20%

18% in 1300s

The Roman Empire BC 500 – AD 400	The Middle Ages	
	400 – 1066	1066 – 1500

Other crimes

Hunting

Being a Christian ▷ Heresy

Forgery

Hooliganism at the chariot races

Vandalism

Car crime

74% in 1600s | 75% in 1800s | 47% in 1997 (not including car thefts)

15% in 1600s | 10% in 1800s | 6% in 1997

Early Modern Britain 1500–1750 | **Industrial Britain** 1750–1900 | **Twentieth Century** 1900–2000

Poaching

Smuggling | Drug dealing

Not attending church

Witchcraft

Computer fraud

Football hooliganism

Avoiding taxes

Not sending children to school

1. Which kinds of crime have been most common throughout history?
2. Has the proportion of violent crime increased, fallen or remained the same?
3. Which crimes that were not committed in earlier centuries are common today?
4. When was the period of greatest change in crime?
5. What is the 'dark figure' in crime statistics?
6. One of the big changes over time is the change in the crimes which are considered serious and those which are not. Put the following crimes in order of seriousness for:
a) the Middle Ages
b) today.

   ■ Heresy
   ■ Murder
   ■ Robbery with violence
   ■ Knocking down someone's garden fence
   ■ Protesting against the government
   ■ Stealing from a market stall
   ■ Racial abuse.

7. Write two paragraphs explaining:
a) the difference in order
b) the reasons why the order is different.

The big ideas

1. There is **great continuity in types of crime** across the centuries. Petty theft dominates.
2. Because of the 'dark figure', **no one knows for sure how much crime** there was at any period.
3. **Fear of crime** has often been greater than the actual amount of crime has justified.

How have punishments changed through history?

THIS PAGE SUMMARISES punishments. Below the timeline are the different types of punishment which were used at different times. Above the timeline are the reasons why these punishments were used.

1. Which methods of punishment were used for the longest time?
2. Choose one punishment not used today. Explain why it is no longer used.
3. When was the period of greatest change in punishments?
4. Here are some of the reasons to punish people. Punishments should:
   a) deter the criminal from committing crime
   b) warn other people away from committing crimes
   c) compensate the victim
   d) protect society
   e) reform the criminal
   f) take revenge against the criminal.
   List two examples of punishment which match each reason.
5. How have ideas about the purposes of punishments:
   a) changed
   b) stayed the same?
6. This graph is attempting to show the development of punishment through history. Do you think it is accurate? Explain why or why not, and if you disagree draw a more accurate version.

The purposes of Punishment

Revenge

Deterrence

The Roman Empire	The Middle Ages
BC 500 – AD 400	400 – 1066

Types of Punishment

Exile

Reparation — Wergilds – payments to victims

Humiliation — Pillory and stocks

Custody — Slavery

Fines

Physical — Whipping

Capital

In public: Crucifixion — Fights to the death between gladiators

By — Stoning

Hanging

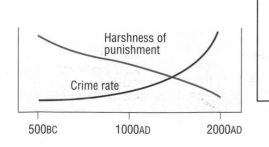

Harshness of punishment

Crime rate

500BC   1000AD   2000AD

190

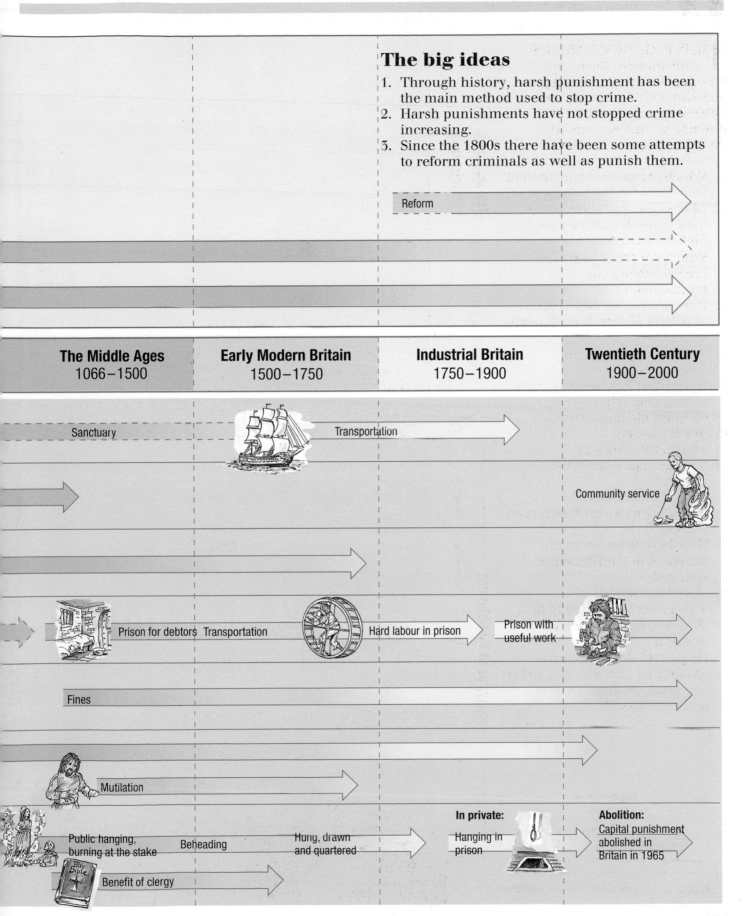

The big ideas

1. Through history, harsh punishment has been the main method used to stop crime.
2. Harsh punishments have not stopped crime increasing.
3. Since the 1800s there have been some attempts to reform criminals as well as punish them.

Reform

The Middle Ages 1066–1500	Early Modern Britain 1500–1750	Industrial Britain 1750–1900	Twentieth Century 1900–2000

Sanctuary

Transportation

Community service

Prison for debtors Transportation

Hard labour in prison

Prison with useful work

Fines

Mutilation

Public hanging, burning at the stake

Beheading

Hung, drawn and quartered

In private: Hanging in prison

Abolition: Capital punishment abolished in Britain in 1965

Benefit of clergy

How have policing and trials changed through history?

FOR CENTURIES IT was the responsibility of individuals and communities to catch and deal with criminals themselves. As society has become more complex, the role of catching criminals and bringing them to trial has been taken over by the police. The top part of this chart summarises the methods that have been used through history to catch criminals and to bring them to court. The lower part summarises the different methods that have been used for trials.

1. Who was responsible for catching criminals and collecting evidence in:
a) Rome
b) Saxon England
c) Late medieval England
d) Tudor and Stuart England?
2. When was the period of greatest change in law enforcement?
3. Why were changes at that time so important?

The big ideas

1. For centuries local communities were expected to catch criminals themselves.
2. A professional police force was a new development in the 1800s, although at first there was a lot of opposition to the idea.

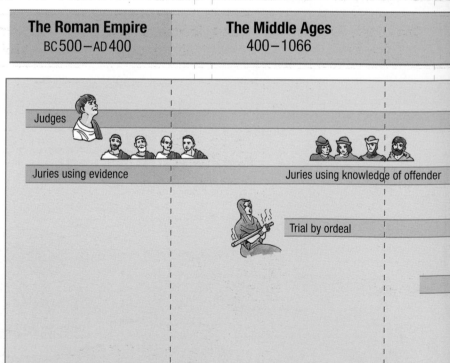

Stopping crime and catching criminals

Legionaries

Vigiles

Tithings

Hue and cry

The Roman Empire	The Middle Ages
BC 500 – AD 400	400 – 1066

Trials

Judges

Juries using evidence

Juries using knowledge of offender

Trial by ordeal

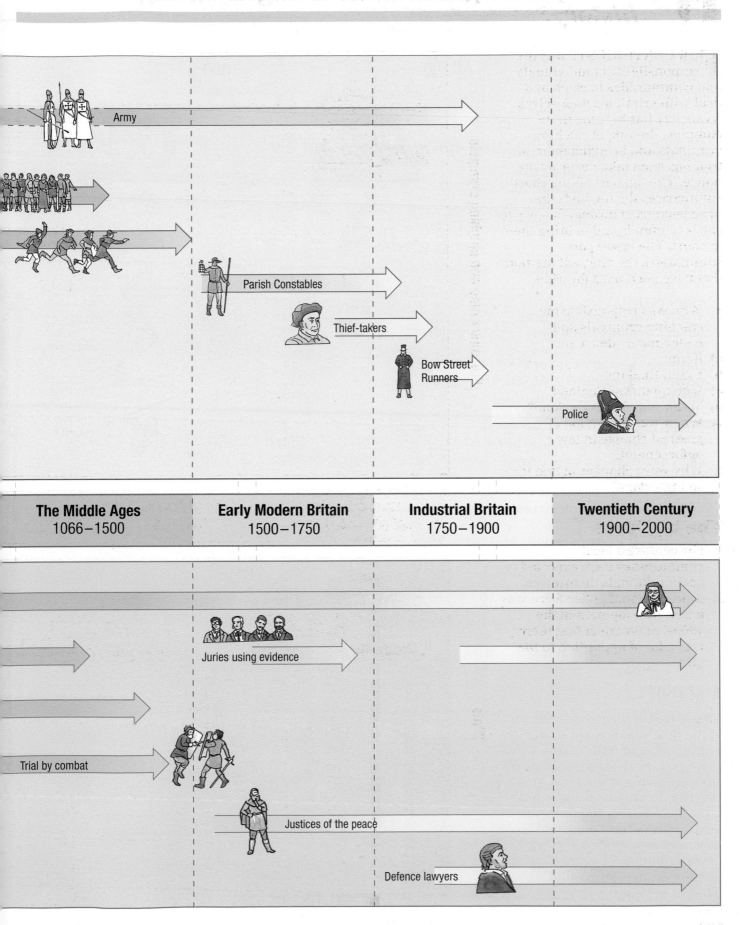

Army

Parish Constables

Thief-takers

Bow Street Runners

Police

| The Middle Ages 1066–1500 | Early Modern Britain 1500–1750 | Industrial Britain 1750–1900 | Twentieth Century 1900–2000 |

Juries using evidence

Trial by combat

Justices of the peace

Defence lawyers

How have explanations of crime changed through time?

THERE HAVE ALWAYS been arguments about what causes crime. While you have been studying crime and punishment you have heard or read politicians' views about why crimes are committed. The diagram below shows you the kinds of ideas that were held at different periods. You have already met all these ideas in earlier chapters but this diagram brings them together.

1. Which ideas about the causes of crime have been held in every period?
2. Which ideas were once held but are no longer so widely believed?
3. Have any new ideas about the causes of crime developed for the first time in the twentieth century?
4. Do you think there has been more continuity than change in ideas about the causes of crime?
5. People's explanations of crime greatly affect the methods of law enforcement or the types of punishment they support. For each of the explanations in the diagram explain what measures of law enforcement or punishment it might lead to.

■ ACTIVITY

Choose one of the periods shown on the timeline. Prepare a two-minute talk about the causes of crime in your chosen period as if you were living at the time. Make sure you do not just list the causes but explain which you think are the most important ones. You also need to choose evidence to back up your opinions. Use the timeline as an index to find material to help you.

AD 200

1300

Poverty drove people to crime.

Poverty drove people to crime.

Laziness, greed or alcohol led people to crime.

Laziness, greed or alcohol led people to crime.

There was no effective police force.

There was no effective police force.

The Devil tricked or tempted people into crime.

Demobilised soldiers turned to crime.

Large towns led people to think they could get away with crimes.

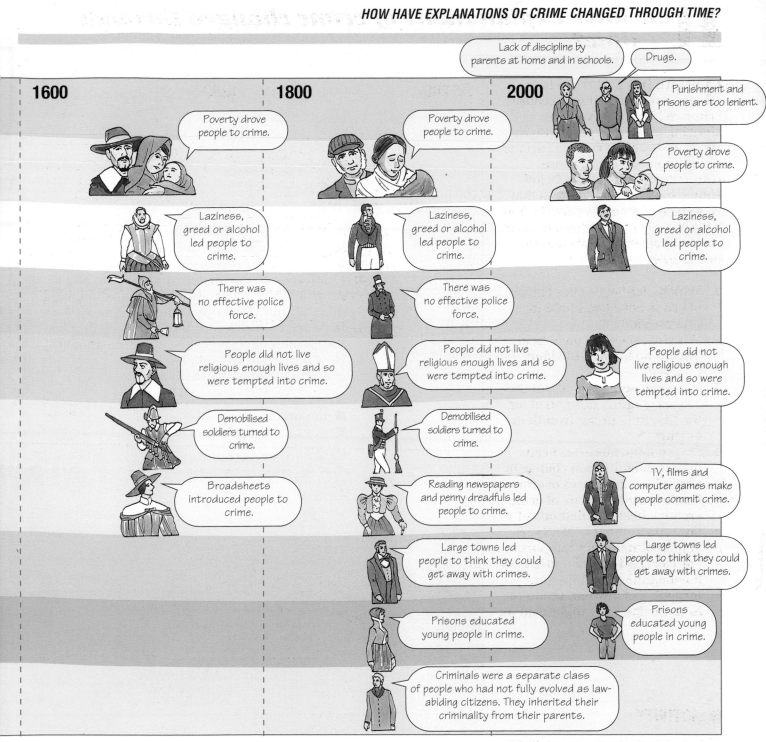

The big ideas

1. These are explanations of crime, not causes of crime. The difference is crucial. The evidence for what actually causes crime is difficult to find.
2. People's explanations of crime are greatly affected by their circumstances and their own beliefs about human nature, politics, etc.
3. People's explanations of crime greatly affect the methods of law enforcement or the types of punishment they support.

Religion

WHILE YOU HAVE been studying the history of crime and punishment you will have noticed a number of 'factors' affecting crime and punishment cropping up again and again. If you didn't notice them by yourself, then some of the questions made sure you did!

Our task in history is not just to list or describe the events in the past – it is also to explain why they happened. Over the next eight pages you are going to explore some of the factors that have 'made things happen' in the history of crime and punishment. The first is religion.

■ TASK

1. The drawings on the timeline are examples of religion influencing crime and punishment. Explain in your own words what each one shows.
2. Using your own research, find other examples of religion influencing crime and punishment. Add them to your own copy of the timeline.
3. In which period do you think that religion had the greatest effect on crime and punishment?
4. How important has religion been in the history of crime, punishment and trials:

   ■ very important
   ■ important
   ■ not very important?

   Explain your answer carefully.

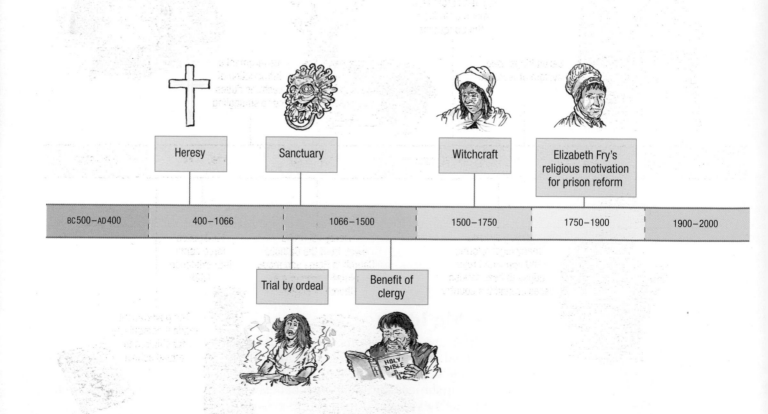

	Heresy		Sanctuary		Witchcraft	Elizabeth Fry's religious motivation for prison reform	
BC 500 – AD 400	400 – 1066		1066 – 1500		1500 – 1750	1750 – 1900	1900 – 2000
		Trial by ordeal	Benefit of clergy				

Government

GOVERNMENTS ARE A massive influence on crime and punishment.

- Governments decide what is a crime.
- Governments set the punishments.
- Governments enforce the law.

■ TASK

1. Complete and fill out a table like this one with examples from each period of governments doing each of these things. You can use the sources on this page.

	Deciding what is a crime	Setting the punishments	Enforcing the law
Saxon period			
Late Middle Ages			
Early Modern Britain			
Industrial Britain			
Twentieth-century Britain			

2. Is the government's influence over crime and punishment greater today than in previous periods?

New Norman laws, e.g. the Forest laws, made by William the Conqueror

Saxon kings used a system of wergilds

Government's introduction of customs duties led to smuggling

BC 500–AD 400	400–1066	1066–1500	1500–1750	1750–1900	1900–2000

Henry II made many legal reforms and appointed royal judges to hear serious cases around the country

Henry VIII broke away from the Catholic Church in Rome and made himself head of the Church of England

First police force came into existence 1829

The government made it compulsory for children to attend school

What other factors have affected crime?

AS YOU LOOKED at the previous pages you probably said to yourself – it's not as simple as this! You can only go so far by looking at individual factors. Investigating any one factor in isolation from others is misleading because they almost always work together to produce change or continuity. It would be extremely unusual for a single factor by itself to create change or continuity. In fact, there is a complex web of factors which influence developments in crime and punishment. Here are some of the factors which have particularly affected crime.

■ TASK 1

1. Make your own copy of this diagram.
2. Using the information on the opposite page, add notes to the boxes to explain the significance of each factor.
3. We have not provided information on Government, Religion and War so you will have to do your own research by looking back to pages 196–197 and earlier in the book (pages 85, 92, 110, 135).
4. Add other factors which you think affect crime.
5. For each factor in your diagram give one other example from this book of how it affected crime.
6. Add lines to show how these different factors relate to each other.
7. Give two examples of changes in crime which resulted from a mixture of causes.
8. Which factor or factors shown here do you think have been the most important in affecting crime? Give evidence to support your choice.

■ TASK 2

'The causes of crime have changed very little throughout history.' Write an essay to explain whether you agree or disagree with this statement. You can get a sheet from your teacher to help you plan the essay structure.

factors affecting crime

Chance

Government

Wealth and poverty

Urbanisation

Religion

Effectiveness of law enforcement

Influence of parents

War

Human nature

Human nature
Some people would say that all crime is caused by human nature – individuals who are greedy, bored, desperate or immoral. Human nature has not changed very much in 2000 years, although the crime rate has risen and fallen, new crimes have appeared and old crimes disappeared. Some crimes have become more common. Some have disappeared altogether. So we need to look at other factors to explain these changes.

Influence of parents and adults
One of the most difficult factors to understand in crime is the influence of parents or other adults on children. This is because it is impossible to prove that the way people are treated when they are children, affects their behaviour when they grow up. Is a child who was beaten regularly more likely to become a violent adult? Are children who were sexually abused more likely to become child abusers themselves when they grow up? We cannot be certain, but if this is an important factor then all the punishments and policing cannot prevent such crimes. The only thing likely to stop such crimes is help for the criminals from specialists such as doctors and psychologists.

Urbanisation
In the Middle Ages most people lived in small communities and were well known to everyone around them. Would they dare steal when they would be easily recognised or shamed by being punished in front of their friends?

As towns grew in the late 1700s and early 1800s, there were more people who lived unknown to their neighbours in the bustling streets. By the early 1800s towns were ideal for thieves. There were plenty of victims, plenty of places to hide and the chances of being identified were slim when there was no effective police force.

From the time of Ancient Rome to the present day, crime has been a particularly urban phenomenon. As cities grew, crime grew and crime rates in cities have usually been far higher than in villages.

However, urbanisation can sometimes help reduce certain crimes. Highwaymen preyed on carriages which travelled on the lonely turnpike roads of the 1700s, but as the empty waste lands, ideal for hold-ups, were built on, highwaymen finally disappeared.

Chance
This probably seems the strangest factor in the list, but some would say it plays a major part. For example, the chance event of **bad weather** has led to poor harvests and this has caused rising food prices. This in turn has lead to increased poverty and sometimes crime.

Effectiveness of law enforcement
Crime increases if criminals do not expect to get caught. It decreases if they expect to be caught and convicted. The effectiveness of law enforcement is a crucial factor in determining the levels of crime. Law enforcement is expensive, and often it is also controversial and unpopular. So efforts to enforce the law, to introduce police forces, to speed up trials, to ensure fair punishments have often been slow and ineffective.

Wealth and poverty
Statistics from various periods in history show that the amount of crime rises when poverty increases. However, there is no simple link between poverty and crime.

1. **Not everyone who is poor commits crime**, even at times of the worst poverty. Indeed, only a tiny minority turn to crime. Therefore, poverty alone is not a cause of crime. Other factors must play a part as well, such as the personality of the individual and whether there is an opportunity for crime.

2. At times of poverty **there has usually been a time-lag before crime has risen** sharply. In the 1590s, for example, it took two or three years of bad harvests and rising food prices before crime reached serious levels. This suggests people may have tried to avoid taking to crime but were eventually driven to it by sustained poverty.

3. **Crime may only appear to have risen at times of poverty.** Through this book you have often heard mention of the 'dark figure' – the amount of unreported crime (see page 44 for example). One theory is that at times of poverty more crime is reported. Fear of crime increases, so victims report every crime, however small, including crimes that they might otherwise have ignored.

4. Some historians say that **inequality of wealth has also helped to create crime**. As societies became richer then some poor people may have stolen in order to gain a share of this wealth.

What other factors have affected punishment?

GOVERNMENTS DECIDE WHAT are serious and lesser crimes, and set the level of punishment accordingly. They introduce new methods of punishment when it is thought necessary. Almost all changes in punishment therefore stem from government decisions. Those decisions will be influenced by a number of factors.

■ TASK

1. Make your own copy of this diagram.
2. Using the information on the opposite page, add notes to explain the significance of each factor.
3. We have not provided information on Social change, Religion and Effectiveness of punishments so you will have to do your own research by looking back to pages 17, 39, 93, 128–129 and 180–183.
4. Add other factors which you think affect punishment.
5. For each factor on your diagram give one other example of how it affected punishment.
6. Add lines on your copy to show how the different factors relate to each other.
7. Give one example of changes in punishment which resulted from a mixture of causes.
8. Which factor or factors do you think have been the most important in affecting punishment? Give evidence to support your choice.

Factors affecting punishment

Individuals

Social change

Political events

Mass media

Religion

Fear of crime

Wealth and poverty

Effectiveness of punishments

Ideas about punishment

Ideas about crime

The people who make decisions about punishment are often greatly affected by ideas and attitudes of the time. They may be religious ideas or political ideas. During some periods, religious leaders have had great influence and punishments have been used to try to make people live 'sin-free' lives. In the eighteenth and nineteenth centuries many people were influenced by the progressive ideas of the Enlightenment. One of these ideas was that people could be taught to use reason and behave rationally, and therefore punishment should try to reform and educate criminals.

Political events

Until the 1770s many criminals were transported from Britain to America, but after the American War of Independence the colonies were lost. This led to changes. The first was the increased use of prisons. The second was the transportation of prisoners to a new colony – Australia.

Wealth and poverty

The history of punishment has been greatly affected by the wealth of the government.

For example, until the nineteenth century, governments did not have enough money to build effective prisons. Even in the 1700s, prisons were still regarded as too expensive, although the government was receiving far more money in taxes. Prisoners were transported abroad because it was a much cheaper option than keeping them in prison.

By the mid-1800s the costs of transportation were rising and this played a part in ending this punishment, as you saw on page 119. However, the costs of running the prison system continued to affect how people were treated in prison. Today in Britain, with 63,000 people in prison, there are experiments to find effective and cheaper forms of punishment, such as house arrest using an electronic tag.

Individuals

Individuals such as John Howard and Elizabeth Fry played a part in changing the nature of the prison system. Both wanted to see reforms that would improve conditions in prisons, but also make punishments more effective. Such individuals were important because they campaigned and persuaded governments to make changes. However, these individuals were not the only reason for the great changes in prisons in the nineteenth century, as you saw on page 133.

Mass media

For 400 years crime has been 'news'. Since the development of the first broadsheets in the 1600s, newspapers have had a strong influence on people's attitudes to punishment. For example, the 'garotting crisis' of the 1860s was a 'media event' which drove the government towards harsher prison regimes.

But the media have also helped to expose miscarriages of justice. The intense media scrutiny of the trial and execution of Derek Bentley and the A6 murderer, James Hanratty (the last person to be hanged in prison), helped to fuel the argument for the abolition of capital punishment.

Fear of crime

Whenever fear of crime has increased, governments have reacted by making punishments more severe to try to prevent crime rising.

From around 1600 most people believed that crime was increasing and this played a part in the introduction of the Bloody Code.

How did factors work together to bring about change?

ONE OF THE greatest changes in punishments was the abolition of the Bloody Code in the early 1800s which greatly reduced the number of crimes punished by execution.

1. Our first task is to identify some of the factors that led to the abolition of the Bloody Code.

Why was the Bloody Code abolished in the 1830s?

Government: the government was reforming many other aspects of British life during this period so the time was right for reforming the punishment system.

Individuals such as Samuel Romilly campaigned against the Bloody Code.

Ideas: the Enlightenment had encouraged the optimistic view that criminals could be reformed.

Attitudes to punishment: the number of executions was going down in spite of the Bloody Code. Courts were reluctant to sentence people to death. They preferred transportation or prison.

Wealth: the government had enough money to find alternative punishments such as prison.

2. Then we must see how these factors worked together.

Were any of these reasons linked?

Yes, a lot of them are very closely linked. Individuals were motivated by the ideas of their time. Individuals could not have persuaded the government to change the Bloody Code if attitudes to punishment had not been changing anyway.

3. Finally we must work out whether some factors are more important than others.

Which reason do you think was most important?

I think that wealth was important. Without wealth the government would not have been able to afford alternative punishments.

No, it was the attitudes to punishment that really mattered. Courts stopped using the Bloody Code long before it was abolished. Abolition of the Bloody Code was just getting rid of laws that the courts were refusing to use.

■ TASK

1. This illustration gives you an explanation for the abolition of the Bloody Code. Your task is to decide whether you agree with this explanation or not. Work with a partner. Take each of the three stages in turn and decide whether the answers in the speech bubbles provide the best possible answers. If you think you can give a better answer, then write out your own alternatives. You can get a sheet from your teacher to record your own ideas.

2. Choose one of the following developments in crime and punishment and draw up your own analysis using the same pattern. How did factors work together to bring about:
   a) witchhunts in the sixteenth and seventeenth centuries
   b) the reform of prisons in the nineteenth century
   c) the setting up of a police force in the nineteenth century.

Patterns of change

THROUGHOUT THIS BOOK you have been studying changes in crime and punishment. Now is the time to think in more detail about some of the patterns of change you have studied in this course. This page introduces the main ideas. Over the next seven pages you will investigate examples of these patterns.

There has been a lot of continuity even though sometimes it looks like change

In history it is important to study continuities as well as changes. There has been great continuity in the nature of crime: petty theft has always been the most common crime while murder or violent assault have always made up a tiny proportion of crime. Every period seems to have had 'new crimes'. For example, the invention of the motor car has made breaking the speed limit a new crime in the twentieth century.

But some so-called new crimes are not new at all. Most computer crime, for example, is simply theft – a very old crime indeed. Only the method used by the criminal has changed.

Sometimes change is rapid; sometimes slow

Sometimes change goes to and fro like a pendulum

REFORM   REACTION

Sometimes change makes things better; sometimes it makes things worse

So it's clear from these figures that our tough new policies are having an effect.

DRUG RELATED CRIME

1990   1995   1997   1999

203

Slow change: Trials

Some aspects of a modern trial and a modern courtroom are very similar to a trial in the Middle Ages.

1. Study the two pictures. They are 600 years apart. List as many differences and as many similarities as you can.
2. From your study of earlier chapters of this book, list any other examples of continuity between a medieval trial and the modern trial.
3. Why do you think the conduct of trials has changed so little since the Middle Ages?
4. a) Give one other example of slow change in the history of crime and punishment.
    b) Explain why this change has been slow.

SOURCE 1 A medieval court: the King's Bench

SOURCE 2 A modern court, 1990s

Judge

Witness

Defence lawyer

Prosecution lawyer

Accused

Jury

Rapid change: The twentieth-century police officer

The courtroom may have changed little, but the work of the police officer has changed beyond recognition in the past 100 years.

100 years ago

Communication

Weapons

Transport

on foot and bicycle

Today

Communication

radio

Weapons

new style truncheon

Transport

S OURCE 3 Developments in the work of police officers since 1900

■ TASK

1. Make your own copy of Source 3. In the boxes provided, add details about how this aspect of policing has changed in the past 100 years. Add more boxes to your diagram to show other changes. Use pages 176–179 to help you.
2. Which aspects of policing have not changed in the past 100 years?
3. Explain why change has been rapid for the police.
4. Why have some aspects of policing changed very little when others have changed rapidly?

Reform and reaction: What kind of prison regime?

IN THE HISTORY of crime and punishment it often appears that change moves in one direction, then it moves back in the opposite direction, and so on, just like a pendulum. Prison reform is an example of this.

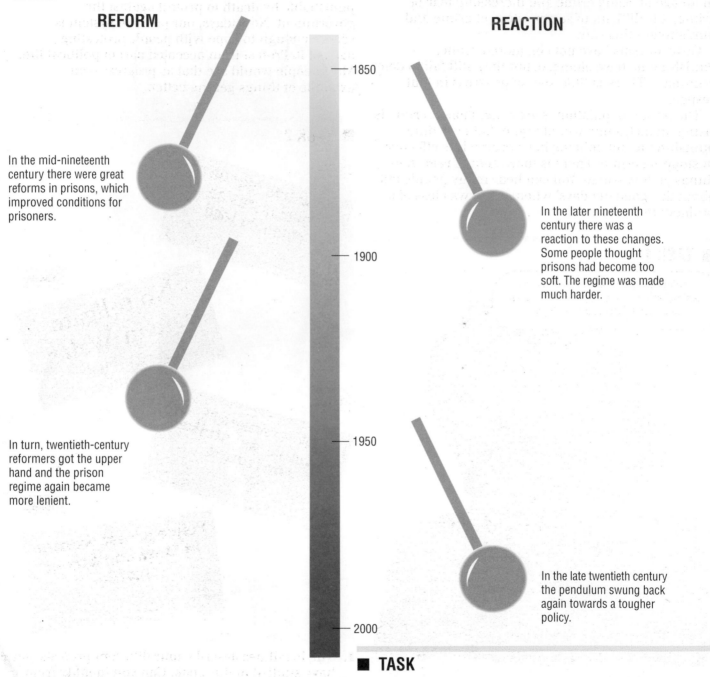

REFORM

In the mid-nineteenth century there were great reforms in prisons, which improved conditions for prisoners.

In turn, twentieth-century reformers got the upper hand and the prison regime again became more lenient.

1850

1900

1950

2000

REACTION

In the later nineteenth century there was a reaction to these changes. Some people thought prisons had become too soft. The regime was made much harder.

In the late twentieth century the pendulum swung back again towards a tougher policy.

■ **TASK**

1. Study the illustration and use it to write your own account of how and why ideas about conditions in prisons changed through the nineteenth and twentieth centuries. You can find out more on pages 128–133 and 180–183.
2. Describe one other example of this same pattern of change in the history of crime and punishment.

Regress and progress

Regress: The story of crime

Some people see history as the story of human progress – things getting gradually better. However, in an age of rising crime and increasing fear of crime, it is difficult to see the story of crime and punishment this way.

Governments have not conquered crime. Punishments have changed, but they still fail to deter criminals. There is little sign of progress in that respect.

The prison population is growing. Violent crime is rising. In fact, some would argue that over time punishment and policing has become less effective in stopping crime. There is more sign of regression – things getting worse. You can hear many people talk about the 'good old days' when crime was less of a problem than it is now.

■ TASK 1

> Crime is getting worse. Nobody is dealing with it effectively. I wish we could get back to the good old days.

1. What evidence could the speaker use to support her view that things are getting worse?
2. What evidence could someone use to challenge her view of crime and punishment?
3. Describe one other example of what you regard as regression in the history of crime and punishment?

Progress: The treatment of protesters

Four hundred years ago in Britain it was a crime punishable by death to protest against the government. Nowadays, our political system is secure enough to cope with people protesting against it. Protest is an accepted part of political life. Most people would see that as progress – an example of things getting better.

■ TASK 2

1549 — Protesters tear down enclosures on common land

1840 — No tollgate safe in Wales

1926 — Rail transport in chaos as strike continues

1909 — Police arrest women in Downing Street scuffle

1. The headlines describe four different protests you have studied in this book. Can you identify from the headline alone who is protesting about what?
2. From your work earlier in this course, record how these protesters were treated.
3. Now use your findings to explain whether you agree with this statement: 'The change in the treatment of protesters through time is an example of progress.'

Turning points and trends: Capital punishment through time

THESE FINAL FOUR pages give you the opportunity to apply your understanding of continuity and change to one topic that has been a central part of the story of crime and punishment: capital punishment or execution.

SOURCE 1 From the Laws of King Alfred the Great, 870–899

> *4. If anyone plots against the King's life he forfeits his life and everything he owns.*

SOURCE 2 From the records of the Royal Courts in Norfolk, 1307–16

> *Hamon, son of John in the Corner, was taken for stealing at night one mare worth 10s and for stealing one horse worth 13s 4d and for robbing Thomas le Neve of goods worth 40s. He stands trial and is convicted. He is to be hanged.*

SOURCE 3 Capital crimes. In the late 1600s the number of crimes that led to the death penalty increased rapidly. This trend continued through the eighteenth century and into the nineteenth

Year	The number of crimes carrying the death penalty
1688	50
1765	160
1815	225

SOURCE 4 A crowd at a public hanging in 1747. These were supposed to deter people from crime. However, there is little evidence that they did so. By the 1700s public hangings had become public holidays. The crowds laughed and drank. A London magistrate said in 1783: 'All the aims of public justice are defeated … the terrors of death, the shame of punishment are lost'

In the 1700s anyone found guilty of murder or theft of goods worth more than one shilling (which, remember, was seen as a serious crime), would, in theory, hang. However, only 25 per cent of those convicted were actually hanged. Many were saved because the jury decided that the stolen goods were worth less than one shilling or women were spared because they were pregnant. Others escaped because they were able to claim benefit of clergy. Those who were hanged were likely to be persistent and/or dangerous offenders. Most who escaped hanging were sentenced to transportation instead.

The Roman Empire 500BC – AD400 (pages 9–22)		The Middle Ages 400–1500 (pages 23–54)	

SOURCE 5 Some significant dates in the history of capital punishment

1789	*Last woman burned for murdering her husband.*
1820	*Last beheading – of the Cato Street conspirators who tried to assassinate the entire government.*
1820s–30s	*Abolition of nearly all capital crimes. Ending of benefit of clergy.*
1841	*Only murder, treason and ... remained as capital crimes.*
1868	*Last public hanging took place.*

	Average number of death sentences per year	Average number executed per year	% of executed who were executed for murder
1805–14	443	66	20%
1815–24	1073	89	18%
1825–34	1218	53	23%
1835–44	199	13	77%
1845–54	57	9	100%

SOURCE 6 This table shows the difference between the number of death sentences given by the courts and the number that were actually carried out, 1805–54

SOURCE 7 Crowds protesting against the execution of Ruth Ellis, the last woman to be hanged in Britain, in 1955. They were campaigning against the use of the death penalty as a punishment

■ TASK

You can use Sources 1–7 on these two pages as the basis for your answers to questions 1–8, but you can also find more sources and information on the pages listed on the timeline index on pages 190–191.

1. Execution has been used as a punishment throughout history.
   a) What continuity has there been in the types of crime punished by execution?
   b) What changes have there been in the types of crime punished by execution?
2. What different methods of execution have been used in the past?
3. Why were different types of execution used for different crimes?
4. Was there more change or continuity in the history of capital punishment up to 1800? Use examples to support your answer.
5. How did the use of capital punishment change:
   a) in the 1800s
   b) in the 1900s?
6. Which of these possible turning points do you think was most important:
   a) the abolition of the Bloody Code
   b) the ending of public executions
   c) the abolition of capital punishment in 1965? Give reasons for your answer.
7. What evidence is there that the abolition of capital punishment for murder in 1965 was a continuation of a trend that had been evident for a long time?
8. Do you regard the abolition of capital punishment as an example of progress (things getting better) or regression (things getting worse)? Explain your answer carefully.

Early Modern Britain 1500–1750 (pages 65–106)	Industrial Britain 1750–1900 (pages 107–142)	The Twentieth Century 1900–2000 (pages 169–186)

Why has there been change in the history of capital punishment?

Execution was a common form of punishment until the 1800s. Then came a series of changes which eventually led to its abolition in Britain in the 1960s. This diagram summarises the reasons.

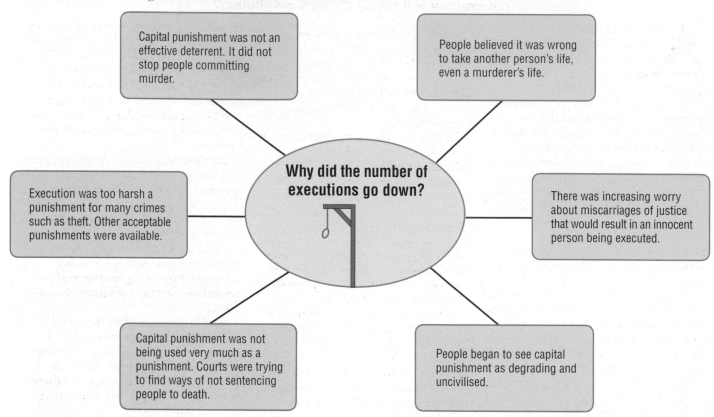

Capital punishment was not an effective deterrent. It did not stop people committing murder.

People believed it was wrong to take another person's life, even a murderer's life.

Execution was too harsh a punishment for many crimes such as theft. Other acceptable punishments were available.

Why did the number of executions go down?

There was increasing worry about miscarriages of justice that would result in an innocent person being executed.

Capital punishment was not being used very much as a punishment. Courts were trying to find ways of not sentencing people to death.

People began to see capital punishment as degrading and uncivilised.

Could Britain ever reintroduce capital punishment?

At the time of writing this book, capital punishment has been abolished for over 30 years. Despite many debates and votes in Parliament, the supporters of capital punishment have never been close to the majority they need to reintroduce it. It may seem therefore that the history of capital punishment in Britain has come to a full stop. However, change is always possible even after a long period of continuity.

In the USA the use of capital punishment ended in 1972. Six hundred people who had been sentenced to death had their sentences changed to life imprisonment. It appeared that there too the history of capital punishment had come to an end, but then certain states decided to reintroduce capital punishment for the crime of murder. In 1976 the executions began again. Between 1976 and 1995, 272 people were executed in the USA. Ironically, the murder rate has not fallen. In the state of Florida where executions began again in 1980, the next

three years saw a 28 per cent increase in murders, to the highest rate in the state's recent history. In Georgia, the year after the reintroduction of execution saw a 20 per cent increase in murders, when the national murder rate fell by five per cent.

If the death penalty can be reintroduced in the USA, it could be reintroduced in Britain too. This might seem unlikely, but to most people in earlier centuries the abolition of public executions would have seemed unlikely, if not impossible.

So history can always surprise us with a change in the pattern of ideas, but we must also be careful in making comparisons with other countries. The death penalty has been abandoned for far longer in Britain than it had been in the USA. Each state in the USA has the power to make its own laws on the death penalty and this makes change easier. There is also a much higher murder rate in the USA, a factor which may push politicians into taking action, regardless of whether capital punishment works as a deterrent.

Should we kill the killers?

Arguments continue over the death penalty. Does it work as a deterrent or is it purely an act of retribution?

After several delays, 31-year-old Nicholas Ingram was finally executed ten days ago as three high-voltage charges of electricity were passed through his body.

In America the relatives of murder victims are able to address the state's parole board, which decides whether to carry out the court's sentence. In Ingram's case, the victim's wife Mary Sawyer – who was also shot in the attack which killed her husband – described how they had 'begged for mercy and were given none. He [Ingram] was judge, jury and executioner, all in a matter of minutes.' The board decided that Ingram's crime deserved the electric chair.

Amnesty International has conducted surveys into American attitudes towards capital punishment. The surveys show that three out of four people support the death penalty. However, when asked if, instead of the death penalty, they could impose a sentence of life without parole (reduction in sentence due to good behaviour) and force offenders to work in prison for money that would go to the families of victims, many changed their minds. In New York, for instance, the 71 per cent who supported capital punishment went down to 19 per cent when the other option was offered.

In Britain, the Police Federation favours a return to capital punishment for premeditated murder. Federation chairman Fred Broughton claims there has been a continual rise in the murder rate since capital punishment was abolished.

This view is refuted by the findings of Roger Hood, the director of the Criminological Research Centre at Oxford University, who found in a survey carried out for the United Nations that there is no scientific proof 'that executions have a greater deterrent effect than life imprisonment'.

In the US, two-thirds of police chiefs do not believe the death penalty reduces murder, and 82 per cent believed murderers do not think about punishment when they kill.

Foremost among British MPs favouring restoration is Sir Ivan Lawrence QC, chairman of the Home Affairs Select Committee. He believes the alternatives to capital punishment have failed 'because too many innocent victims have been murdered'.

But one innocent person whose life was saved by the abolition of the death penalty is Judith Ward. In 1973 she was convicted of the murder of 12 soldiers in a coach explosion on the M62. She served 18 years in prison for a crime she did not commit before winning her appeal in 1992.

'If the death penalty had still been in force in Britain I would have been executed,' she says. 'No country which resorts to legalised murder can claim to be truly civilised.'

In the US, researchers have estimated that 350 innocent people have been wrongly convicted of murder this century. For 23 of the prisoners, the evidence establishing their innocence appeared after they had been executed.

The death penalty in America also appears unfairly biased against certain races. More than 40 per cent of those on death row are black even though they make up just 12 per cent of the nation's population. In addition, 84 per cent of those executed since 1977 were convicted of murdering a white victim even though black and white people are murdered in roughly equal numbers. It appears that the taking of a white life is more serious than taking a black life.

For those sentenced to death, there can be a long wait. William Andrews was executed in 1992, 17 years after he entered death row at the age of 20. The average time on death row for those who do not consent to their execution is eight years.

Right until the moment of death, things have gone wrong. On many occasions those being electrocuted have needed several bursts of electricity before dying.

And in Texas in 1988, Raymond Landry was being executed by lethal injection when the line leading to the syringe burst. The deadly chemicals sprayed around the chamber, and those observing the killing were forced to flee for their own lives.

© The Guardian, April 1995

SOURCE 8 An article from the *Guardian*, April 1995. The photo shows Judith Ward

■ TASK

1. Study the diagram on page 210 and sort the reasons into three categories:
   a) reasons why the number of executions went down so rapidly in the 1800s
   b) reasons why execution was eventually abolished in the 1960s
   c) reasons that apply to both the 1800s and the 1960s.
2. Read Source 8. What developments do you think would have to take place for the death penalty to be reintroduced in Britain?

Glossary

adultery a sexual relationship with someone other than the marriage partner

aediles officials in Ancient Rome, responsible for upholding minor laws of the city

arson deliberately setting fire to a building

assassination the murder of an important or well-known person, often a political figure

blacklegs workers who do not join a strike and continue to work

Bloody Code the harsh laws gradually introduced between 1500 and 1750

blood feud the legal right of a murder victim's family to hunt down and kill the murderer in revenge

brigands robbers

capital punishment the death penalty. Crimes carrying this punishment are known as capital crimes

community service an alternative punishment to imprisonment, whereby offenders have to perform certain duties for the community, such as repairing or decorating work

commuted a punishment being made less severe

compurgation the oath taken by witnesses in favour of the accused in a medieval court

conditional pardon a pardon that is conditional on future good behaviour and can be withdrawn if any further offences are committed

constables men from every village or town who were appointed to uphold law and order. They did this in their own time and received no payment for it

counterfeiting forgery

coroner an official responsible for investigating violent or suspicious deaths

crucifixion an ancient method of putting someone to death, by nailing or binding to a cross

cut-purses pickpockets

defendant the person on trial in a court of law

deterrent a measure that frightens or prevents people from committing crime

discharge allowed to go free

duffers slang term for the men who bought goods from smugglers and sold them on to the public

exile banishment from one's home or country

freemen peasants who were not under the control of the lord of the manor

gallows wooden frame from which the hanging noose is attached

Habeas Corpus literally means 'you have the body'. It is an order for an accused person to be brought before a judge or court to establish on what charges he or she is being held. This prevents unlawful imprisonment

heretic a person who holds different beliefs from the authorised teachings of the Church

hierarchical describing a system of government organised according to each person's rank

hue and cry the practice of raising the alarm (by means of loud shouts and cries) when a crime had been committed. Everyone within earshot had to join the hunt for the suspect

hulks ships used as prisons in nineteenth-century Britain

King's approver a criminal who became an informer and helped the authorities to convict others. In return, the 'approver' escaped punishment

magistrate's court a court presided over by a judge called a magistrate

neck-verse the passage from the Bible that people had to read to claim benefit of clergy

non-conformist person who does not conform to the generally accepted patterns of behaviour

outlawed cast out of society

pardoned forgiven for a crime and released from any punishment

patricide the murder of one's own father

pillory a wooden frame with holes for the head and hands. Convicted offenders were sentenced to be put in the pillory, where they would be publicly humiliated and ridiculed. The **stocks** held the feet only

poaching illegally hunting animals, birds or fish on someone else's property

posse a group of men who called on to help the sheriff track down a criminal

probation a system where offenders are allowed their freedom on condition of good behaviour. If they break the probation rules they can be imprisoned

prosecuting bringing a legal case against someone accused of a crime

quarter sessions courts held every three months by Justices of the Peace

reform to improve and change criminals so that they would no longer commit crime

repeal reverse or cancel laws

reprimanded severely scolded

sanctuary a safe place within a church or cathedral. Once a person claimed sanctuary they could not be removed by force

scolds name for women who were accused of being quarrelsome or noisy in public or disobedient to their husbands

sergeants official appointed by the king to uphold the law during the Middle Ages

sheriff the chief law officer of each county during the Middle Ages; sheriffs were appointed by the king and had wide ranging powers

solitary confinement kept separate from other people

stocks see **pillory**

suffragettes women who campaigned to win the vote

tithings groups made up of ten men who were responsible for each other's behavior. If a member of a tithing broke the law, the others had to bring him to justice or pay a fine for his crime

transportation sending convicted criminals overseas

treason disobedience or disloyalty to the monarch (or government)

trial by ordeal a test which an accused person had to undergo if the courts could not decide on a verdict due to lack of evidence. The test involved great physical pain, such as carrying a red-hot iron; if the resulting wound healed cleanly it was taken as proof that the accused was innocent

vagrancy wandering from place to place without a settled home or job

vigiles officials who patrolled the streets of Rome, fighting and preventing fires

the watch men who patrolled the streets during the night, trying to prevent crime

wergild a form of compensation paid to the victims of crime in Saxon times

workhouses institutions where the poor were sent if they could not support themselves; they were provided with basic food and shelter, but were forced to work very hard